152.4
moy

+QP401 .M65

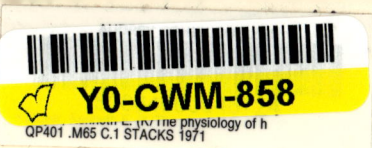

QP   Moyer, Kenneth E.
401   The physiology of hostility
M65

COLL. FOR
201 VARICK ST. N.Y.C.

The Physiology of Hostility

The Physiology of Hostility

K. E. MOYER
Carnegie-Mellon University

MARKHAM PUBLISHING COMPANY / Chicago

MARKHAM PSYCHOLOGY SERIES

ALLEN, ed., *Psychological Factors in Poverty*
DUKE and FRANKEL, *Inside Psychotherapy*
MOSCOVICI, ed., *The Psychosociology of Language*
MOYER, *The Physiology of Hostility*
SAHAKIAN, ed., *Psychology of Learning: Systems, Models, and Theories*

COPYRIGHT 1971 BY MARKHAM PUBLISHING COMPANY
ALL RIGHTS RESERVED
PRINTED IN U.S.A.
LIBRARY OF CONGRESS CARD CATALOG NUMBER 78–136620
STANDARD BOOK NUMBER: 8410–5012–0

*To "Dusty," Rob and Cathy
who have given my life meaning.*

Preface

Most of the papers in this volume were written for presentation to particular audiences and in each an attempt has been made to amplify a specific aspect of the general problem of the physiology of aggressive behavior. Because at the time each of these papers was originally presented, most of the others were not generally available, it was necessary to include much of the earlier material to relate the concepts in context. As a result, there was considerable redundancy, which has been reduced by editing without destroying the continuity of the individual work. Unfortunately, it has not been feasible to eliminate all of it. To do so would have required rewriting and integrating all of the papers. The result would have been a text rather than a collection of writings, as requested by the publisher. That project will be saved for a later day. I hope the reader will be able to skim lightly the repetitive portions of the material and bear with this inconvenience.

The information presented has been documented to enable the serious scholar to consult original sources and thereby verify a point or determine whether his interpretation of the data agrees with mine. To avoid duplication, the references for all of the individual papers have been compiled into a single list at the end of the book. I have used the number notation form to minimize the interference of documentation with the ease of reading.

Throughout the writing of all of the papers in this volume, bibliographic assistance was received from the UCLA Brain Information Service, which is part of the Neurological Information Network of NINDS and is supported under Contract #DHEW PH-43-66-59. That assistance is gratefully acknowledged.

Schematic diagrams of the brain have been included for the student who has a limited knowledge of neuroanatomy and wishes to get an idea of the "geography" of the brain areas under discussion.

I began to concern myself with the problems of the physiology of aggressive behavior in September of 1966 while I was on leave from Carnegie-Mellon University, supported by a grant from the Ford Foundation to the Graduate School of Industrial Administration for studies in the behavioral sciences. The National Science Foundation supported this work in part by Grant No. GB6652 from July 1, 1967 to June 30, 1969, and is currently continuing support by Grant No. GB12918. The opportunity to pursue my research on aggressive behavior has been further aided by a sabbatical leave from Carnegie-Mellon University during the 1969–1970 academic year. Without this most generous support from the Ford Foundation, the University, and the National Science Foundation, this work could never have been completed, and I am most grateful.

As with most academicians, I have had the good fortune to be able to test my ideas by presenting them informally to my colleagues and graduate students. Their responses have constantly influenced my thinking. Although many have helped me to clarify my ideas, I particularly appreciate the discussions I have had with Len Jarrard, Jim Korn, and Dick Bandler.

Mrs. Elinor Wilkes deserves thanks because she has struggled with the first drafts of most of these papers, made sense out of my filing system, and contributed greatly to help keep the research program running smoothly. I also appreciate the work of Barbara Gourley, who did the final typing, and the help of Judy Parkman and Mike Crabtree, who were helpful in many ways.

Finally, and perhaps most important, thanks to "Dusty," who understands me.

Contents

	Preface	vii
1	Brain Research *Must* Contribute to World Peace	1
2	Internal Impulses to Aggression	11
3	Kinds of Aggression and their Physiological Bases	25
4	A Preliminary Physiological Model of Aggressive Behavior	52
5	The Physiology of Aggression and the Implications for Aggression Control	81
6	The Physiology of Affiliation and Hostility	109
7	Maternal Aggression: A Failure to Replicate	128
8	Aggressive Behavior in the Rat: Effects of Isolation and Olfactory Bulb Lesions	135
	References	147
	Index	175

1

Brain Research *Must* Contribute to World Peace

K. E. MOYER

A brief, concise statement of my ideas on aggressive behavior, presented in this first short paper, may serve well as an introduction to this collection of readings. The remaining papers elaborate and develop in detail the concepts briefly cited here.

Man's capacity for total world destruction is a constant threat that makes peace between nations essential to the survival of the species. If peace cannot be maintained, other problems are of little importance. How an understanding of the physiology of aggressive behavior will reduce international conflict is not yet clear. Obviously, wars are the result of a complex of interacting social, political, economic, and other factors, forces that ultimately act on individuals. Thus, any increase in our understanding and control of human behavior may contribute to our understanding and control of the behavior of nations. Anthony Storr expresses it well when he says ". . . if stability in world affairs is ever to be achieved, the psychological point of view deserves equal consideration with the political, economic, and other aspects. The study of human aggression and its control is, therefore, relevant to the problem of war although alone, it cannot possibly provide a complete answer (369)."

"World peace," however, involves more than the absence of

conflict among nations. A peaceful world must include a general reduction in man's hostility to man in all human interactions. Individual hostile behavior must be reduced if man is to achieve his potential for a quality life. The argument that some hostility is of value, or may be, is irrelevant. Men of introspection must agree that much of their anger and irritability is neither rational nor of value. Control of individual irascibility will contribute to world peace, broadly defined, and an understanding of the physiological substrates of that behavior has much to contribute to such control.

In addition to providing a brief outline of a model of aggression and some of the implications for control indicated by the model, this paper offers a warning of the potential dangers associated with such controls. Power-oriented men have always tried to achieve absolute behavior control. Such a potential exists, and all men should be aware of it.

This paper was presented at the Symposium on Brain Research and Human Behavior in the Plenary Session on "How Brain Research Can Contribute to World Peace" under the joint sponsorship of UNESCO and the International Brain Research Organization, March 11–15, 1968, in Paris, France. It was written as a discussion of four previous papers in that session by Professor O. Adrianov of the USSR Academy of Medical Sciences at the Brain Institute, Moscow, USSR; Dr. P. Karli from the Institut de biologie medicale of the Université de Strasbourg, Strasbourg, France; Dr. B. F. Skinner, of Harvard University, USA; and Dr. R. Thapar of the International Center of New Delhi, India.

A tape recording of these remarks, broadcast by UNESCO RADIO over its worldwide network, was heard by Dr. Gilchrist of the Medical School of the Fiji Islands, who requested and received permission to transcribe the tape and publish the remarks in the Fiji School of Medicine Journal. It appeared in Vol. III, No. 11, November, 1968, pp. 2–5 and is reprinted here with the permission of the editor. I wish to express my appreciation to the Honorable Professor Chagas, Brazilian Ambassador to UNESCO, to Dr. Fernandez de Molina for the invitation to participate in this symposium, and to Carnegie-Mellon University, which made the trip financially possible.

Mr. Chairman, Professor Chagas, and ladies and gentlemen: I am sure that I reflect the feelings of the entire audience when I express our appreciation to the speakers for their well thought out, important and provocative papers. It has been my assigned task to attempt to integrate this material and then to speak to the problem of how brain research can contribute to a peaceful world. I will attempt to be brief so that we will have time to discuss this most important topic.

I must first say that I believe that brain research can contribute to a peaceful world. It will; and in fact, it must.

We have learned this afternoon that aggressive behavior has many and complex causes. Professor Thapar has outlined some of the sociological mechanisms which produce aggression. He has referred particularly to the meaningless affluence which results in a vast wastefulness which in his words, "sparks explosive psychological tensions." We can gather from the remarks of Dr. Skinner that there are psychological causes of aggressive behavior. An individual who has been reinforced for aggressive behavior will become more aggressive. From Professors Adrianov and Karli we learn that aggressive behavior also has a physiological basis. Professor Adrianov has emphasized the importance of the cortical control over lower brain centers. Dr. Karli has summarized for us 15 years of excellent and painstaking work in which he has defined progressively more discretely the detailed neurology of one particular kind of aggressive behavior in the rat.

We have much to learn in each of these disciplines, but it appears clear that as we increase our understanding of the details of these multiple causes of aggressive behavior, we will ultimately be able to bring it under control. Each speaker has already offered suggestions as to how that control might be achieved. Dr. Thapar would educate man to a different set of values which would decrease the tensions resulting from the current socioeconomic structure. Dr. Skinner suggests that aggression can be controlled by properly manipulating the contingencies of reinforcement. Both

4   The Physiology of Hostility

Professors Adrianov and Karli would attempt to control aggression through the activation of the beautifully complex circuits of the cortex which send inhibitory fibers to the limbic system where hostility resides.

There is, in a sense, a communality in what each of our speakers has said this afternoon. Essentially, it is that the brain is sufficiently flexible that man can be taught to inhibit aggressive tendencies. This is, of course, a hopeful and an optimistic statement. A peaceful world must ultimately come from the control of hostile tendencies. Our speakers also agree that a peaceful world depends not only on the control of the hostile tendencies that lead to war, but also on the control of those hostile tendencies that set neighbor against neighbor, and husband against wife.

So far, our conclusions about the role of brain research in peace are that it is sound neurophysiology to believe that education can be a useful tool in the inhibition of overt aggressive behavior. Nothing has been said as yet about the control of hostile feelings. However, there is reason to believe that hostile feelings may become sufficiently intense that overt aggression will result regardless of the manner in which the contingencies of reinforcement have been arranged and regardless of the individual's prior education and training.

There may be yet another answer to the question, "How can brain research contribute to a peaceful world?" Brain research may devise methods which will enable man to gain the physiological control of his aggressive tendencies. It may, and it must, contribute to man's understanding of some of the implications of that kind of control. As soon as we answer that question in that way we are faced with a multitude of moral and ethical problems. We are forced to make value judgments and we would be well advised to give them much careful thought.

Professor Karli has expressed the concern that such a cure for aggression may be worse than the disease. Professor Nuttin, in the round table on Wednesday, asked the question, "Would it indeed be progress if we learn to control aggressive behavior by physiological manipulation?" I submit to Professor Karli, to Professor Nuttin and to the assembled audience that it is already too late to ask those questions. The control of aggressive behavior by physiological means is already here. I speak here not of what should be or what might be, but of what is. It also seems to me to be inevitable that the scope of that control is going to increase as our understanding of the brain increases. The continuing accumulation of knowledge cannot be terminated. We can only hope to consider wisely the manner in which that knowledge will be used. It appears that the scientists in brain research stand on a threshold similar to the one on which the atomic physicists stood in the early 1940's.

Sufficient data have accumulated (and much of it has been presented at these meetings) to permit us to see at least an outline of a model of aggressive behavior in animals as well as in man. I would like to sketch very briefly the outline of this model because I think it leads to the inevitable conclusion that physiological controls for hostile behavior will continue to be developed, and at an accelerated pace.

First, it appears clear that aggression is not a unitary concept. There are, in fact, a number of kinds of aggressive behavior and each has a different physiological basis. Since time is short, I shall give just two examples. The work coming out of Dr. Flynn's laboratory has shown that if a very friendly cat is stimulated in the lateral hypothalamus through an implanted electrode, it will ignore the experimenter and attack an available rat. However, if the cat is stimulated in the medial hypothalamus, the cat will ignore the rat and attack the experimenter (113).

Another implication that may be drawn from the studies of Dr. Flynn as well as those of Hess, Fernandez de Molina, Karli and many others, is that animals have well organized circuits in the brain which, when activated, result in well integrated attack behavior on particular kinds of stimuli (122; 185).

Although the evidence is slim, it appears clear that man, for all of his encephalization, is not free of those aggressive circuits. King reports the case of a mild-mannered female patient who became aggressive, verbally hostile, and threatened to strike the experimenter when she was electrically stimulated in the region of the amygdala. When the current was turned off, she again became mild mannered and apologetic for her behavior. Her hostile feelings and aggressive behavior could be turned on and off at the flick of a switch. Her interesting comments were that she felt no pain but that she did not like to feel so hostile (217).

There is also evidence from several sources that, like many other systems in the brain, there are suppressor circuits which are antagonistic to the aggression circuits. Professor Karli has told us of aggressive inhibitory circuits in the brain of the rat. When he interrupts these suppressor circuits, a peaceful rat is turned into a killer. There are similar findings for other animals (417; 425).

Fortunately for man and animal alike, the aggressive circuits are not active most of the time. We must therefore consider how they become active. Very briefly, there is good reason to believe that these different hostility circuits are sensitized or desensitized as a function of certain blood constituents, particularly, though not exclusively, the hormones. It has been known for centuries that the raging bull can be converted into the gentle steer by lowering its androgen level through castration. This finding has been verified experimentally in a variety of animals (38; 79).

Endroczi and his colleagues in Hungary have shown that maternal aggression in the rat can be directly manipulated by experimentally shifting the hormone balance. Lactating rats will attack frogs which are placed in their cages and this aggressive behavior can be blocked by the administration of estrogen and reactivated by the administration of hydrocortisone (118).

The many details of the neuro-endocrine interactions in the various kinds of aggression must be worked out, but the general pattern appears to be emerging rather clearly. Certain hostility circuits appear to be sensitized by particular hormone balances and when these circuits are sensitized, a variety of environmental conditions will evoke hostile feelings and behavior. These environmental situations may involve frustration, stress in many forms, pain, or, if these circuits are highly sensitized, simply the presence of an attackable entity. What types of entity will be attacked will depend in part on the reinforcement history of the organism and in part on the particular aggression circuit that is sensitized.

Now that we have the bare bones of this model, which I do not have time to elaborate, let us look at the kinds of aggressive controls that are available now and the potential for further controls.

First of all, we have the educational or training process that my colleagues on the panel have suggested. The individual may learn to inhibit his aggressive behavior. It is frequently difficult; it is frequently tension producing; but it is also frequently possible. Obviously it is not always possible (333).

We should also have several physiological means of control at our disposal. As Karli has told us, we can interrupt some of the aggressive circuitry and reduce hostile behavior by surgery. It has been demonstrated that the wild cat Lynx rufus rufus can be made tractable and friendly by an amygdalectomy (331). Man is no exception. There are wild men as there are wild cats, men who have so much spontaneous firing of the aggressive circuits that they are a constant danger to all around them and to themselves. A few bold surgeons throughout the world have performed operations to permit these men to lead peaceful, if not profitable, lives. Dr. Sano at the University of Tokyo has had good success with lesions in the posterior hypothalamus (327). Le Beau, here in France, recommends cingulectomy in intractable cases of anger, violence and permanent agitation (233). These are examples of the control of man's hostile behavior by physiological manipulations. Incidentally, man's hostile feelings are also controlled. A patient of Dr. Sawa with temporal lesions reported that he could not get angry if he wanted to (398).

We should also be able to control aggression by the physiological activation of the aggression suppressor areas. Let's take an example from Delgado's laboratory. He placed a radio-controlled electrode in the caudate nucleus of the boss monkey in a colony. Whenever the boss monkey began to attack another monkey, Professor Delgado would activate the electrode by remote control and turn him immediately into a peaceful and benevolent despot. He went one step farther and made the electrode activator available in the cage. One of the submissive monkeys who was short on weight but long on intelligence soon learned the value of the activator. Whenever the boss monkey showed signs of threat and irascibility, the submissive monkey would look the boss straight in the eye and press the lever, thus stimulating the boss's caudate nucleus and making him again peaceful and benevolent (93).

Irascible man is subject to the same control. Dr. Heath, in New Orleans, reports that he has implanted permanent electrodes in the septal region of violent psychotics. The patient can then be brought into the clinic, paranoid, raging, violent and threatening.

8 The Physiology of Hostility

He is plugged in and stimulated, having no awareness of the stimulation. His response is immediate. He relaxes, his hostility dissipates, he smiles and is at peace with the world. It is a short step from here to give the patient his own transistorized power pack with an anti-hostility button that he himself can press whenever he feels his intolerable hostility coming on. The technical problems have already been solved (174). Again, this is the control of aggression by physiological manipulation.

It is also possible to control hostile tendencies by the chemical manipulation of the aggressive circuits through the use of drugs. The savage rhesus monkey is readily tamed, not sedated, but made friendly, by giving it Librium® (301). In a study by Scheckel and McConnell, (cited in Zbinden and Randall, 436), rats were trained to press a lever for a food reward at the sound of a high-pitched tone. They were also trained to press a second lever on presentation of a low-pitched tone. In 10 percent of the rodents' responses to the low-pitched tone, foot shock resulted as well as a reward. Thus, the low-pitched tone created a conflict situation. After administration of Librium,® latency of response to the low-pitched tone was markedly reduced, but there was no change in response latency for the high-pitched tone, where no conflict was involved. Dr. Kalina has reported excellent success with the use of the drug diazepam for the control of the destructive rampages of psychotic criminals (202). Again, this is the physiological manipulation of aggression. It should be emphasized that these are essentially anti-hostility agents, not sedatives in the usual sense.

The control of man's aggressive behavior by physiological manipulation is here now. It is here whether we like it or not and whether we consider this kind of control to be progress or not. We should take a little more time to consider the implications of these facts.

It seems fairly clear that the man who is ill with pathological aggressive tendencies, as in the cases described so far, should have available to him the cures developed by brain research; but what of the normal person? What are the implications for you and me? I once had a neighbor who met all of the accepted criteria of free-

---

® Registered trademark for chlordiazepoxide-HCl, Hoffman-LaRoche Inc., Nutley, N.J.

dom from pathology. She certainly should not and could not have been committed. However, her aggression circuits were easily fired. She felt hostile much of the time. She was irascible and uncomfortable, and though she reported that she tried very hard to inhibit her hostile behavior, she found herself frequently shouting at her children and her husband. Certainly, most men would agree that she should be freed of this unreasonable hostility if she is able to find a drug that will help her control it. Drugs that would help her handle her feelings of hostility may be available now, and if they are not, they will be within a few years. These seem to be clear and unmixed blessings of brain research. It will be a more peaceful world when each of us has the opportunity, if we choose, to reduce our irrational irritability by physiological means.

That, however, is not the end of the story. Knowledge is accumulating at an ever-increasing rate. Airplanes that are longer than the initial flight of the Wright brothers are now being built. If there is a comparable advance in our understanding of the chemistry and physiology of aggression, and there is every reason to believe that there will be, what manipulations will be possible sixty-five years from now? It is not inconceivable that specific anti-hostility agents could be placed in the water supply to make a peaceful population. This is frightening, but the potential is there whether we are frightened by it or not; it will not disappear just because we ignore it.

Would this cure for war be worse than war? At the moment, we just don't know, but we had better find out as soon as possible. It appears to me that brain research can and must contribute to world peace by finding some of these answers. There are many questions to be answered. I will mention just a few.

Is it possible to reduce hostility specifically without also affecting the intellect and ambition? We do not know.
Is it possible to reduce hostility without reducing initiative and creativity? We do not know.
Is it possible to reduce hostility without reducing man's resistance to injustice and oppression? We do not know.

Research, however, can provide us with these answers. But, what are the broad implications of these answers once we find them? What are the philosophical, the ethical, the sociological and the psychological implications?

Professor Miller has suggested that UNESCO or the United Nations should have special research agencies that would bring together from all disciplines and all countries scientists dedicated to increasing knowledge about peace. This is a necessity.

We have already heard the quotation, "war is too important to be left to the generals." I submit that the physiology of peace is too important to be left to those of us who do brain research.

2

Internal Impulses to Aggression

K. E. MOYER

The title of this paper reflects my reaction against the influential school of thought that proposes that aggressive behavior is fundamentally different from other basic behavior because it is purely and simply a learned response and is never more than a reaction to external stimulation. Such a conception of aggressive behavior is part of a much broader position suggesting that man has no innate behavioral tendencies and that all human behavior is based on learning. Konrad Lorenz (246) said that this doctrine "lies at the root of most of the fallacies which threaten humanity with extinction." I do not feel the position is either that powerful or that pernicious; I do believe it is unsound and leads to faulty predictions and inadequate behavioral controls.

The arguments both for and against this school of thought have usually been presented without reference to or knowledge of the physiological substrates of behavior, but a new dimension is added to our understanding when the physiology is considered. In this paper, I have attempted to demonstrate the remarkable similarity of the physiological processes underlying aggressive behavior and those underlying eating behavior and to show that the differences are more superficial than real. I believe that an equally good case could be made for the similarity of the physiological bases of aggressive behavior and sexual or drinking behavior. Most people concede without argument that there are internal impulses to eat, mate, and drink. Since the basic mechanisms are essentially the same, there must also be internal impulses to aggression.

This paper, illustrated with slides, was presented at a meeting of the Section of Biological and Medical Sciences of the New York Academy of Sciences. It was published in the *Transactions of the New York Academy of Sciences, Series II*, Vol. 31, No. 2, pp. 104–114, © The New York Academy of Sciences; 1969; reprinted by permission. Subsequently, it was condensed for publication in *Mental Health Digest* 6, 1969, 19–22.

The first paper in this volume was combined with this paper and published in the *Carnegie Review*, 1968, No. 17, pp. 4–17. It was then reprinted in *Introduction to the Behavioral Sciences* by John H. Sandberg, New York, Holt, Rinehart and Winston, Inc., 1969.

My thanks are extended to Dr. Leonard Lerner, who invited me to address the distinguished group at the New York Academy of Sciences.

The internal impulses to aggressive behavior and the implications this information has in the area of aggression control will be considered here. A discussion of the internal impulses to aggression necessitates a consideration of the current controversy over whether or not there is an aggressive drive.

Some investigators maintain that there is no drive for aggressive behavior in the same sense that there is a drive for eating, drinking, or sex behavior (10; 188; 256). J. P. Scott, who has done excellent and extensive research on the problem of aggression, is an enthusiastic proponent of this position (337; 338; 339; 340; 341). In 1965, he said, "All that we know (and this comprises a considerable body of information in certain species) indicates that the physiological mechanisms associated with fighting are very different from those underlying sexual behavior and eating. There is no known physiological mechanism by which spontaneous internal stimulation for fighting arises" (339: 820).

Another group studying this problem has arrived at exactly the opposite conclusion. Lorenz (245), on the basis of ethological studies, Lagerspetz (231), on the basis of behavioral studies with mice, and Feshbach (124), on the basis of experiments with humans, have concluded that there is indeed a drive for aggressive behavior.

Much of this controversy stems from the looseness of the various definitions of drive. The concept means very different things to different people. Drive is frequently given the status of an intervening variable that is essentially an expression of ignorance or lack of concern with what is going on inside the organism. Dr. Ethel Tobach and others have expressed the view that to be useful, the term drive must be given a sound physiological basis (342). However, the more I investigate the physiological basis of behavior, the less need I find for the concept of drive. The difficulties with this construct have been considered elsewhere (42; 49;

77), so I need not detail them here. In addition to the criticism offered in those sources, there are certain philosophical problems with the term drive as it is sometimes used. I find the implied mind-body interaction neither necessary nor useful in making predictions about behavior. Furthermore, the drive concept frequently implies a hedonistic interpretation of behavior (the pleasure principle of psychoanalytic thinking and Young's affective arousal theory are examples), which is neither necessary nor useful.

To avoid further confusion, I think it is time to reject the term drive. There are certain basic circuits in the nervous system. When they are active, certain complex behaviors occur. The problem for the student of behavior is to determine the internal and external variables that activate and deactivate these circuits. Certainly, there are differences in the mechanisms for turning the basic neuronal circuits on and off. There are also remarkable similarities. The evidence seems to indicate that there are basic (in a sense, "built in") circuits for aggressive behavior just as there are for consummatory and sexual behavior.

Much of the discussion about the similarity of aggressive behavior and other basic behaviors seems to revolve around whether aggression is endogenously or exogenously determined (385). Scott and Fredericson (343: 820) have suggested that "There is no evidence for any sort of spontaneous internally arising stimulation which would cause a 'need for fighting' per se. Instead, we have a mechanism that will produce fighting in response to predictable external stimulation." However, the same statement can be made about all basic behavior patterns. Behavior does not occur in a vacuum. A deprived animal neither makes random chewing movements nor attempts to eat all available objects. Regardless of the intensity of the internal state produced by deprivation, the animal responds to a very limited set of stimuli with an eating response. It eats only food. In the same manner, the aggressive subject behaves aggressively only toward a very limited number of stimulus objects. Conversely, an animal will not engage in eating behavior or in aggressive behavior to an appropriate stimulus unless a certain characteristic physiological state is present. Some of these physiological mechanisms will now be examined.

FACILITATION OF CONSUMMATORY AND AGGRESSIVE BEHAVIOR BY BRAIN STIMULATION

It has been demonstrated repeatedly that when certain areas of the brain are activated, an animal will become restless and engage in exploratory behavior. If that behavior brings it into contact with food, the animal, though satiated, will begin to eat (5). An extensive series of experiments by Miller and his colleagues (263; 264) has shown that the eating behavior evoked by brain stimulation has many of the characteristics of normal deprivation-induced behavior. A rat that is stimulated in the lateral hypothalamus will eat lab chow or lap milk, but it will not drink pure water. Thus, the response is stimulus bound.

In a similar manner, an animal can be induced to display aggressive behavior by the stimulation of specific brain areas. Cats that normally do not attack rats will do so during electrical stimulation of the hypothalamus (409). If the lateral hypothalamus is stimulated, the cat ignores the experimenter and quietly and efficiently stalks and kills the rat, usually by biting it in the neck region, as is characteristic of the species. In my own laboratory, Richard Bandler has been able to induce a similar predatory mouse killing in rats by carbachol stimulation of the lateral hypothalamus. If there is no stimulus object available, the animal may explore in a restless manner, but it will not behave aggressively. A cat that has been stimulated in the lateral hypothalamus shows distinct and evidently unlearned preferences in the types of stimulus objects it will attack. An anesthetized rat will be attacked more quickly and persistently than a stuffed rat, and there is little tendency for the cat to attack a foam rubber block about the size of a rat (238).

Stimulation of the medial hypothalamus produces a very different kind of aggression. The cat shows pronounced sympathetic arousal and attacks with a high-pitched scream, tearing at the stimulus object with unsheathed claws. It may ignore an available rat, but viciously attack a person (113).

Just as food is reinforcing to the animal whose "feeding system" is activated, the opportunity to attack is reinforcing to an animal whose "predatory system" is activated. Cats that had attacked rats during hypothalamic stimulation learned a Y maze "to obtain a rat they could attack." (309: 187).

Care must be used in applying data obtained from animal research to humans. For obvious reasons, there is a limited amount of data on the effects of brain stimulation in man. We know nothing about how stimulation of the human brain affects eating behavior. Somewhat more is know about aggression. King (217) describes a patient who became angry, verbally hostile, and threatened to strike the experimenter when stimulated with a current of 5 milliamperes by means of an electrode implanted in the amygdaloid region. When the current was reduced or turned off, she became mild mannered and apologetic of her aggressive behavior.

There is also indirect evidence that spontaneous activity of the neurones in the temporal lobe, as well as of other areas of the brain, causes aggressive behavior. In some individuals, spontaneous firing of the cells in the temporal lobe and thalamus leads to subjective feelings of rage and the execution of incredibly violent behavior (140; 391). A number of studies have shown that aggressive behavior, such as fire setting, aggressive sex behavior, and murder, and other acts of violence are associated with 14/second and 6/second positive spikes in the EEG record (333; 334; 427). This assaultive aggressive behavior may or may not be associated with epileptic motor seizures. Even when it is, there is reason to believe that the neurohumoral substrates underlying the two behaviors are different in that they are differentially affected by brain lesions and drugs (F. R. Ervin, 1968, personal communication).

It might be suggested that "spontaneous neurological rage reactions" are abnormal and that they have little to do with the bulk of human behavior. However, "abnormal" is a statistical, not a neurological, concept. Good evidence indicates that some individuals are born with a tendency for certain neurones to fire spontaneously and that the amount of spontaneous firing is on a continuum, occurring more in some individuals than in others. The most relevant question is not whether internal activation of certain brain areas can trigger spontaneous aggressive action, but how frequently does this occur? A mechanism for internally activating aggressive behavior appears to exist. Perhaps it occurs in many people, but more frequently in a few. (See Reference 196 for a further discussion of this point and an excellent review of the literature.)

REDUCTION OF CONSUMMATORY AND AGGRESSIVE BEHAVIOR BY BRAIN LESIONS

The above evidence indicates that there exist in the brain of man as well as of animals well integrated mechanisms, which, when activated, result in complex, well-organized, well-directed behavior. Whether the behavior is consummatory or aggressive depends on the particular circuit involved. Both types of behavior are directed toward particular stimuli. As one might suspect, when these brain mechanisms are damaged, the individual is unable to respond appropriately to the relevant stimuli.

Damage to the lateral nucleus of the hypothalamus produces an animal that does not show the slightest interest in food. Left alone, it will starve to death in the midst of plenty. If tube fed (in some cases for several months), it may respond, but to only the most preferred taste stimulation (272; 375).

Damage of the brain mechanisms governing aggression can accomplish a dramatic reduction in aggressive behavior. It has been shown that bilateral lesions in the amygdala will surgically tame the untameable wildcat (*Lynx rufus,* 331), the fierce, wild Norway rat (426), and a variety of other innately hostile animals including the agouti, cat, monkey, hamster, and cotton rat (see 275 for details). These normally vicious animals can be handled without gloves immediately after the operation. Lesions in a number of other brain areas will also reduce aggressive tendencies (275).

In man, the data are limited, but do exist. Ursin (398) summarizes several cases of hostility control through brain surgery. He refers to one of Sawa's patients (328) who reported that after the operation he could not get angry even if he wanted to. Lesions in the temporal lobe (297), dorsomedial thalamus (363), posterior hypothalamus (325; 327), and the anterior cingulum (390) have successfully reduced uncontrollable hostility in man. Le Beau

(233; 315) suggests, "Cingulectomy is specially indicated in intractable cases of anger, violence, aggressiveness, and permanent agitation."

FACILITATION OF CONSUMMATORY AND AGGRESSIVE BEHAVIOR BY BRAIN LESIONS

There are neurological mechanisms in the brain that prevent the manifestation of both excessive eating and aggressive behavior. When these mechanisms, located in well-defined areas of the brain, are destroyed, the individual's reaction to a particular kind of stimulus becomes excessive. Lesions in the ventromedial nucleus of the hypothalamus, for example, frequently cause the well-known syndrome of hypothalamic hyperphagia (115). Soon after recovery from surgery, the animal begins to eat voraciously, doubling or tripling its food intake and increasing its weight correspondingly. However, the animal is finicky (155) and its excessive eating response is elicited only by certain preferred taste stimuli.

Bilateral destruction of either the basal or central nucleus of the amygdala will convert a friendly, affectionate, domestic cat into an animal that will attack without provocation (425). Wheatley (417) has produced extremely vicious cats by lesioning the ventromedial hypothalamus. Increased aggressive behavior has also been produced by destruction of the septal region, frontal lobes, cingulum, and portions of the hippocampus. These aggressive responses are well directed, stimulus oriented, and are not comparable to the sham rage produced by decerebration (see 275 for specific studies).

Specific brain lesions in man will also increase hostile tendencies (407; 417).

INHIBITION OF CONSUMMATORY AND AGGRESSIVE BEHAVIOR BY BRAIN STIMULATION

Irritative scars caused by lesion experiments make the evidence difficult to interpret. However, brain stimulation experiments produce further evidence on the role of inhibitory mechanisms in the control of both eating behavior and aggressive behavior. there is considerable evidence that the types of physiological mechanisms underlying eating behavior are similar to those underlying aggressive behavior.

Eating can be inhibited by stimulation of the "satiety" center in the ventromedial hypothalamus (431). Septal stimulation can block eating behavior in the deprived monkey (91).

Brain stimulation can also block aggression without interfering with normal motor responses. Amygdaloid stimulation can block the normal mousing in cats as well as predation induced by hypothalamic stimulation (113). Stimulation of the caudate nucleus will inhibit aggressive behavior in a dominant male monkey (93). In humans, Heath (174) has reported that stimulation in the septal region immediately reduces agitated, violent psychotic behavior. The patient's behavior changes almost instantly from disorganized rage to happiness and mild euphoria. Heath indicates further that this phenomenon has been observed in a large number of patients.

INFLUENCE OF BLOOD CHEMISTRY CHANGES ON CONSUMMATORY AND AGGRESSIVE BEHAVIOR

There is a generally held theoretical conviction that eating behavior is regulated by the action of certain components in the bloodstream which, in turn, increase sensitivity in particular brain circuits. Glucose changes have been suggested as important in the short-run control of eating (259) and lipids in long-run control (213).

In light of the available evidence, it is not unreasonable to postulate a similar mechanism in the regulation of aggressive behavior. However, since there may well be various kinds of agression (275), there must also be a variety of contributing regulators. Androgens in the bloodstream are undoubtedly critical to the development of intermale aggression (38; 240; 347; 352; 397). There is recent evidence that these androgenic effects may be masked or inhibited by estrogens, at least in isolated male mice (372). Female irritability is cyclical and increases in the shrew (292) and the guinea pig (219) during estrus. Further, aggressiveness in the ovariectomized female guinea pig can be inhibited by a series of estrogen injections followed by an injection of progesterone (219).

Changes in the hormone balance in the bloodstream can also inhibit maternal aggression. The domesticated mother rat will attack and kill a frog that is put into her cage only during the period of lactation. Maternal aggressiveness can be completely abolished without interfering with the rat's care of her young if she is given a few days of oestrone therapy (118). Some of the test rats that failed to show the frog-killing response did so when injected with hydrocortisone. Hydrocortisone injections also overcame the killing inhibition produced by oestrone.

Clinical endocrinology reinforces support of the importance of blood components in the regulation of aggressive tendencies. Care must be exercised in the interpretation of these data because they are not from controlled laboratory studies. Certainly, however, the data are suggestive and can result in hypotheses which should be followed up in the laboratory.

Irritability is a frequent component of the premenstrual tension syndrome in the human female and is successfully treated by the administration of progesterone (85; 158). It has been shown that crimes of violence committed by women are related to the menstrual cycle. A study of 249 female prison inmates showed that 62 percent of the crimes of violence were committed during the premenstrual week as opposed to 2 percent at the end of the menstrual period (273). Diandrone (dehydroisoandrosterone) increases confidence in adolescents with feelings of inferiority and promotes aggressive responses (324). In patients with a history of aggressiveness, diandrone is likely to produce excessive irritability and outbursts of rage (323; 370). On the other hand, castration reduces the number of asocial acts of individuals convicted of sex crimes (170; 234), and the administration of stilboestrol, in some cases, provides dramatic control of both hypersexuality and irritable aggression (111; 323).

It is generally recognized that frustration and stress, particularly if prolonged, are likely to result in increased irritability and aggressive behavior. Frustration-induced irritability may stem from sensitization of certain brain areas by the particular hormone balance that characterizes the stress syndrome. Both the adrenal cortex and the thyroid are intimately involved in the stress syndrome, and dysfunctions of either gland result in increased irritability (76; 143).

INFLUENCE OF LEARNING ON CONSUMMATORY AND AGGRESSIVE BEHAVIOR

The influence of learning on aggressive responding has received considerable emphasis (337; 338; 343). Scott and Fredericson (343: 306) suggest that training can overcome hereditary predispositions, concluding that "training includes by far the most important group of factors which affect agonistic behavior." The implication is that aggressive behavior is set apart from other basic behaviors in some way because learning has a strong influence on it. However, learning has a strong influence on all basic behavior patterns. Psychiatrists' couches are filled with individuals who have learned hypo-, hyper-, or deviant sexual behavior. Learning also has a potent influence on consummatory behavior (429). Eating behavior reinforced by shock termination results in excessive food consumption with marked obesity (422).

Training can inhibit all consummatory behavior (241; 258). In one study, negative reinforcement in the form of sublethal doses of poison produced a complete inhibition of eating behavior with the result that the subjects (rats) starved to death (308). Since training can completely inhibit consummatory behavior and cause the death of an organism, one might conclude, as Scott and Fredericson (343) did about aggression, that training can overcome hereditary predispositions and that it includes by far the most important factors that affect consummatory behavior.

Further, while there is good evidence that all eating behavior can be completely inhibited by training, there is some doubt that training can completely inhibit all aggressive behavior. Swade and Geiger (333) conclude that the aggressive behavior that is correlated with the 6- and 14-per second positive spiking on the EEG can no more be controlled by the individual than a grand mal seizure can be controlled by an epileptic. After a study of over 1,000 cases, these authors (334: 616) characterize that form of aggressive behavior as follows: "The control by rage is so absolute that parents fear for their lives and those of others. Typical complaints are: extreme rage outbursts, larceny, arson, violent acts without motivation, sexual acts (aggressive), threats to stab, shoot, mutilate or beat, poor social adjustment (not schizophrenic), rage reactions, mutilation of animals, and total inability to accept correction or responsibility for the act."

AGGRESSION CONTROL

As Tinbergen (385) suggests, the argument concerning whether or not aggression is a drive is very much a matter of emphasis and the two theoretical positions are not as far apart as it seems. The entire argument might be purely academic and of little consequence were it not for the implications as to further research and the control of aggression. One certainly need not conclude with Scott (340) that the instinctual analysis of behavior is a complete explanation of behavior and, as such, offers no new leads for research. The term instinct has a confused history and may not be the best term. Since most authors who postulate instinctive aggression agree that it has a physiological basis (41: Chap. 1), innumerable suggestions for research emanate from this point of view. If there is an "instinctual urge to aggression," there must be a physiological basis, and that basis can be delineated experimentally. Further, there are many hypotheses to be tested to determine the specific neural and endocrine mechanisms underlying various kinds of aggressive behavior.

The theoretical position as to the determinants of aggressive behavior strongly influences the type of control measures considered. Manipulation of the internal environment is not mentioned by either Scott (338) or Hinde (188) when they deal with the problem of aggression control. Lorenz (245) certainly accepts the idea of internal impulses to aggression, but he conceives of them in terms of the rather vaguely defined energy concept. Since he also considers that "aggressive energy" is closely linked with the energy of ambition, love, and other socially acceptable attributes, he confines his recommendations for aggression control to suggestions for the redirection of "aggressive energy" and does not consider reducing aggressive tendencies per se.

The evidence presented indicates that aggressive behavior is determined by both external and internal variables, and aggressive response tendencies can be modified by learning. This provides at least three approaches to the most important problem of aggression control. The external environment can be manipulated to reduce the number of stimuli which instigate aggression; the individual can be taught to inhibit aggressive responses; and the internal environment can be manipulated directly. The fact that only the last approach will be dealt with here does not imply that the others are unimportant.

Physiological control of aggressive tendencies may be accomplished by brain stimulation, brain lesions, hormone administration, and the administration of drugs. As noted above, continuing aggressive behavior in the monkey can be blocked immediately by direct stimulation of the caudate nucleus (93). In man, direct septal stimulation transforms a violent, profane, destructive individual into one who is calm, friendly, and sociable. At the moment, very little is known about this method of control, but there seems little doubt that it is possible. How practical it will become is a matter of conjecture. Two developments could make it eminently practical: development of a method of pinpoint brain stimulation without opening the skull (387), and the discovery of a drug which selectively stimulates these nuclei. Both developments are well within the realm of possibility.

As already mentioned, selective brain lesions may reduce or eliminate aggressive behavior. The reader will recall Sawa's patient (328) who, after the operation, felt that he could not become angry if he wanted to. Currently, brain surgery is being used effectively for the control of extremely assaultive individuals.

Control of aggressive tendencies can also be achieved through the adjustment of hormone balances. Progesterone is frequently used to reduce the irritability associated with premenstrual tension (158). Maternal aggression in the rat has been controlled by the administration of oestrone (118). Stilboestrol has been used clinically to diminish irritable aggression in the male (111; 323). Further understanding of the role of hormones in aggressive behavior should lead to a rational endocrine therapy for certain kinds of aggressive behavior. Dr. Lerner's work with androgen antagonists may be particularly important (236).

Finally, drugs are a useful and practical means of altering the internal environment in order to reduce aggressive tendencies. There are a number of chemical agents that appear to be specific inhibitors of hostility and reduce aggression without appreciably affecting the individual's alertness or motor coordination. The vast literature on this topic cannot be reviewed here, but a few examples will illustrate the point. The use of Dilantin® for the control of aggressive tendencies has recently received national publicity (317). Dr. Turner (394) has presented numerous case studies demonstrating the effectiveness of this drug for that purpose and has offered a theoretical statement that may guide research on this problem. Scheckel and Boff (329) have shown that chlordiazepoxide and diazepam reduce aggressiveness in squirrel monkeys at doses that do not interfere with other behaviors. Diazepam has been used with "remarkable success" in eliminating the destructive rampages of psychotic criminals (202).

Research on drugs to control behavior is in its infancy and there is good reason to believe that the judicious use of the fruits of this research can help to control the minor, but uncomfortable, irritability of such dysfunctions as premenstrual tension as well as the major assaultive crimes of individuals afflicted with discontrol syndrome.

In summary, we must conclude that aggressive behavior is determined by an interwoven complex of internal, external, and experiential factors. The solution to the multifaceted and critical problem of the control of destructive, aggressive tendencies will be approached only when all of these factors are given adequate consideration.

® Registered trademark for diphenylhydantoin, Parke, Davis & Co., Detroit, Mich.

3

Kinds of Aggression and Their Physiological Bases

K. E. MOYER

The thesis of this paper is that there are different kinds of aggressive behavior, just as there are different kinds of consummatory behavior. Both eating and drinking can be classified as consummatory behavior. These behaviors share certain similarities in the kinds of responses and physiological mechanisms involved. It is obvious, however, that the details of the neurological and blood chemistry substrates for these two kinds of consummatory behavior are very different. Any attempt to find a single physiological basis for consummatory behavior would therefore lead to confusion and a rash of contradictory and unreproducible experiments. Just that kind of confusion has existed in much of the research on aggressive behavior. *Kinds of Aggression and Their Physiological Bases* is a first attempt to sort out the different kinds of aggression, provide operational definitions, and review what is known about the physiological substrates of each kind.

This paper was originally published in *Communications in Behavioral Biology*, Part A, Vol. 2, No. 2, August 1968, pp. 65–87, Abstract No. 08680058 (1968); Copyright 1968 by Academic Press, Inc., and is reprinted here by permission.

I particularly wish to thank James Korn and Leonard Jarrard for a critical reading of this manuscript.

The term aggression is usually applied to behavior that leads or appears to lead to the damage or destruction of some goal entity. However, the stimulus situations that elicit destructive behavior and the patterns of behavior that result in damage and destruction are so diverse that there must be a variety of physiological substrates involved. It therefore seems fruitless to search for a single physiological basis of aggression.

Several authors have suggested that aggression is not a unitary concept (47; 193; 337; 402). To date, however, there has been no systematic attempt to sort out the various kinds of aggression and indicate a reasonable basis for classification. Those are two objectives of this paper.

If, as suggested here, there are several kinds of aggression, progress in understanding the general phenomenon of aggressive behavior can be made only when the various aggressions are carefully and operationally defined. The definition phase must then be followed by research in which experimental manipulations are applied to the subjects who are then tested in a variety of situations which define the various classes of aggression. A given manipulation may very well facilitate one kind of aggression, suppress another and have no effect on a third.

This paper is particularly concerned with the physiology of aggression and will therefore attempt a review of what is known about the physiological processes involved in each class of aggressive response. Although the neural and endocrine bases of some kinds of aggression may overlap, it is proposed here that they are essentially different and that it is possible to discriminate among these physiological substrates experimentally.

There are some obvious differences in the response patterns that animals show in different aggressive-inducing situations. Several authors (190; 309; 409) have pointed out that the topography of behavior in predatory attack by the cat is quite different from aggression which has been called "affective." The former involves relatively little emotional display. The cat does not hiss or growl, but slinks close to the floor and makes a silent, deadly attack on the rat. In "affective" aggression, however, there is evidence of pronounced sympathetic arousal. The back arches, the tail fluffs out, the ears lay back against the head, the animal hisses and growls and may attack in a flurry of scratching and biting. Tinbergen (384) has said that deer use their antlers when engaged in conflict with other male deer (inter-male aggression) but use their front hooves in defense against predators. When more detailed ethological analyses have been made, response topography may become a useful method of differentiating among the various kinds of aggression. At this point, however, the observations are too limited to permit a general classification on this basis.

Types of aggression may also be differentiated on the basis of the kinds of stimulus situations that elicit destructive behavior. This is the basis for the classification system used in this paper. Aggression is generally stimulus bound, and in many classes of aggression, the stimulus situation to which the S will react with hostility is highly specific. The male mouse, for example, will attack another male, but it will not generally attack a female (343). The rat will attack a strange rat but seldom a member of its own group (30; 116). Certain rats will attack mice, but will not attack rat pups (285).

Aggression evoked by brain stimulation is also stimulus bound. Cats stimulated in the hypothalamus attack rats persistently and effectively. The attack on a dead rat, however, is less sustained and only brief transient attacks are made on a stuffed rat or a block of wood about the size of a rat (238; 409).

OPERATIONAL DEFINITIONS

I will now attempt to define several classes of aggression operationally, on the basis of the stimulus characteristics that will evoke them. This system of classification is tentative. Much more research must be directed toward the problem of distinguishing the various kinds of aggression if a classification scheme of maximum usefulness is to be achieved. However, this system is a start and can be modified later as research findings dictate. There may also be aggressive responses that do not fit neatly into any of these classifications but have been left out because they are quite species specific.

The classes of aggression defined here are: predatory, inter-male, fear-induced, irritable, territorial defense, maternal and instrumental.

Predatory Aggression

This type of aggressive behavior is evoked by the presence of a natural object of prey. Movement on the part of the prey, though not essential, increases the probability of attack. Predatory aggression is differentiated from the other classes of aggression by its relative stimulus specificity and the general irrelevance of the particular test environment. It is differentiated from inter-male and irritable aggression on the basis of the object of attack. It can be differentiated from fear-induced aggression if the S is given an opportunity to escape from the stimulus object. Territorial defense and maternal aggression are excluded if the test is conducted away from the animal's home territory and in the absence of young to be protected.

Inter-Male Aggression

The most potent releaser of this aggressive response in most species is the presence of a male conspecific to which the attacker has not become habituated. The general environment in which the stimulus is presented is not particularly important and the attack is made without provocation on the part of the victim. Inter-male aggression is differentiated from the other classes on the same basis as indicated for predatory aggression.

Fear-Induced Aggression

In its purest form, fear-induced aggression is always preceded by attempts to escape. Thus, one of the components of the stimulus situation eliciting fear-induced aggression is a degree of confinement in which the defensive animal is cornered and is unable to escape. In that situation, the animal turns and attacks the attacker.

A second component of the stimulus situation is, of course, the presence of some threatening agent. This type of aggression is differentiated from all others in that it is always preceded by escape attempts.

Irritable Aggression

The stimulus situation that evokes an irritable aggression response is the presence of any attackable organism or object. The range of stimuli that will elicit irritable aggression is extremely broad and may involve inanimate as well as animate objects. The epitome of this type of aggression is usually described as anger or rage. The fact that the general environment is not relevant to the evocation of irritable aggression differentiates it from territorial defense and maternal aggression. Irritable aggression is differentiated from fear-induced aggression in that it is not preceded by attempts to escape and therefore does not involve a "fear" component. Irritable aggression is differentiated from predatory and inter-male aggression by its inclusiveness. The animal showing irritable aggression will attack prey, other males and many other available stimuli. Predatory attack and inter-male attack, however, are limited to the relevant objects.

Territorial Defense

In this case, the stimulus situation involves an area in which the animal has established itself and an intruder. A conspecific is most likely to be attacked but some species will attack an intruder of any type. The stimulus of the territory is essential to this class of aggression and differentiates it from other types. The attack is provoked simply by the presence of the other animal in the territory and the probability of attack decreases as the attacking subject gets farther from its own territory.

Maternal Aggression

In most mammalian species, this type of aggression is the particular province of the female. The stimulus situation involves the proximity of some threatening agent to the young of that particular female. Both the young and the threatening agent as part of the necessary stimulus complex distinguish this class of aggression from the others. As the mother gets farther from the young, the tendency toward aggression decreases.

Instrumental Aggression

Any of the above classes of aggression may result in a change in environment that constitutes a reinforcement for the animal and the probability that the aggressive behavior will occur in a similar situation. Feshback (124) considers this position in detail. Instrumental aggression is a learned response and the stimulus situation that evokes it may be any of those described above.

For the sake of completeness, it should at least be mentioned that sex-related aggression is probably also a class of aggression. These are the aggressive responses elicited by the same stimuli that produce the sexual response. The existence of sex-related violence is obvious to anyone who reads the newspaper, but very little is known about the variables of which it is a function. There is some experimental evidence to show that sexual and aggressive motivation are related (26). Since little more is known about this class of aggression, it will not be discussed further.

The above classes of aggression are certainly not mutually exclusive. It is entirely possible, in the real world, that a particular instance of aggression may involve more than one of the above classes. Thus, irritable aggression may augment inter-male aggression, thereby increasing the intensity of the aggressive response. The position taken here, however, is that there are different neural and endocrine bases for each of the above aggression classes and the manipulation of the physiological variables will inhibit or facilitate the classes of aggression differentially. Also, our understanding of the interactions among these various classes of aggression should be enhanced as we understand the details of the neural and endocrine bases. The physiology of the above classes of aggression will now be reviewed.

Generalizations will be made in the discussion below, but it should be recognized that these generalizations do not necessarily apply to all species since there is a considerable amount of interspecies variability.

PHYSIOLOGICAL BASES

Predatory Aggression

Predatory responses are aggressive in that they lead to the injury or destruction of the prey. Aside from that, predatory aggression has little in common with the other classes of aggression listed above (71; 96). The physiological basis of predatory aggression in mammals has been most extensively studied in the cat and the rat, and experimental evidence is rapidly accumulating to indicate that the neurological basis of this kind of aggression is distinct from that of other kinds.

Wasman and Flynn (409) and Egger and Flynn (113) differentiate qualitatively between predatory attack and "affective attack" in the cat. If the animal is stimulated in the area of the lateral hypothalamus, it will ignore the experimenter and attack a rat. However, if stimulated in the medial hypothalamus, the cat will ignore a rat and attempt to attack the experimenter. They also report that the topography of the two types of response is different in that predatory attack involves only "minimal signs indicative of feline rage." A number of other studies have also shown that stimulation of the lateral hypothalamus of the cat produces predatory aggression (190; 238; 250; 309; 409). Stimulation of the rat in the lateral hypothalamus does not induce a non-killer to attack a mouse but it does reduce the killing latency of a natural killer (208).[1] In the cat, predatory attack induced by hypothalamic stimulation is augmented by the simultaneous activation of the midbrain reticular formation either through direct elec-

---

[1] Since this paper was written, there have been several demonstrations of the induction of predatory behavior in the non-predatory rat. King and Hoebel (218) have induced mouse killing in a certain percentage of non-mouse killers by electrical stimulation of the lateral hypothalamus. Bandler (22; 24) has reported a reproducible mouse killing in a non-killer with the application of crystalline carbachol directly to the lateral hypothalamus, as have Smith, King and Hoebel (355). Frog killing can be facilitated by either electrical (104) or chemical stimulation of the lateral hypothalamus (22; 24). However, the same lateral hypothalamic stimulation that facilitates frog killing rarely elicits mouse killing in a non-mouse killer. DeSisto and Huston (104) have, in fact, shown that the same hypothalamic stimulation which facilitates frog killing will cause the rat to bite objects in its cage while completely ignoring an available mouse.

trical stimulation or by the administration of amphetamine (349; 350).

The role of the amygdala in predatory aggression will be discussed later, but interruption of the fibers running between the amygdala and the hypothalamus virtually eliminates that behavior (206). There is also evidence that the hypothalamic predatory system is inhibited by portions of the prepyriform cortex, the lateral olfactory stria (205), the olfactory bulbs (205), and particular stimulation points in the midbrain (350).

All types of aggression, including predatory, are dramatically reduced by lesions in the lateral portion of the upper midbrain. These cats show a variety of sensory defects and the reduction in aggressive tendencies seems due primarily to the animal's inability to receive and interpret sensory input (364).

Lesions of the frontal lobes will induce mouse killing in some non-killer rats (203). However, the topography of this lesion-induced killing appears to differ from normal mouse killing and may involve irritable aggression instead of, or in addition to, predatory aggression. The attack is particularly ferocious and involves continued biting after the mouse has been killed. Unfortunately, Karli did not test the aggressiveness of these rats against other stimulus objects.

Little is known about the endocrine basis of predatory aggression. Testosterone, which is of considerable importance in inter-male aggression (38; 229), has relatively little influence on predatory aggression. Castration and subsequent adrenalectomy does not reduce the tendency for killer rats to kill mice and the administration of testosterone to non-killers does not increase the tendency to kill (204). However, castration at an early age reduces the percentage of non-killing rats that can be converted to killers by an olfactory lobe ablation. The killing response may then be activated in these operated animals by testosterone administration (108).[2]

There appears to be a relationship between the physiological status that produces eating behavior and that which produces predatory aggression but the relationship is not yet clear. Eating

---

[2] Recent evidence from our own laboratory seems to indicate that the aggressive behavior resulting from olfactory ablation is irritable, rather than predatory, aggression. See the paper by Bernstein and Moyer (45).

and predatory attack can both be induced by stimulation of the same area of the lateral hypothalamus (190). However, more intense stimulation is required to induce aggression than to induce eating. Thus, the same neurones are not necessarily involved. The more intense stimulation may spread and activate additional neurones.

The Hutchinson and Renfrew study demonstrates that there is an anatomical proximity for the predatory and eating response patterns, but there is evidence that predatory behavior is not based on hunger. Bilateral lesions in the lateral hypothalamus that abolish feeding behavior in the rat only temporarily inhibit predatory aggression (206). It has also been shown that non-killer rats will not kill mice even though they are starved (203). Similar results have been reported by Clark (73) for the predatory mouse Onychomys. However, either cyclic food deprivation (416) or competition over food (180; 181) tends to increase the percentage of rats that kill mice.

Hunger is evidently not essential for the manifestation of predatory behavior since many predators will continue to kill long after their capacity to eat the prey has been exhausted and will kill even when satiated. However, it is possible that the same factors that influence eating behavior influence predatory behavior. Food deprivation in the killer or in the hypothalamically stimulated predatory animal may shorten the killing latency or lower the required stimulation threshold. This hypothesis has not yet been experimentally tested.

Some work has been done on the definition of the stimulus situation that will elicit predatory aggression. Rats that kill mice will not generally kill rat pups (285). The odor of the pups has an inhibitory effect on the predatory behavior (282). In cats that will promptly attack rats during stimulation of the lateral hypothalamus, the intensity and persistence of attack decreases as the dissimilarity of the stimulus object and a rat is increased. The cats seldom attacked a styrofoam or foam rubber block and would make only half-hearted attacks on a toy dog or a stuffed rat (238). The persistence of the attack appears to be related to the type of sensory feedback derived from the region of the mouth. Stimulation of particular areas of the hypothalamus produces a sensory field in the muzzle area of the cat that varies in size in proportion to the intensity of the stimulation. When this sensitized muzzle area is stimulated, there is a resultant opening of the mouth (249). This pioneer study helps to define the mechanisms underlying the relatively specific stimulus control of aggressive responses. MacDonnell and Flynn (250) also have specified the particular senses involved in the cat's ability to locate and bite the rat under the influence of hypothalamic stimulation. Olfaction plays little role, but vision and tactile cues from the forepaws and snout are essential.

In summary, the evidence seems to lead to the conclusion that predatory aggression can be differentiated from other forms of aggression on the basis of both the topography of the response and the relatively specific stimulus situation that will elicit the response. The physiological mechanisms underlying predatory aggression also appear to be different from those underlying other types of aggression.

Inter-Male Aggression

Inter-male aggression is elicited by a very specific pattern of stimulation and, therefore, should probably be considered as a separate class of aggression. In some species, the male odor appears to be the primary eliciting stimulus (30; 117). Inter-male aggression in the mouse is eliminated by removal of the olfactory bulbs and is drastically reduced if the animal's natural odor is masked by an artificial scent (314). Vision, however, may not be critical to this response (88). Males that have been together for some time seldom fight (30; 156; 343). This may be the result of an habituation to the odors of the other animals or to inhibitions learned during the formation of the social hierarchy. Animals may learn, because of the punishment of defeat, to respond to the cues of dominant individuals with a submissive posture. The submissive posture of a conspecific inhibits aggressive behavior on the part of an opponent. This inhibition of aggression by particular postures is unique to inter-male aggression. Aggression-inhibiting postures of the rat have been described in detail (30; 347) as have those of other species (87; 116; 245; 256).

Androgens appear to be critical to the manifestation of aggressive behavior in males. Inter-male aggression does not appear in either mice (133) or rats (347) until after sexual maturity. However, androgens have little influence on female behavior. Testosterone administered to castrated mice results in a dramatic increase in the fighting of males but not of females (389). Testosterone injections given to immature mice increase the aggressive behavior of males (240) but not of females (239). There have been reports of increases in irritability of females given androgens, but these are difficult to evaluate because, in general, they have been unsystematic observations made in connection with studies conducted for other purposes (20; 35; 189).

Mice castrated in prepuberty do not develop inter-male aggression. When testosterone pellets are implanted in the same mice, the aggressiveness appears. However, it disappears when the pellets are removed (38). Similar results have been reported by others (36; 46; 48; 397).

Aggressiveness in rats and mice can be increased by prolonged isolation. This aggressive behavior is complex but probably involves inter-male aggression. Isolation-induced aggression is prevented either by castration or hypophysectomy prior to isolation. It is restored by testosterone injections. Adrenalectomy has little effect. Thyroxine tends to shorten the period of isolation required to produce aggressiveness but thiouracil lengthens it (353; 433).

Many experiments involving the study of neurological manipulations on dominance relationships have been conducted. It is difficult to isolate the neurological basis of inter-male aggression from these studies because the prior social experience influences the effect of the experimental manipulations. It has been shown, for example, that septal lesions enhance the aggressiveness of a dominant hamster. However, the same lesions increase the submissiveness of a submissive hamster (375). In the socially naive hamster however, septal lesions specifically facilitate inter-male aggression. Septal hamsters, unlike septal rats, do not show hyperemotionality and are not aggressive toward human handlers (357; 358).

Chemical stimulation of the septal area in the naive hamster indicates that submissive behavior is increased by catacholaminergic stimulation while inter-male aggression is increased by catacholamine antagonists. Cholinergic stimulation decreases aggression without increasing submissive responses, and an anticholinergic agent increases aggressiveness (356).

In summary, inter-male aggression appears to be elicited by a relatively narrow range of sensory stimuli and is inhibited by specific sensory stimuli. It is particularly dependent on the male hormone for its manifestation. The evidence indicates that intermale aggression can be characterized as a relatively unique class that can be differentiated from other classes of aggression on a variety of dimensions.

Fear-Induced Aggression

Conjecture about the physiological basis of fear-induced aggression must be tentative at best. The limited number of conditions in which animals are usually studied makes it difficult to determine from published reports whether the aggression being studied is fear-induced or irritable because it is frequently not possible to determine whether the animal would have tried to escape prior to developing aggressive tendencies had the opportunity been available. Both of these kinds of aggression have strong affective components that lead to further confusion between them.

Since fear-induced aggression is always preceded by escape attempts, any experimental manipulation that reduces the number of stimuli from which the animal tends to escape should also reduce the tendency to that particular kind of aggressive behavior. This seems to account for part, although not all, of the reduction in aggressiveness in animals with amygdaloid lesions. A number of studies have shown that fear reactions (escape tendencies) are drastically reduced in a variety of animals after amygdalectomy; this is true of the monkey (320; 331), the cat (330; 331; 348), and the wild Norway rat (203; 425), as well as of the lynx and agouti (331). Conditioned fear reactions learned prior to the operation extinguish more rapidly in amygdalectomized monkeys than they do in control-operated animals (412). The amygdala and fear-induced aggression will be discussed in more detail later.

Fear-induced aggression has also been reduced in monkeys (392) and in phalangers (4) by lesions in the temporal lobe not involving the amygdala.

The cingulate gyrus also appears to be involved in fear-induced aggression. Anterior cingulectomy in the monkey produces a temporary reduction in fear and an increase in docility (146; 211; 408). These animals are variously described as being tame, uncompetitive, socially indifferent, and having lost their shyness of man. Stimulation in the same region, however, makes monkeys anxious and irritable (13). Brain lesions may also facilitate fear-induced aggression. Septal lesions in the rat cause hyperemotionality, including increased escape tendencies and aggressive behavior (54; 55; 215; 216). The threshold for escape and the threshold for aggression in a social situation are both lowered by septal ablations (61; 63). However, it is not clear in these studies whether the aggressive behavior is the result of blocking the escape response.

The hypothalamus is involved in both fear-induced aggression and irritable aggression but the details are not yet clear. According to Kling & Hutt (221), lesions in the ventromedial hypothalamus in cats result in aggression only if escape is blocked. Wheatley, however, has shown that these lesions may result in extreme savageness without escape tendencies (417). Stimulation in the anterior hypothalamus results in aggression only in the cornered cats, whereas stimulation of the ventromedial hypothalamus produces rage that is uncontaminated by escape tendencies (432). It is evident that attempts to separate the functions of such a very small and functionally congested area as the hypothalamus will cause confusion. Romaniuk (313) indicates that aggression and escape are organized in the hypothalamus on a dorsal-ventral basis. He has found that stimulation of the ventral part of the medial hypothalamus produces aggression in the cat whereas stimulation of the dorsal part of the medial hypothalamus produces an attempt to escape. He did not, however, corner the escaping animals to determine whether they would become aggressive.

A large number of studies have shown that stimulation of various brain areas results in escape behavior on the part of the subject. These studies have been well summarized in a variety of reviews (5; 53; 57; 122; 185) and need not be reviewed in detail here. In general, however, it is not possible to determine whether these escape behaviors would have caused aggression if the subject had been cornered or prevented from escaping.

Extreme fear does not always produce aggression, of course. The animal may continue to cower, may assume submissive postures, may freeze, may faint, or may enter a cataleptic state. It is not safe to assume that brain stimulation that produces escape behavior will always cause fear-induced aggression. Future research is needed to resolve this problem. In order to study the neurological basis of this particular kind of aggression, it is necessary to locate brain areas that will elicit escape behavior on stimulation, stimulate the behavior, permit the animal to escape, and then continue to harass or threaten it to determine whether the resulting response will be aggressive.

Essentially, nothing is known about the endocrine basis of fear-induced aggression. It seems likely, however, that certain endocrine balances might sensitize the brain areas that control this type of response to external stimulation. A combined approach using brain stimulation and peripheral endocrine manipulation may turn out to be a sensitive tool for the investigation of this problem. When we locate brain areas that produce escape behavior followed by fear-induced aggression, endocrine manipulations can be undertaken to determine whether the involved brain areas are sensitized or desensitized by the endocrine changes.

In summary, it appears that the stimulus situation that produces fear-induced aggression can be readily differentiated from the stimulus that produces other types of aggression. Although little research has been directed specifically toward this problem, evidence indicates that the neurological basis of this class of aggression is different from that of predatory aggression and that further research will differentiate it from irritable aggression as well as from other types. Little is known about the endocrine basis of this type of aggression.

Irritable Aggression

In its pure form, irritable aggression involves attack without attempts to escape from the object being attacked. The most extreme form of irritable aggression is exemplified by destructive "uncontrollable rage" directed against either animate or inanimate objects. In less extreme forms, it may involve only "annoyance" or half-hearted attack.

The tendency to irritable aggression is increased by several antecedent factors.

Frustration has classically been cited as one of the major causes of this class of aggressive behavior (110). Two detailed reviews, pro (41) and con (66), deal with this concept in detail.

Therefore, only two recent studies which indicate this relationship are mentioned. Thompson and Bloom (381) showed that rats frustrated by non-reward during the first extinction session attacked other rats with sufficient severity to produce lacerations. Pigeons will attack a stuffed pigeon during extinction periods (16).

Although it is apparently not true for all species (145; 360), it is generally true that irritable aggression is increased as any of the drive states are increased. This occurs during competition for food (336) as well as under non-competitive conditions (89). Fatigue increases irritability in humans (382, quoted in 77). Sleep deprivation increases verbal hostility in man (232). The drive state produced by morphine withdrawal increases aggressive behavior in addicted rats (50).

An extensive series of studies by Azrin, Hutchinson, Ulrich and their collaborators have shown that irritable aggression can be induced in a variety of species by aversive stimulation. This "pain-induced aggression" is general in regard to the object of attack and may involve the same or different sex or species, or even inanimate objects. This research has been well summarized by Ulrich (395).

It appears that irritability and thus the tendency to irritable aggression is increased by any stressor. Whether all these antecedent causes of irritable aggression can be subsumed under the general term "frustration," as argued by Berkowitz (41), is a semantic problem.

As indicated in the discussion of fear-induced aggression, it is frequently difficult to determine from experiments designed to deal with other problems what particular kind of aggression is being observed. It is therefore not possible to delineate the neurological basis of irritable aggression with any confidence. There are, however, a number of experiments from which tentative conclusions may be drawn. In the interpretation of these studies, it is necessary to keep in mind the studies on aggression induced by aversive stimulation (395). It is always possible that a given experimental manipulation may activate neuronal circuits comparable to those that produce the conscious experience of pain when activated in man. Thus, the aggression produced may be secondary to the activation of "pain" circuits. Delgado (96: 679) has considered this problem in some detail and concludes that "the cerebral mechanisms for the perception of pain and for aggressive behavior have a different anatomical and physiological organization . . ." This conclusion is based on a number of experiments showing that animals stimulated in certain brain areas make responses similar to those made when they are subjected to external aversive stimulation. Aggression does not necessarily follow brain stimulation in those areas. Stimulation in other areas elicits aggressive behavior that is not accompanied by behavior resembling response evoked by aversive stimulation. However, whether the animals feel pain or anger can never be more than conjecture.

Several investigators have reported aggressive behavior with evidence of considerable sympathetic arousal on stimulation of the ventromedial hypothalamus (VMH), thus implicating this brain area in irritable aggression. The stimulated animal may attack either the experimenter or another animal (2; 150; 286; 350; 410; 432).

Occasionally, attacks on a "hallucination" during VMH stimulation have been reported (57; 432). However, the majority of evidence indicates that aggressive responses are stimulus bound and that some stimuli are preferred. A live rat is preferred to a dead one and attacks on a stuffed rat or toy dog are not sustained (409). In the absence of an object for attack, only pupillary dilation and slight snarling occur during stimulation (286).

Irritable aggression produced by VMH stimulation is enhanced by simultaneous stimulation in the midbrain reticular formation as is predatory aggression produced by lateral hypothalamic stimulation (350). There are also areas in the midbrain that, when stimulated alone, result in irritable aggression (96; 354).

As noted, irritability without escape tendencies is produced in many animals by VMH lesions (11; 151; 192; 200; 260; 417). Irritable aggression has also been reported in humans with tumors in the hypothalamic regions (407; 417). Whether the hyperirritability produced by VMH lesions is due to irritative scar tissue, "denervations sensitivity" (150), or because of the interruption of a suppressor circuit cannot as yet be determined. However, cats made "savage" by VMH lesions were again made docile by lesions in the midbrain, specifically in the medial lemniscus and the spinothalamic tracts, or in the central gray. In the latter case, however, the docility was temporary (151; 200).

The cingulum is involved in aggressive behavior but there are species differences. Irritable aggression is increased in cats by either stimulation or lesions in the cingulum (13; 211; 212). An increase in aggression as the result of cingulectomy may have an irritative focus. Cingulate lesions also produce irritable aggression in dogs. This irritability may be caused by hypersensitivity to tactile stimulation (58). Cingulectomy reduces fear in monkeys and makes them more docile (211). Cingulectomy has been used to treat uncontrollable violence in man. Although these patients are more easily irritated after the operation, their outbursts are milder and less sustained (233; 390; 418).

The amygdala is involved in the neural circuitry for several kinds of aggressive behavior and the effects of stimulation and lesions operate through the hypothalamus and midbrain. The details of the relationships among the various brain levels and the different kinds of aggression remain to be worked out, although beginnings have been made (114; 123). There have been some conflicting reports and some indications of species differences, but studies on the amygdala exemplify the different neurological bases of various kinds of aggressive behavior and support the contention that it is possible to facilitate one kind of aggression and suppress another with the same manipulation. It would seem, for example, that stimulation of an area in the lateral portion of the basal nucleus of the amygdala of the cat would facilitate fear-induced aggression but inhibit both predatory and irritable aggression.

Early studies showed that total bilateral amygdalectomy raised the threshold for at least three different kinds of aggressive behavior. Irritable aggression is dramatically reduced. Amygdalectomized cats do not act aggressively even when suspended by their tails or generally roughed up (330). Amygdalectomy also eliminates predatory aggression in the cat (373) and in the rat (425). Fear reactions (escape tendencies) are also reduced by amygdalectomy in a variety of animals with a consequent reduction in fear-induced aggressive behavior. This is true of the monkey (320; 330; 331; 348), and the wild Norway rat (203; 425), as well as the lynx and agouti (331).

Some reports of increases in irritable aggression after amygdalectomy (27; 330) lead to confusion about the role of the amygdala in aggressive behavior. More recent research involving the manipulation of specific amygdaloid nuclei (n.) has helped clarify the situation. Some of these research results are summarized in Figure 3-1.

Stimulation of the central n. (F. in Figure 3-1) results in fear and escape responses in the dog (130) and cat (13; 425). The cat will escape if it is possible but becomes aggressive when cornered. Its reaction to stimulation in the basal nuclei (D. and E.) is similar. Fonberg (130), however, has reported that stimulation of the more ventral portion of the basal and lateral n. results in fear inhibition of dogs.

Lesions in the central n. produce irritable aggression in cats (425) and in dogs (130). The cat will cross the room in order to find another cat to attack. The dog does not attack spontaneously, but shows great irritability to normal restraints and once started in a rage response becomes more and more wild exhibiting what Fonberg calls an avalanche syndrome. Both Woods and Fonberg have suggested that the central n. may have inhibitory functions that release aggressive behavior when it is lesioned.

Stimulation of the medial nucleus (G.) seems to cause irritable aggression without escape tendencies in both the cat and the dog. Since the cat was tested without a particular object of attack, the results are somewhat difficult to interpret, but the responses included hissing, growling, claw extention and pupillary dilation (251). Lesions in this same general area in the dog produce tameness (130), while stimulation of the same area in the dog causes ferocity. Fonberg refers to the reaction as defensive, but makes no mention of escape tendencies.

In general, experiments conducted by Ursin and Kaada (401), using stimulation in cats, support the findings listed above but seem to show more overlap of irritable and fear-induced aggression, particularly in the central n. (F.). Their general conclusions were that fear reactions are located in the rostral part of the lateral nucleus and the central nucleus and anger reactions lie in the more ventromedial and caudal parts of the amygdala. Ursin's (399) lesion experiments have, in general, supported those findings and clearly show that fear and anger reactions are anatomically separable. Conversely, Allikmets (7) was unable to differentiate among the amygdaloid nuclei that produced fear and anger reactions on electrical stimulation. He suggested that the reaction to stimulation

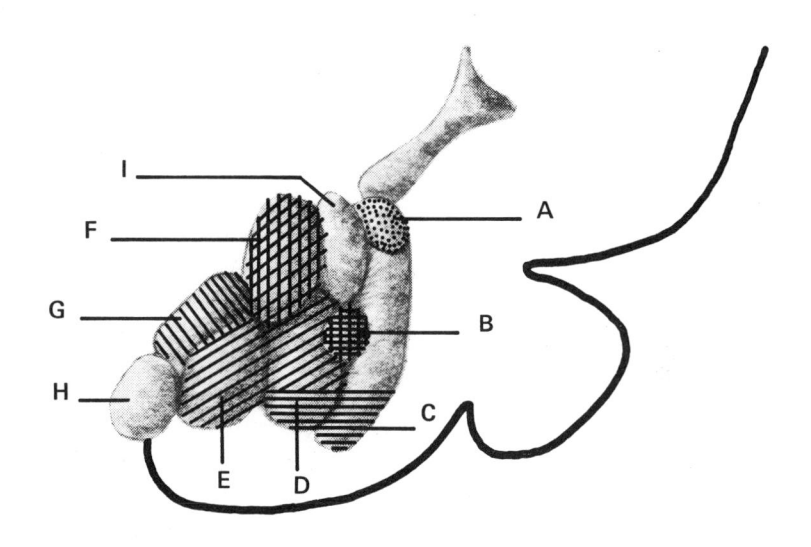

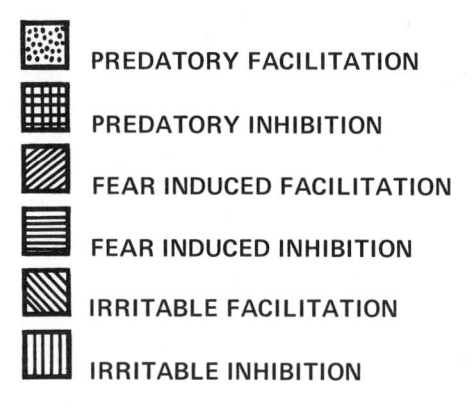

FIGURE 3-1

Schematic of the nuclei of the amygdala associated with different kinds of aggression (explanation in text). A.—dorsal portion of lateral n., B.—medial part of lateral n. and lateral part of basal n., C.—lateral n., D. and E.—basal n., F.—central n., G.—medial n., H.—cortical n., I.—putamen central amygdaloid complex.

depended on the individual differences in the cats. Docile cats showed fear while the resistive ones showed signs of strong aggression.

Predatory aggression in the cat produced by stimulation of the lateral hypothalamus is enhanced by stimulation of the dorsal portion of the lateral nucleus of the amygdala (A.). The same response is inhibited by stimulation of the medial part of the lateral n. and the lateral part of the basal n. (B.) (113). Lesions of the suppressor areas above produce response facilitation on hypothalamic stimulation (114). Killer rats with ablation of the central nucleus completely lose the tendency to kill mice, indicating that predatory aggression is facilitated there (207). This central n. control is conveyed to the lower brain areas through the ventral amygdalofugal system (405). Mouse killing by rats is also inhibited by amygdaloid stimulation, but this appears to be a generalized motor inhibition and is not restricted to particular nuclei (208).

Interpretation of the above findings must remain tentative until further research identifies the types of aggression and tests for them specifically while manipulating the particular amygdaloid nuclei. It does not appear possible to reconcile the results of all of the studies done on the amygdala, but several points seem to stand out. Fear-induced, irritable, and predatory aggression are probably controlled by separate but overlapping anatomical areas. In general, fear-induced aggression originates mainly in the dorsal, lateral and rostral areas, whereas irritable aggression resides in the ventral, medial and caudal regions. Predatory aggression control is located in the more dorsal portion of the amygdala.

Results of research by Fonberg (130), Woods (425) and Egger and Flynn (114) suggest the likelihood that a portion of the amygdaloid area controlling fear also has inhibitory functions in relation to the irritable and predatory areas. There is no indication at the moment whether inhibition acts through the facilitating areas of the amygdala or through the lower brain areas.

Irritable aggression has seldom been produced in man by stimulation of the temporal region (152; 398). However, one case of clear-cut irritable aggression in the human is described in some detail by King (217). When stimulated with a current of 5 ma. by means of an electrode implanted in the amygdaloid region, the patient became angry, verbally hostile and threatened to strike the experimenter. When the current was reduced or turned off, she became mild mannered and apologetic for her aggressive behavior.

Evidently, a number of other brain areas are involved in the neural circuitry of irritable aggression, but considerably more research is needed before it will be possible to understand the interrelations among these areas. Hippocampal lesions increase the aggressiveness of cats toward conspecifics and toward the experimenter (156). That this result may be due to irritative effects of the lesions is supported by the finding that the aggressiveness decreases over time, and at least one study indicates that stimulation of the rostral hippocampus by means of acetylocholine injection produces irritable aggression (251). Irritable aggression is also produced by stimulation of the following brain areas of the monkey: the central gray, posteroventral nucleus of the thalamus (94), Forel's field, midline thalamus (96), the superior colliculus (92) and the tip of the temporal lobe (12; 13).

Irritable aggression can be inhibited by the stimulation of several brain areas but only a limited amount of work has been done in this area. Stimulation at some points in the head of the caudate nucleus reduces aggressive behavior in the monkey (91; 93) and stimulation of certain areas of the midbrain suppresses attack induced by hypothalamic stimulation in the cat (350). Heath (174) reports that stimulation in the septal area in humans produces an immediate change from psychotic disorganized rage to happiness and mild euphoria.

There is evidence that both the endocrine and the nervous system are involved in the control of irritable aggression but little is known about interactions between the two. In one study, it was shown that castration controlled both the hypersexuality and the aggressive behavior of amygdalectomized cats (330). These same experimenters reported a drastic increase in irritable aggression in two docile, spayed, but otherwise normal female cats after administration of daily doses of diethylstilbestrol. However, this finding has never been replicated. Although there are wide individual differences, some normally docile cats become vicious during estrus and may snarl, spit and strike at a male introduced into the cage (156).

Androgenic hormones appear to play a role in irritable aggression. It is well known that castration reduces this type of behavior in domestic animals such as the bull, but there has been little systematic study of the problem. Hutchinson, Ulrich and Azrin (191) found that castration reduced, but did not eliminate, irritable aggression produced in rats by foot shock. It is possible that amygdalectomy produces a reduction in aggression through the endocrine system. A number of studies have shown that amygdalectomy produces testicular atrophy and thus the output of androgenic hormones (152). There is, however, no work that bears directly on this hypothesis.

The literature on the effect of population density on the pituitary-adrenal axis has been well summarized (72; 161; 379). Increased adrenal weight and, evidently, increased adrenal function covary with increased irritable aggression under the pressure of greater population density. The causal relationship among these variables is not yet clear. Fighting is a stressor and must, therefore, influence endocrine changes. Thus, many of the glandular changes that occur are likely to be the result of fighting, as suggested by Scott (341). It also seems likely, however, that the hormonal changes resulting from stress sensitize the brain areas that are related to irritable aggression. This hypothesis, however, has not been tested experimentally.

There are a number of suggestions from clinical endocrinology that implicate endocrine mechanisms in irritable aggression. It seems that irritability may result from any significant disturbance of the endocrine balance (303). Irritability is increased by hypo- and hyperfunction of the adrenal cortex (76) as well as by hypo- and hyperthyroid states (143).

Diandrone (dehydro-isoandrosterone) has been shown to increase confidence in adolescents with feelings of inferiority and to promote aggressive responses (324). In patients with a history of aggressiveness, diandrone is likely to produce excessive irritability and outbursts of rage (323; 370). On the other hand, castration has been shown to reduce the asocial acts of individuals convicted of sex crimes (170; 234 are representative of a large number of studies). It has also been shown clinically that, in some cases, administration of stilbestrol provides dramatic control of both hypersexuality and irritable aggression (111; 323).

It is well documented that irritability is a part of the premenstrual syndrome (85). A study of female prisoners revealed that 62 percent of crimes of violence were committed in the premenstrual week, and that behavior in the institution during the premenstrual period was improved by B complex and ammonium chloride therapy (273).

The above studies are, of course, clinical in nature, but they do serve to suggest hypotheses which can be tested in the laboratory.

Funkenstein, King and Drolette (135), have offered the interesting hypothesis that the hormone noradrenaline is involved in the "anger out" response, which would seem to be irritable aggression as it is used in this paper. Except for one study, however, there is little evidence to support the proposition that there is a causal relationship between norepinephrine and aggression. Marrone, Pray and Bridges (257) have shown that addition of norepinephrine into an aquarium containing Betta splendens produces significant increases in the threat display of males. Baenninger, however (personal communication), indicates that if a mirror or conspecific is present when either adrenalin or noradrenalin is placed in the aquarium, aggressive displays by the Betta are suppressed. Further research on this problem with higher organisms is certainly in order.

In summary, irritable aggression can be reasonably differentiated from the other classes of aggression discussed. States of the organism that are sufficient to produce it are frustration, increase in drive, and pain. The ventromedial hypothalamus and the medial nucleus of the amygdala are particularly involved as a part of the neurological basis of this class of aggression, although stimulation and lesions in other areas of the brain have also produced irritable aggressive behavior. It can also be inhibited by brain stimulation and lesions. Although the endocrine experiments do not provide clear-cut answers, there is little doubt that a variety of endocrine dysfunctions alter the organism's tendencies to irritable aggression.

Territorial Aggression

Relatively little space will be devoted to this class of aggression because virtually nothing is known about the physiology involved. Reviews of the concept of territoriality (14; 69; 70) indicate that a large number of species will behave aggressively toward any unfamiliar intruder who enters a more or less well defined territory in which the organism has established itself. The aggression appears to be specific to the stimulus situation that involves the territory and as the animal gets farther from the territory, the probability of aggression decreases. In the few studies done on the physiology of this problem (unfortunately none on mammals), it has been shown that the gonadal hormones may be involved in this response, but even that is not well established. Testosterone given to ring doves causes them to enlarge their territories (39) but gonadectomy does not affect the territorial defense of pigeons (68; 70). Furthermore, in many species, territorial aggression is not restricted to the male.

Maternal Aggression

Although many animals are capable of intense aggression in defense of the young (162), little is known about the physiology of this class of aggression. Incidental observations have indicated that female aggression increases during lactation (343), but systematic investigations of this phenomenon are rare. In one study, it was shown that a female albino rat will kill a frog placed in its cage only if the rat is lactating. The frog-killing response is not apparent in the male, in the non-lactating female, or in the lactating female who is separated from her litter. This maternal aggression can be suppressed by three days of treatment with oestrone, which does not appear to decrease lactation. If hydrocortisone is administered to lactating rats that are relatively non-aggressive, the maternal aggression is increased after three or four days of treatment (118).[3] There is some indication that maternal aggression in the lactating rat may be abolished by lesions in the amygdala, the septum or the pyriform area (244).

It is possible that the hormonal changes accompanying delivery and lactation serve merely to increase the generalized irritability of the female. The limited observations so far reported, however, seem to indicate that the stimulus of the young is a significant contributor to the aggressive response. It is on that basis

---

[3] We have been unable to replicate any aspect of this study. See the paper by Revlis & Moyer (306).

that maternal aggression is here designated as a separate class of aggression. Further research will have to determine the validity of this hypothesis.

Instrumental Aggression

This class of aggression does not have a particular definable physiological basis, except as learning and reinforcement have a physiological basis. It consists merely of an increase in the tendency of an organism to engage in destructive behavior in a particular situation because that behavior has been reinforced in the past (124). If the particular situation involves another animal, the cue complex of that animal tends to elicit an aggressive response. On this basis, over a period of time, dominance hierarchies will develop. In some species, each animal in a group tends to respond to each other animal in an aggressive or submissive manner. Thus, there will be a large habit component in the interanimal interactions in an established dominance hierarchy. Any study of the physiological basis of aggression that uses changes in the dominance hierarchy as a dependent variable must take into consideration the influence of habit factors and the kinds of cues presented to the experimental subject. This interaction of habit factors and physiological changes has been well demonstrated in a series of experiments in Bunnell's laboratory (60; 62; 357; 358) and by Delgado (94).

Inasmuch as this paper is primarily concerned with the physiological basis of aggression, the problem of learned aggression and the vast literature on dominance will not be elaborated here. Guhl (161) has done an extensive review of the literature relating to hormones and dominance.

Interactions among the Classes of Aggression

To clarify the underlying physiological bases of aggression, the discussions above have dealt with the classes of aggression in their pure form as much as possible. There is every reason to believe, however, that the different kinds of aggression interact with each other, and differentially with other drive states. For example, in an excellent paper by Baenninger (18), it was shown that a learned fear response and pain have a differential effect on predatory aggression in the rat. A conditioned emotional response was developed in mouse-killing rats by giving them tone-shock trials. Testing rats in the presence of a mouse showed that the conditioned stimulus of the tone inhibited mouse killing, but the unconditioned stimulus of shock overcame the inhibition and produced killing. This appears to be the interaction of predatory and irritable aggression.

Since the classes of aggression have not previously been systematically sorted out, little is actually known about the interactions among them. Such understanding can only come from further research in which the behaviors being dealt with are carefully and operationally defined.

It is trite to say that more research is needed. More research is always needed. In this case, however, more research is needed soon. Aggressive behavior is one of the critical problems facing man. Whether it is the collective aggressive tendencies that lead nations to war or the irritability of a mother who slaps her child without justification, aggressive tendencies are significant contributors to man's unhappiness. It seems only reasonable to assume that the widely predicted population explosion is going to lead to an explosion in inter-personal aggressiveness. One of the principal things to be learned from the study of increases in population density in animals is that aggressive behavior increases with the rise in population (72; 161; 379). Thus, there are practical and urgent, as well as scientific, reasons for increasing the attention given this problem.

SUMMARY

The physiological bases of aggressive behavior have been reviewed and the concept that aggression is not a unitary phenomenon has been developed. There are several kinds of aggression, each of which has a particular neural and endocrine basis. The type of aggression may be classified on the basis of the stimulus situation that will elicit it. Although the classes of aggression may overlap, different experimental manipulations will differentially affect the various kinds. These classes of aggression and what is known about the neurology and endocrinology of each are briefly summarized below.

Predatory aggression is elicited by a narrow range of stimuli. The topography of the response is different from that for other types of aggression. The lateral hypothalamus is particularly involved in predation. Predatory aggression is inhibited by amygdalectomy and is probably facilitated by frontal lesions. It is little influenced by either the presence or absence of gonadal hormones.

Inter-male aggression is elicited by a strange male of the same specie and is inhibited by particular "submissive" postures of that male. It is particularly dependent on the male hormone for its development. Little is known about the neural basis of this class of aggression except that the septal area is probably involved.

Fear-induced aggression occurs only in cases where escape has been attempted but is not possible. In general, it is reduced by lesions in the amygdala and some other temporal areas and, perhaps, is facilitated by lesions in the septum and ventro-medial nucleus of the hypothalamus. It is increased by stimulation in the hypothalamus anterior to the ventro-medial nucleus. Little is known about the endocrinology involved.

Irritable aggression may be increased by frustration, deprivation, and pain. The ventro-medial hypothalamus is particularly involved and, paradoxically, irritable aggression is increased by either stimulation or ablation of that area. It is reduced by amygdalectomy, castration, and stimulation of the caudate nucleus and the septum. A wide range of stimuli will elicit irritable aggression.

Both territorial and maternal aggression appear to be specific to the situation involved and what little evidence there is indicates that the reproductive hormones are involved. Essentially, nothing is known about the neural basis of these kinds of aggression.

Instrumental aggression may be based on any of the above classes. It consists of an increase in the tendency of an organism to engage in destructive behavior when that behavior has been reinforced in the past.

4

A Preliminary Physiological Model of Aggressive Behavior

K. E. MOYER

The earlier papers in this volume have implied a particular point of view that differs markedly from the other major theoretical statements on aggressive behavior. The first very briefly sketched a model for aggressive behavior and that model was projected to the second without being explicitly stated. In "Kinds of Aggression and their Physiological Bases," much of the substantiating evidence on the neural and endocrine substrates was presented. In the paper that follows, an attempt is made to make the model more explicit and to consider the manner in which a large number of factors interact to facilitate or inhibit aggressive responses. Several points that were not considered in the earlier papers are made, and the model is more inclusive. It is, nonetheless a *preliminary* model and, as such, leaves a number of questions unanswered. Like all models, it was built to be altered or, perhaps, destroyed by further research. However, if it serves to stimulate and to guide some of the research that ultimately leads to its modification, perhaps beyond recognition, it has served its purpose.

This paper was initially presented at a symposium on the "Physiology of Fighting and Defeat" sponsored by the Animal

Behavior Society at the annual meeting of the American Association for the Advancement of Science held in Dallas, Texas in December of 1968. A transcript of that Symposium is to be published by the University of Chicago Press under the editorship of B. E. Eleftheriou and J. P. Scott.

The original manuscript has been substantially altered in the interest of reducing the overlap with other papers in this volume thereby enabling the inclusion of more recent research in this very fast-moving field.

I thank Dr. J. P. Scott, whose invitation to participate in this symposium provided the opportunity to discuss some of our theoretical differences.

After a consideration of the evidence presented in the previous papers in this volume, we are led to the inevitable conclusion that a number of different kinds of aggression can be identified. The particular classification system suggested above may not be, and probably is not, the one that will ultimately be the most useful. It is probable that further research will clarify these kinds of aggression and further define the physiological distinctions among them. However, although we may argue about the most efficacious classification system, the fact that there are different kinds of aggression seems now to be indisputable.

It is obvious that if each of these kinds of aggressive behavior has a different physiological basis, it will not be possible to construct a model that will fit each in detail. It may, however, be possible to identify mechanisms or types of mechanisms which, although differing in detail, are similar for all aggression types. An attempt will now be made to elucidate some of these mechanisms.

NEURAL SYSTEMS AND AGGRESSION

The first premise of this model indicates that the brains of animal and man contain innately organized neural systems. When these systems are active and particular complexes of stimuli are present, the organism tends to behave destructively toward those stimulus complexes. Also, as suggested in earlier papers, the different kinds of aggression are elicited by activity of different, although sometimes overlapping, systems. The factors that determine whether or not these tendencies will result in overt action will be discussed below.

A corollary of this proposition is that a particular aggressive behavior will not occur if its neural system is suppressed, interrupted, or in some way deactivated.

55

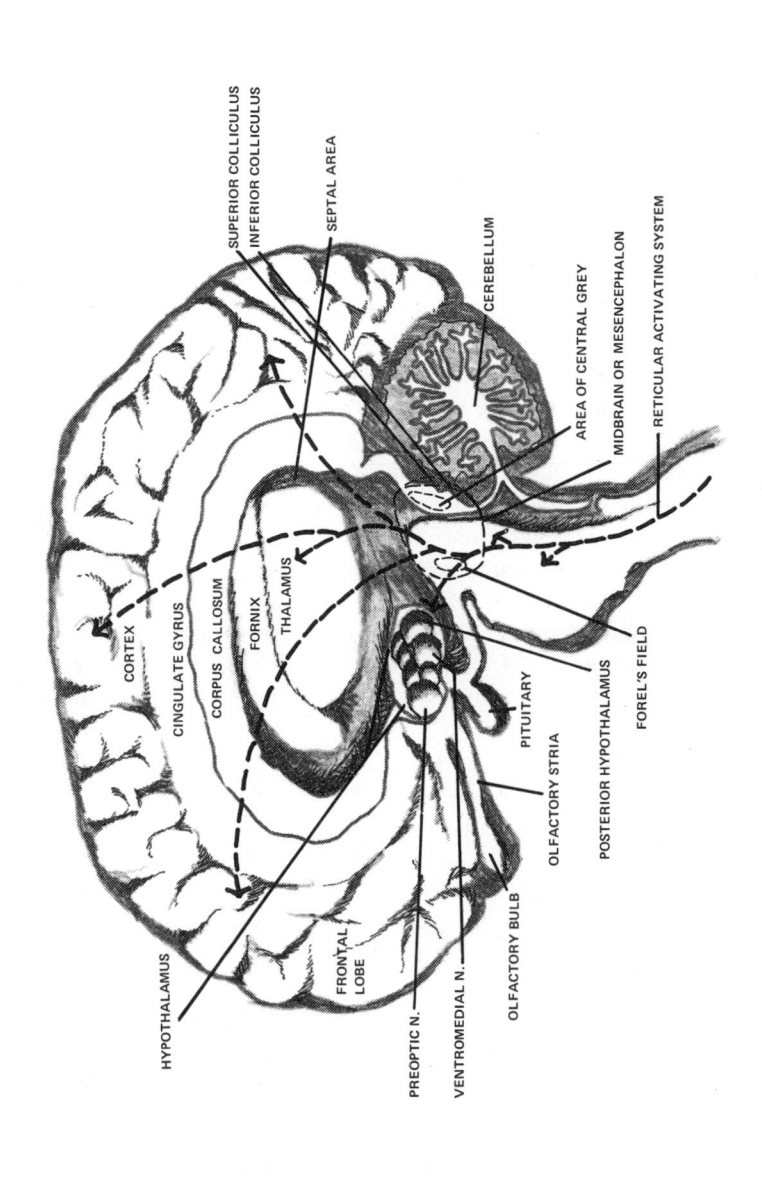

A second corollary of this premise is that since aggressive behavior is stimulus bound, the activation of a neural system in the absence of the appropriate stimulus complex will generally not result in aggressive behavior.

There is now, I believe, a massive amount of data to support this basic premise. Much of it has been presented in the three previous papers in this volume. Numerous studies clearly demonstrate that it is possible to activate a number of different locations in the brain electrically and produce a well-organized attack on particular target entities. Further, which target entity is attacked will depend on the particular portion of the brain that is stimulated.

In addition to the data already cited, several papers that summarize much of the available evidence on the neural substrates for aggressiveness are now available. The excellent and extensive series of studies by J. P. Flynn and his colleagues that has now been compiled provides an overview of some eight years of work on the neurology of both predatory and irritable aggression in the cat (129). Brown and Hunsperger (57) have surveyed a number of studies showing that attack behavior in the cat (most probably what has been termed here "irritable aggression") is caused by stimulation of the amygdala, hypothalamus and midbrain. Kaada (198) has provided an extensive review of the literature on brain mechanisms related to aggressive behavior. He cites numerous studies that differentiate between attack behavior (irritable aggression), defense behavior (fear-induced aggression) and flight. On the basis of both stimulation and lesion studies he concludes that, "All three behavior patterns appear to have their separate, although somewhat overlapping representations in the brain."

The neurology of the predatory system in the rat has been studied by Karli and his colleagues for the past fourteen years and worked out in considerable detail. Karli, Vergnes, and Didier-georges (208) have summarized this impressive series of studies. Richard Bandler (22; 23; 24), has now completed a series of studies that contribute further to an understanding of the particular brain sites involved in the predatory neural system of the rat. He has also convincingly demonstrated that the system is cholinergic. Direct stimulation of the lateral hypothalamus with carbachol by means of an implanted cannula facilitated both frog killing and mouse killing by the rat. This carbachol-induced facilitation could also be blocked by peritoneal injections of atropine sulfate. The atropine sulfate also significantly increased the attack and kill latencies. When atropine sulfate was applied directly to the lateral hypothalamus a reliable and consistent attack suppression was produced. Bandler's findings on the cholinergic nature of predation in the rat were recently confirmed by Smith, King and Hoebel (355). The lateral hypothalamic sites reported by Bandler to be positive for the facilitation of predation by carbachol appear to correspond well with those at which King and Hoebel (218) elicited mouse killing by electrical stimulation (23).

The interactions between the activity of the particular brain systems and the external stimulus have also received experimental support. Except for the few studies mentioned in the Kinds of Aggression paper (57; 432) in which brain-stimulated cats attacked the empty air (hallucination?), most of the evidence supports the view that aggressive behavior that is induced by brain stimulation is clearly stimulus bound.

The importance and the specificity of the target stimulus for aggressive behavior is well demonstrated in a study reported by Robinson, Alexander and Browne (310). A submissive male monkey under the influence of radio-controlled electrical stimulation of the anterior hypothalamus repeatedly attacked a dominant male in the cage but did not attack the female. Under repeated stimulation, the dominance relationship between the two males was changed. The stimulated monkey showed no generalized hyperirritability and did not manifest any increased proclivity to attack inanimate objects. Further, the aggression evoked in this experiment cannot be attributed to pain. At least one of the positive electrode placements produced self-stimulation when the opportunity was provided.

Both the nonstimulated male and the female reacted to the hostility of the stimulated monkey as though they were bona fide natural attacks. The dominant unstimulated male defended himself and counterattacked. The female initially showed aggressiveness toward the subordinate stimulated male but as the fortunes of war began to shift, the fickle female adopted a nonviolent, noninvolvement policy, and when the dominance hierarchy was reversed, she shifted her allegiance to the victor.

It should be emphasized that the aggressive behaviors produced by activation of particular neural systems in the brain are not similar to the sham rage of the decorticate animal. These behaviors are well-organized, well-directed and directly related to the relevant environmental stimulus. As Wasman and Flynn (409: 62), in their description of the cat's behavior during stimulation, state:

> The cat's responses were clearly directed. It would pursue and invariably catch a fleeing rat. If the rat leaped in the air the cat waited and caught the rat in mid-air or when it landed. The effectiveness of the attack was attested to by the frequent deaths and injuries to rats.

There is also now a large amount of experimental data that supports the first corollary of the initial premise of this model. Many studies have shown that lesions in particular portions of the various neural aggression systems virtually eliminate the specific aggressive behavior involved. Thus, the animal with lesions in the proper place does not respond aggressively to stimuli that it would viciously attack just prior to the operation. This material is covered in the earlier papers and presented in detail in the section in this volume on aggression control.

NEURAL SYSTEMS, AGGRESSION, AND MAN

In spite of man's remarkable flexibility, his ability to profit from experience, and his extensive capacity for cognitive processing, he comes equipped with the same kinds of physiological determinants of behavior as do other animals. It has already been pointed out that hostility in man can be turned on and off with the flick of a switch if that switch closes a circuit that sends stimulating current to the appropriate neural system (217). Examples of aggression induced in man by brain stimulation continue to accumulate. It is no longer an extremely rare or chance phenomenon.

Electrical stimulation in the posterior hypothalamus and the tegmentum of the mesencephalon in man has resulted in a report of pain and intense feelings of rage (173). The direct application of atropine to the brain of man in the area of the septum and hippocampus resulted in psychotic reactions including agitation and irritability (175). When one of Heath's patients was stimulated in the hippocampus at a rate of four stimuli per second, spike and slow wave activity was recorded from the septal region and an intense rage reaction was observed (176).

The surgical team from Massachusetts General Hospital (102; 253), implanted electrodes in the brains of four patients and brought the leads out to a radio receiver that was attached to the patient's head and covered by the head bandages. It was thus possible to stimulate these patients from a considerable distance by activating a properly tuned radio transmitter. The patients were free to move around with no restraining wires. In one patient, outbursts of rage and assaultive behavior, similar to her spontaneous episodic anger responses, resulted from stimulation of the right amygdala.

In another patient, electrodes were implanted bilaterally in the amygdala to produce chronic stimulation in an attempt to relieve intractable pain. Stimulation of the left amygdala resulted in a sharp rise in blood pressure that was maintained for over an hour after stimulation had been stopped. About twenty minutes after cessation, the patient became enraged, climbed out of bed and attacked indiscriminately. On the following day, stimulation in the right amygdala was subsequently followed by a belligerent and assaultive disturbance. It was reported that these aggressive episodes were completely at variance with the patient's usual courtly and dignified manner (119).

There is also evidence in man that there is an interaction between the neural activity and the stimulus situation in which the individual finds himself. This seems to indicate that aggressive behavior in man also may, in effect, be stimulus bound. One dangerously hostile patient with an array of twenty electrodes chronically implanted in both temporal lobes did not manifest any aggressive tendencies when the stimulation was carried out in the relatively sterile laboratory environment. Only restlessness was reported. However, when this same patient was stimulated in the hippocampus remotely by radio control when she was "chatting amiably with her psychiatrist," she showed a loss of contact and, after many seconds, exhibited a furious, directed attack against the wall (374). The second instance is perhaps best described in the author's own words, "A similar kind of attack with the same electrical features (EEG) was provoked by such stimulation in the most anterior electrode in the amygdala on the following day. This time she suddenly swung her guitar past the nose of her astonished psychiatrist, smashing the expensive instrument against the wall. On each of the two occasions, the electrical buildup of abnormality followed the same crescendo pattern, about 2 minutes elapsing in both instances before the maximal electrical, typical seizure outburst coinciding with the furious attack" (374: 340).

Clinical evidence for the spontaneous firing of the neural systems for aggression in man as a result of tumors, psychomotor epilepsy and other brain dysfunctions has already been covered (276). In addition to the evidence cited earlier on the correlation between excessive hostility and the 6 and 14 positive spike in the EEG record in children and adolescents, there is further evidence that spontaneous activity in the brain as reflected in the EEG record is correlated with habitual, violent, hostile behavior. As indicated in the discussion on instrumental aggression, habitual, hostile behavior may be a learned response in that hostility is in some way reinforced. However, it appears that a significant number of habitual aggressives have this unfortunate pattern of behavior because of some disorder in the neural systems.

In a study of 151 psychopaths, Hill and Watterson (187) found that 48 percent had abnormal EEGs whereas only 15 percent of normal individuals show similar abnormalities. Sixty-five percent of *aggressive* psychopaths show EEG abnormalities. Jenkins and Pacella (195) came to the conclusion that whereas delinquency does not show any relationship to EEG abnormalities, the habitual expression of aggressiveness does.

Williams (421) has recently studied the EEG records of individuals who were in custody for having committed crimes of aggression. He compared the EEG records of individuals who were habitually aggressive with individuals who had committed a major violent crime but not repeated crimes of violence. EEG abnormalities were found in only 24 percent of the latter group, but in 65 percent of the group of habitual aggressives. He reports the percentage of abnormalities of the population at large to be 12 percent. When he eliminated those individuals in his population who manifested mental retardation, epilepsy or had had a major head injury, 12 percent of the individuals with a single violent crime on their records showed EEG abnormalities, the same as the population at large. However, 57 percent of those individuals who were considered habitual aggressives showed EEG abnormalities. In all of the latter group, the temporal lobe was affected and the anterior portion of that lobe was 3 times as likely to be involved as the posterior. Over 80 percent of those individuals showed rhythms characteristic of temporal lobe dysfunctions.

Mark and his colleagues neatly summarize additional evidence on the relationships between electroencephalographic abnormalities and such behavioral dysfunctions as poor impulse control, assaultiveness and low violence thresholds (254).

The rapidly accumulating evidence on the alleviation of chronic aggressive and assaultive behavior in man by the surgical interruption of particular neural systems has already been mentioned and will be considered in more detail in the next paper. These lesion studies, although not conclusive, certainly lend credence to the idea that in man, as in animals, activation of certain brain systems results in aggressive behavior, and when these systems are rendered nonfunctional, the aggressive behavior is controlled or reduced.

As far as I know, there is no good evidence for a differential physiological basis for the different kinds of aggression in man. This may be due in part to the lack of attention on the concept of different kinds of aggression. It may also be due in part to man's rich symbolic behavior and the ability symbolically to substitute one stimulus complex for another so that any differentiation of the kinds of aggression on the basis of specific stimulus situations evoking them is bound to have severe limitations. Further, there is clearly no necessity for assuming that all of the kinds of aggression identifiable in the various animal species are necessarily identifiable in man. Until more work is done on this problem, however, further consideration will be highly speculative.

DETERMINANTS OF BRAIN SYSTEM ACTIVITY

The initial premise of this model simply states that when a given brain system is active in the presence of a given stimulus complex, destructive behavior will occur. It is obvious, however, that aggressive behavior in both animals and men is a relatively rare occurrence compared with the variety of other manifest behaviors. It is therefore essential that consideration be given to the mechanisms that provide for the activation and deactivation of the neurological systems that result in hostile behavior.

It is proposed here that there are three possible states (which blend into a continuum) of any aggression system. First, the system may be inactive and insensitive. In this condition, it cannot be fired by the usual stimulation that will provoke attack. One example of this state can be found, as indicated above, in the immature or castrated male rat. Neither will respond with aggression or threat postures to the stimulus complex of a strange male conspecific although that stimulus complex is adequate to elicit inter-male aggressive behavior in the normal adult animal.

If the immature or castrated rat is administered testosterone, the adequate stimulus for inter-male aggression will, in fact, elicit fighting behavior (38; 240). Thus, it appears that the testosterone in some way sensitizes the brain system involved in inter-male aggression so that it is fired by the adequate stimulus complex. This then, is the second state: the system is sensitized, but is inactive until it is activated by the appropriate stimulus. If the sensitivity is slight, fewer cells may be activated by the stimulus situation and the resultant attack may be half-hearted, elicited only by a narrow range of the most appropriate stimuli. On the other hand, if the sensitivity is high, the subject will respond to a wider range of stimuli and the attack behavior will be relatively more intense.

In the third state, the particular aggression system may be spontaneously active in the absence of the appropriate stimulus. In this case, the cells of the system are firing and the organism is in a restless state, is aroused and may engage in exploratory behavior. It does not, however, make aggressive motor movements. It will respond more readily to the appropriate stimuli because activity in that system sensitizes relevant sensory modalities so that the receptors are more easily fired. The MacDonnell and Flynn (249) study, which showed that the sensitivity of the muzzle area of the cat is increased during electrical activation of the hypothalamic area that produces predatory aggression is relevant here. In humans, it seems likely that activity in certain of the aggression systems is accompanied by subjective feelings of anger and hostility (333; 391; 427). The individual may engage in extensive aggressive fantasies and a large number of stimuli will elicit aggressive thoughts. It is unknowable, of course, whether animals have any comparable subjective state.

Although the above paragraphs are a reasonable extrapolation of the available experimental data, it must be recognized that it is an extrapolation. Experimental confirmation would require that particular aggression systems be located by implanted electrodes and that activation of those electrodes result in aggressive behavior. It would then be necessary to record from those electrodes to determine the relationship between the activity of the system and the behavior of the organism in both the presence and absence of the appropriate external stimulation. This is a feasible technique for freely moving animals (225), but little use has been made of it in the study of aggressive behavior as yet.

Adams (1) has shown that there are certain cells in the midbrain of the cat that are active only when the cat is engaged in fighting behavior. He also indicated that stimulation at the sites of the cells related to fighting produced hissing behavior in the cats. Repeated electrical stimulation in the amygdala of the cat at 5-second intervals for an hour a day for one to fifteen days results in long-lasting EEG seizure patterns. Some of these animals showed considerable increases in aggressive behavior (8).

HEREDITARY INFLUENCES

There are a variety of factors that contribute to the sensitization of the aggression systems in the brain, and the evidence suggests that some of these factors may be inherited. There are clear-cut strain differences in predatory tendencies. Seventy percent of wild Norway rats kill mice, whereas 12 percent of the domesticated Norways kill mice (203). In our own laboratory, we have shown that a significantly higher percentage of Long Evans hooded rats kill frogs, chickens and turtles than do Sprague Dawley albinos (25).

Hereditary influences have been clearly demonstrated in intermale aggression. Scott (335) has shown that different inbred strains of mice differ consistently and widely in their tendencies to engage in inter-male fighting and that these differences were genetic and could not have been learned. A number of experimenters have shown that through selective breeding, it is possible to develop aggressive and nonaggressive strains of animals: again, the aggression dealt with was inter-male (163; 230; 368; 434).

Although I know of no study that demonstrates the inheritance of aggressive tendencies in man, there is little reason to believe that such tendencies are not inherited. Certainly, there are vast inherited differences in the human nervous and endocrine systems (423). If, as suggested in this model, human aggressive behavior is partly determined by neural and endocrine mechanisms, it is only reasonable to assume that aggressive tendencies in man are inherited, just as the tendency to epilepsy is inherited (235).

Man has chromosomal abnormalities that appear to cause excessive aggressiveness and lack of impulse control. One is Klinefelter's syndrome (65). The other, about which there is considerable debate, is the XYY syndrome (299; 300; 376). See Kessler and Moos (214) for a recent review of this evidence and a discussion of some of the methodological and conceptual considerations essential to its interpretation.

ENDOCRINE INFLUENCES ON NEURAL DEVELOPMENT

Evidently, the sensitivity of the aggression system and the consequent tendency to behave aggressively is permanently influenced by the endocrine, particularly gonadal, status of the organism shortly after birth. A recent study by Conner and Levine (80) indicates that rats castrated as neonates fight less under conditions of shock (irritable aggression) than do either weaning-age castrates or intact rats. Further, the fighting level of the weaning-age castrates can be brought up to normal by exogenously administered testosterone, but the fighting behavior of the rats castrated as neonates remains unaffected by testosterone. Conner and Levine conclude from this that the neural substrates that are modulated by the androgens in later life are permanently changed by the early castration. Recent evidence also indicates that these same neural substrates can be altered by administration of testosterone propionate to female mice on the day of birth. When female mice are so treated and subsequently isolated, they respond to testosterone in the same manner as males castrated at weaning—that is, with increased fighting (inter-male aggression). However, females treated with oil within the first 24 hours after birth do not fight when isolated and given testosterone (112). Edwards thus concludes, "One may presume that the stimulation by endogenous testosterone in the male (and exogenous testosterone in the female) can 'organize' or cause the differentiation of a neural substrate for fighting."

INCREASED SENSITIVITY FROM NEURAL FACILITATION

Aggression circuits can also be sensitized or made more susceptible to being fired by the appropriate external stimulation by the facilitating effect of the activity of other neurone systems. Stimulation of particular sites in the midbrain reticular formation at a particular intensity will produce only mildly alerting responses in the cat. Activation of those sites will, however, facilitate the attack of a cat on a rat when attack is initiated by stimulation of the lateral hypothalamus (349; 350). Sheard has shown that hypothalamically induced predatory attack is also enhanced by intraperitoneal injections of amphetamine and suggests that the amphetamine action is similar to direct electrical stimulation of the reticular system (349). There are also other areas in the brain that have been shown to have a sensitizing or facilitating effect on hypothalamically induced predatory behavior (113; 248; 409).

The research showing the sensitizing effect of the activity of other neurone systems on those neural substrates concerned with aggression has been primarily confined to predatory aggression. However, it seems likely that a similar mechanism exists for all kinds of aggression and that these facilitating mechanisms are probably associated with the neurological substrates of other behavior systems. Although studies to demonstrate specific increases in neural sensitivity in the irritable aggression system have not yet been done, one can draw such an inference from certain behavioral studies. Aversive stimulation (395), as well as a variety of deprivation states, including food deprivation (89; 336), sleep deprivation (232), morphine deprivation in addicted rats (50) and extinction-induced aggression (frustration produced by withdrawal of reinforcement) (16; 381), increases the subject's tendency to manifest irritable aggression in the presence of an appropriate stimulus. All of the above conditions function as stressors and, if long continued, may produce endocrine changes capable of influencing the sensitivity of aggression systems (see below): however, the relatively rapid onset of aggression after some of these stressors implies a neural facilitation.

DECREASED SENSITIVITY FROM NEURAL INHIBITION

As indicated in the Internal Impulses paper, the sensitivity of the aggression systems appears to be influenced by inhibitory input from other systems, although the experimental evidence on this point is, as yet, limited. It is frequently a difficult problem to determine whether activity in the aggression system itself is blocked or whether some particular group of motor responses is being inhibited by the action of a given system. Flynn, et al. (129) have elaborated on the brain areas in the cat that tend to decrease the sensitivity of the hypothalamic portions of the predatory system (and to some extent the system for what is probably irritable aggression). These include the dorsal hippocampus and the baso-medial-lateral amygdala, as well as portions of the midbrain and the thalamus. These, along with the systems that facilitate aggressive behavior, are referred to by Flynn as modulating structures (129). Other examples of the inhibition of aggression have already been noted on pages (6, 7, 8, 19, 23, 41, 44, and 45).

It will be recalled that stimulation of the central nucleus of the amygdala of both the cat and the dog results in escape reactions, but lesioning of that same nucleus produces a highly irritable animal—suggesting that the same neural system that produces the fear or escape also serves to inhibit irritable aggression. It should be noted further that when the hostile behavior of Heath's patients is blocked by septal stimulation, disorganized rage is replaced by happiness and mild euphoria.

There is much more to be done on the neural inhibition of aggression, but the work that has been done seems to lead to the conclusion that the inhibitory neural influences may also be related to the activation of other motivational or motor predispositional systems. These mechanisms may function in a manner similar to the reciprocal innervation mechanism in muscle control. Thus, intense activation of the neurological substrate for the euphoric or fear response may be neurologically incompatible with the simultaneous activity of the irritable aggression circuit because activation of one circuit involves inhibition in the other. (This will be covered in more detail in Chapter 6.)

The model proposed in this paper implies that the modulating systems discussed above are a constant influence on any naturally occurring aggressive behavior. Whether aggression will occur or continue in any given stimulus situation will depend on the interactions of a variety of facilitating and inhibitory influences on the particular aggression system involved. A particular stimulus situation may activate two incompatible neural systems at the same time with the result that behavior is blocked. For example, the fear system and the irritable aggression system may both be activated. The behavior of the animal in that situation may be static or it may vacillate between aggression and escape. As the stimulus situation changes, either as a function of the animal's own behavior or because of changes in the stimulus objects themselves, the new information may differentially influence the ultimate behavior pattern. Significant changes in the stimulus situation may produce a shift in the predominantly active system at any time with a resulting change in behavior.

BLOOD CHEMISTRY INFLUENCES

Considerable evidence indicates that the tendency to various kinds of aggressive behavior varies as a function of changes in the organism's blood chemistry. As indicated above, it is proposed in this model that certain blood constituents act on the brain's aggression systems either to increase or decrease their sensitivity so that they are consequently more easily or less easily fired by the relevant stimuli.

At the moment, it is not clear whether the endocrine changes in the bloodstream, implicated above, increase the sensitivity of the aggression systems directly or whether they do so indirectly by differentially influencing the amounts of neurotransmitters in particular portions of the brain with a resulting change in the sensitivity of particular circuits. There is good evidence, for example, that the brain chemistry of aggressive animals (isolated mice) is different from that of normal animals, including differences in turnover rates of serotonin (139), norepinephrine and dopamine (414). Sigg, Day, and Colombo (353), however, have shown that isolation-induced aggression does not develop in castrated mice. The endocrine-brain chemistry interactions and the causal relationships to the aggressive behaviors remain to be worked out.

In light of the experimental evidence, there can be no doubt that different kinds of aggression are, in part, a function of particular hormonal balances and that the levels of aggressiveness can be directly manipulated by endocrine changes. It is inferred here that the endocrine-induced changes in aggression are the result of direct or indirect sensitization or activation of particular brain circuits. That hypothesis is, however, readily testable, although the testing techniques require considerable technical skill. Sheard (349) has shown that the attack latency and attack intensity resulting from brain stimulation can be manipulated by the peripheral administration of amphetamine. A similar technique could be used to study the sensitization of particular brain circuits by the peripheral administration of endocrines suspected to be important in the various kinds of aggression. This model would predict that the various kinds of aggression as defined above would be differentially sensitized by different endocrine balances, although it is reasonable to suspect some overlap, as in the influence of androgens on both inter-male and irritable aggression.

SATIATION AS A DESENSITIZER

Aggression systems may also be desensitized by the expression of aggressive behavior, although the underlying physiological mechanism for this phenomenon remains completely obscure.

Experiments currently in progress in my laboratory clearly indicate that predatory aggression, at least, can be satiated even though consumption of the prey is not permitted. Further, the predatory tendency reoccurs after a period of predation deprivation. All of the data on this experiment have not yet been analyzed, but it seems safe to make the following general points. If a killer rat is given a mouse once a day, the latency of the kill will become progressively shorter until it stabilizes at less than a minute, generally a few seconds. The rat will continue to kill a mouse each day for prolonged periods even though it is never permitted to eat the prey. It kills quickly and efficiently, with little effort. However, if the rat is presented with a mouse one minute after each kill, the kill latency gets progressively longer, and after 5 or 10 mice, the rat no longer attacks the mice but will even permit the exploring mouse to walk over it and nestle with it. The killing response is also inhibited 24 hours later. If the rat kills, it will kill only one mouse. Perhaps even more interesting, there is some indication that the rat's tendency to kill frogs also seems to be reduced after satiation of the mouse-killing response (Bandler and Moyer, unpublished).

Whether the concept of inhibition of aggression by satiation applies to any kind of aggressive behavior other than predatory is, at the moment, an open question because the relevant experiments have not been done. There is, however, some indication that the concept may be relevant to inter-male aggression. Scott and Fredericson (343) suggest that trained fighter mice are less effective as fighters if they fight more often than every other day. Although these authors attributed the decrease in fighting tendency 24 hours after an encounter to fatigue produced by the initial fight, an equally plausible explanation would be made in terms of some kind of satiation phenomenon. Welch (413) reports that in the situation where mice live together in uncrowded conditions with abundant food, dominant animals will, over a period of weeks or months, make periodic unchallenged attacks on the subordinates. He says, "It is almost as though the aggressiveness of the dominant is repeatedly, if temporarily, reduced by the stimulus of attacking, but seldom for very long."

LEARNING AND THE MANIFESTATION OF AGGRESSIVE BEHAVIOR

Aggressive behavior, like all other basic behaviors, is strongly influenced by experience. Just as an animal can be taught to overeat (422) or undereat (241; 258) through the use of reinforcement, regardless of the state of deprivation, animals can also be taught to exhibit or inhibit aggressive behavior by similar means. It is not appropriate here to survey the vast literature on learning and aggressive behavior. These studies, particularly those on rats and mice, have been reviewed in some detail by Scott (341; 343) and dealt with earlier in this volume. However, some of the implications of the role of learning in aggressive behavior as they relate to this model should be explored.

It is possible to increase the probability of occurrence of any aggressive or destructive response, no matter what its initial motivational source, if that response is followed by a positive reinforcement. The law of effect operates just as effectively in the facilitation of motor responses that are labeled aggressive as in those that are not. In the classification system outlined above, aggressive behavior, so determined, is termed instrumental aggression.

A particularly pure case of instrumental aggression is demonstrated in the study of Stachnik, Ulrich, and Mabry (365; 366). By reinforcing successive approximations to aggressive behavior in rats through positively reinforcing brain stimulation, these investigators were able to induce rats to attack other rats, monkeys and even cats. They note, however, that the occasional pain-elicited aggressive attacks resulting from counterattack by a control rat presented a noticeable contrast to the topography of the conditioned attack. We have used the same procedure to reinforce the attack on a mouse by a nonpredatory rat. It is relatively easy to induce the rat to chase, harass and nip at the mouse. However, although we have tried repeatedly, we have been unable to induce mouse *killing* by this procedure. Because the typical predatory response of the rat biting through the spinal cord of the mouse just never occurs in the nonpredatory rat, it is impossible to reinforce that response.

Another experiment from our laboratory illustrates the distinctiveness of instrumental aggression. Karli (203) has shown that nonpredatory rats will starve to death with a live mouse in the cage. However, it is possible to induce mouse killing in nonpredatory rats by gradually teaching the rat that the mouse is a source of food (Moyer, 1968, unpublished). When food deprived, most rats will eat a dead mouse with the skin of the back slit. After a series of trials with that food object and subsequently with an intact dead mouse, and a live but totally anesthetized mouse, it was found that these rats will attack and kill a lightly anesthetized mouse that is still mobile but sluggish in its behavior. Again, however, it is easy to distinguish this instrumental behavior that results in the death of the mouse from the typical predatory response, either natural or chemically induced. These rats almost never kill by biting the back of the neck. Their attack is directed at the tail, the feet and the belly of the mouse. The approach is tentative, and the latencies of attack and the time between attack and kill are much longer than in the natural predatory response. It is unlikely that any manipulation of the physiological basis for predatory aggression would have much effect on this instrumental response.

Various types of aggression have been both classically and instrumentally conditioned (395). There is also evidence that the opportunity to behave aggressively is, in itself, rewarding. Monkeys, when shocked, will learn a chain-pulling response in order to obtain a tennis ball that they can bite (17), and a pigeon during extinction (a situation that in itself, produces aggressive behavior) will learn to peck a key that will produce another bird that is then attacked (15). Predatory rats will learn a maze to obtain a mouse whereas non-killer rats will not (285) and cats during stimulation of the lateral hypothalamus in the area that produces predatory aggression will learn a Y-maze if an attackable rat is used as reinforcement (309). Berkowitz has summarized an impressive amount of evidence to show that "stimuli are capable of eliciting aggressive responses to the extent that they have been associated with aggression in the individual's past" (43).

Just as aggressive behavior can be facilitated by reward, so can it be inhibited by punishment. Predatory aggression can be readily suppressed by punishment of the attack response (283). In spite of the fact that noxious stimulation produces irritable aggressive behavior (395) it can also, if sufficiently intense, inhibit aggressive tendencies. Aggressive behavior is suppressed in monkeys if the punishing shock is more intense than the shock that elicited the fighting (15). The negative reinforcement involved in defeat during inter-male aggression results in a decrease in aggressive tendencies (201; 230). Miller, Murphy, and Mirsky (265) have clearly shown that it is possible to manipulate social hierarchies in monkeys by punishing a dominant animal in the presence of a subordinate, and Ulrich indicates that when a monkey is severely bitten by an opponent, there is an obvious decrease in the aggressiveness of the bitten subject.

In an established colony where animals have a frequent opportunity to interact, it is easy to see that the learning mechanisms indicated above could account for the development of dominance hierarchies. A given animal could easily learn to respond to the cue complex of one animal in the colony with aggressive responses but to another with avoidance, submissive or aggression inhibitory responses. One would certainly expect these learned responses to interact with the other internal states of the organism, such as the activity of particular aggression circuits. If an animal is punished in the presence of food, the eating responses of that animal in the presence of the cues associated with punishment will be inhibited regardless of the amount of deprivation (and presumed activity in the hunger or consummatory circuits) (241). One would expect no less an influence of learning on the manifestations of aggression. As Plotnik and Delgado (296) and Delgado (93; 96) have shown, the brain-stimulation-induced aggressive behavior of monkeys is related to the animal's prior experience. The effects of lesions involving the aggression circuits are also influenced by the prior learning of the animal (320; 357; 358). It is rare for the activity of the aggression circuits to be so intense that they appear to override well-established habit patterns, although this does appear to occur in humans (333), and Robinson, et al. were able to change the dominance hierarchy by the electrical activation of the neural substrate for inter-male aggression (310).

There is little experimental evidence on the neural mechanisms involved in learned inhibition of an aggressive response. According to this model, it could occur at any one of several levels. As indicated above, the inhibition may occur at the level of the integrating aggression system itself. For example, the subjective feeling of anger in the human (which would be indicative of activity in a system for irritable aggression) could be replaced by fear of sufficient intensity that the irritable aggression system is inhibited and the individual no longer has the subjective experience of anger. The inhibition could also occur at the muscular level producing the extreme tension state of inhibited rage in which the muscles in opposition to the ones used in attack are contracted to a point at which they prevent attack behavior. In this situation, however, the central integrative aggression system would continue to fire, and the human would continue to experience the subjective state of anger.

Man, of course, learns better and faster than all other animals. It is, therefore, reasonable to expect that the internal impulses to aggressive behavior would be more subject to modification by experience in man than in any other animal. Also, because of man's additional ability to manipulate symbols and to substitute one symbol for another, one would expect to find a considerable diversity in the stimuli that will elicit or inhibit activity in the aggression systems. One would also expect the modes of expression of aggression to be more varied, diverse and less stereotyped in man than in other animals.

SUMMARY

Aggression is not a unitary concept. Aggressive behavior can be classed as follows: predatory, inter-male, fear-induced, irritable, territorial, maternal, instrumental and sex-related. These types of aggression may be differentiated on the basis of the stimulus situations that elicit them. Although the physiological bases of the various kinds of aggression may overlap, they are essentially different, and it is possible to discriminate these physiological substrates experimentally.

Experimental evidence is examined to support the proposition that the brain contains innately organized neural systems for the various kinds of aggression. When these systems are active in the presence of particular stimuli, the organism behaves aggressively. Thus, aggressive behavior is stimulus bound and dependent on the functional integrity of the aggression systems.

Man, like all other members of the animal kingdom, is subject to the biological determinants of aggressive behavior. Activation of certain brain areas in man results in aggression. This occurs whether the activation is the result of direct electrical stimulation, stimulation by tumor growth, or spontaneous activity as is found in certain types of epilepsy. Chronic aggressive and assaultive behavior in man can be alleviated by the surgical interruption of particular brain circuits.

A variety of factors contributes to whether or not particular aggression systems will be inactive and insensitive, sensitive, and thus easily fired, or spontaneously active. There is evidence that some of the determinants of the sensitivity of the aggression systems are hereditary and that the development of these systems can be influenced by neonatal endocrine changes.

A number of neural systems in the brain that do not result in aggressive behavior when stimulated, do facilitate ongoing aggressive behavior when activated and, thus, seem to increase the sensitivity of the neural substrates for aggression. It is suggested that these facilitating systems may be activated by environmental changes that result in such states as deprivation, pain, and frustration.

Sensitivity of the aggression systems may also be reduced by activation of other neural systems in the brain. These inhibitory effects may come from other behavior systems in the brain that are neurologically incompatible with the aggression systems. One example might be euphoria. The sensitivity and/or activity of the aggression systems is constantly being modulated by the facilitating and inhibiting input from other systems.

Changes in the blood chemistry, primarily, but not exclusively, hormonal, also have an effect on the sensitivity of the neural circuits for aggression. The experimental evidence leaves little doubt that different kinds of aggression are, in part, a function of particular hormonal balances, and that the levels of aggressiveness can be directly manipulated by endocrine changes.

Aggressive behavior, like all basic behaviors, is strongly influenced by learning. Thus, the tendency to behave aggressively to any stimulus complex may be either enhanced or inhibited, depending on the nature of the reinforcement that follows the behavior.

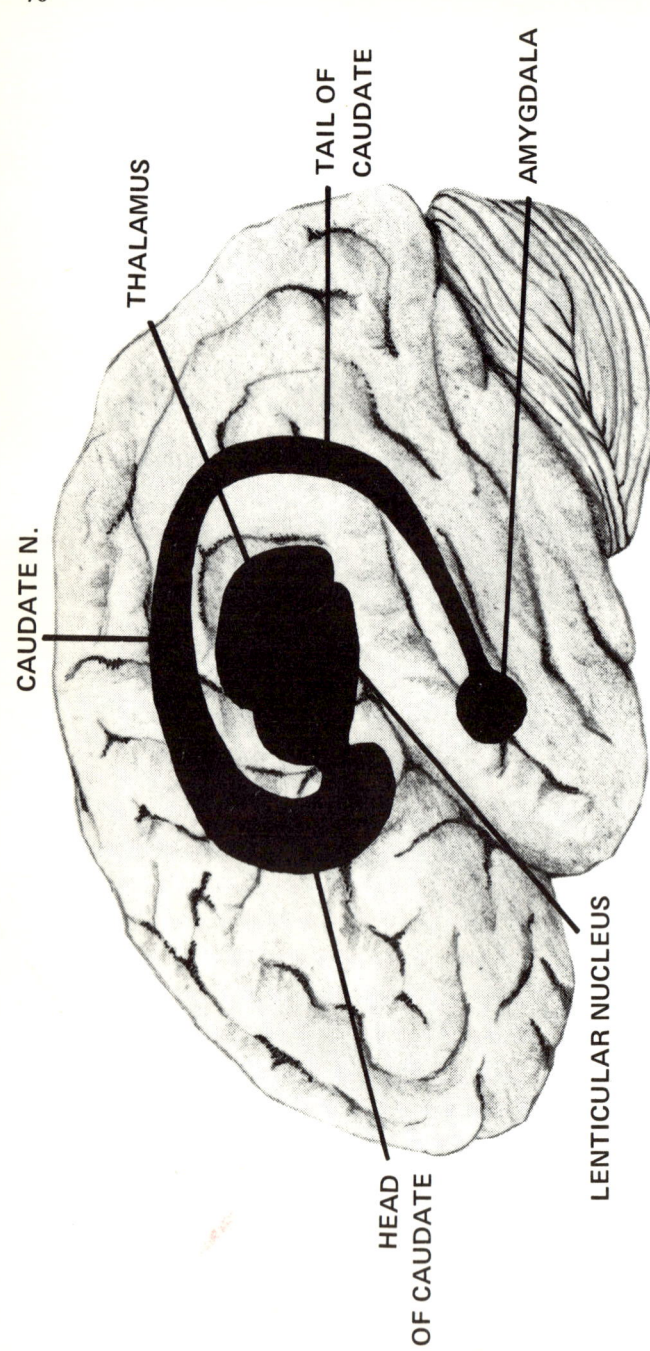

CAUDATE NUCLEUS
AMYGDALA RELATIONSHIP
WITH REST OF BRAIN

LATERAL ASPECT,
LOBES OF THE BRAIN

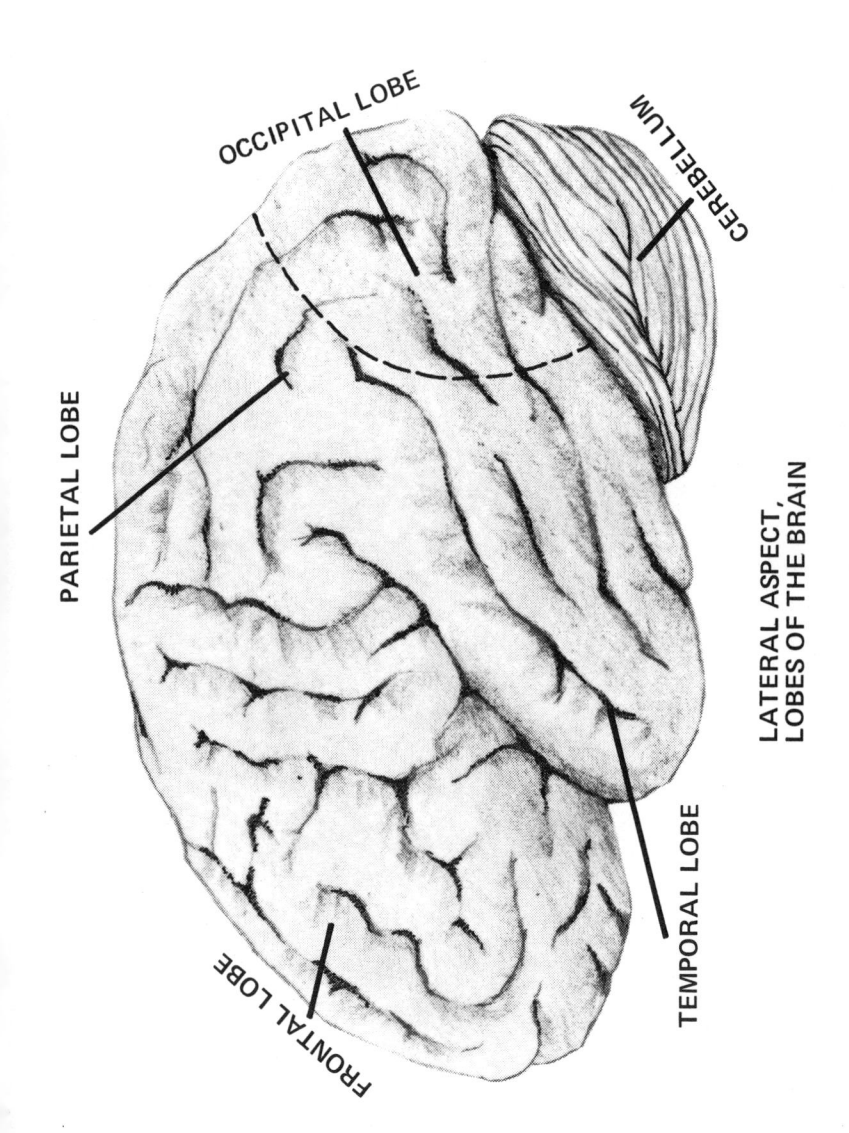

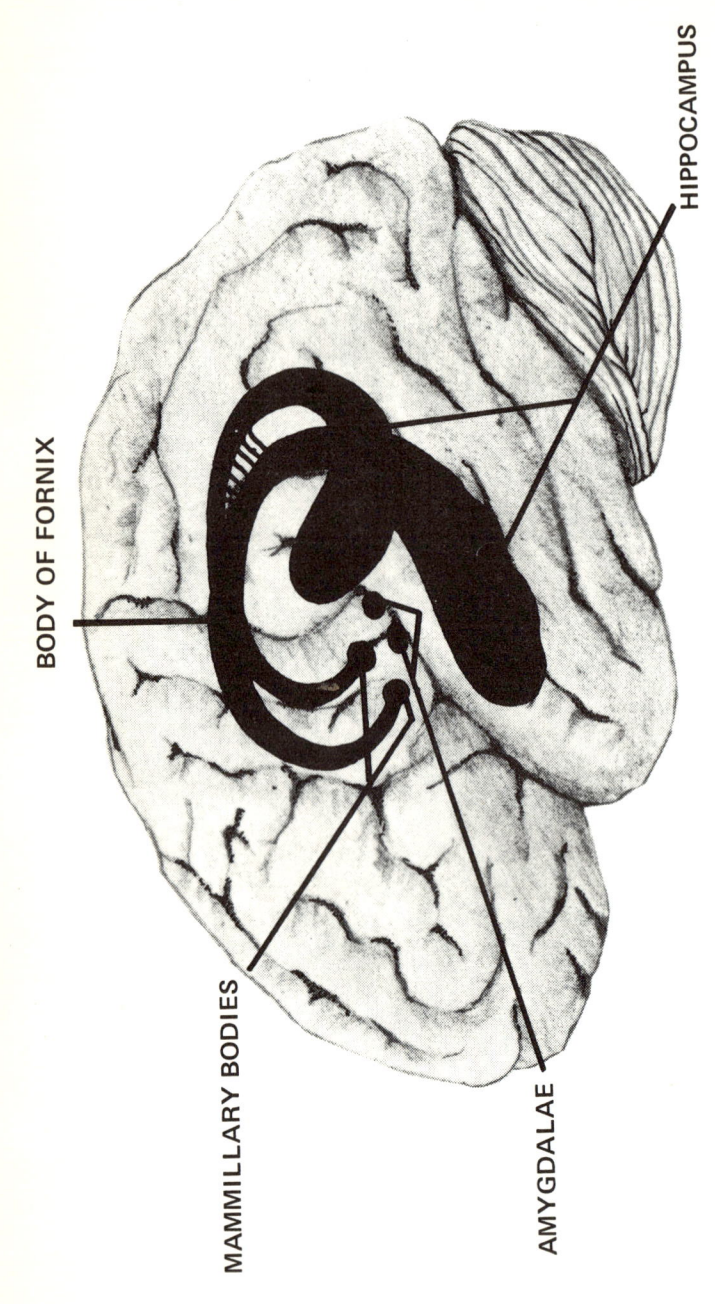

MAMMILLARY BODIES
FORNIX, HIPPOCAMPUS
RELATIONSHIP WITH
REST OF BRAIN

FRONTAL LOBES

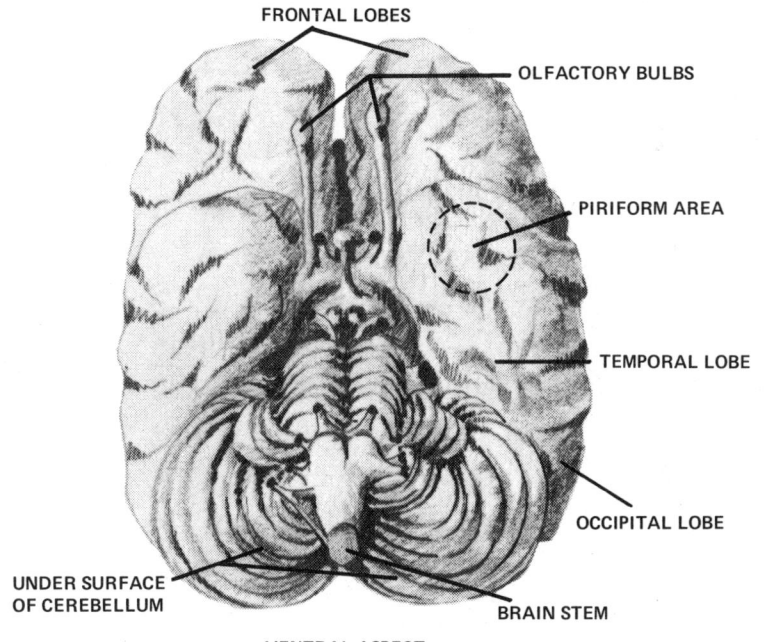

OLFACTORY BULBS

PIRIFORM AREA

TEMPORAL LOBE

OCCIPITAL LOBE

UNDER SURFACE
OF CEREBELLUM

BRAIN STEM

VENTRAL ASPECT

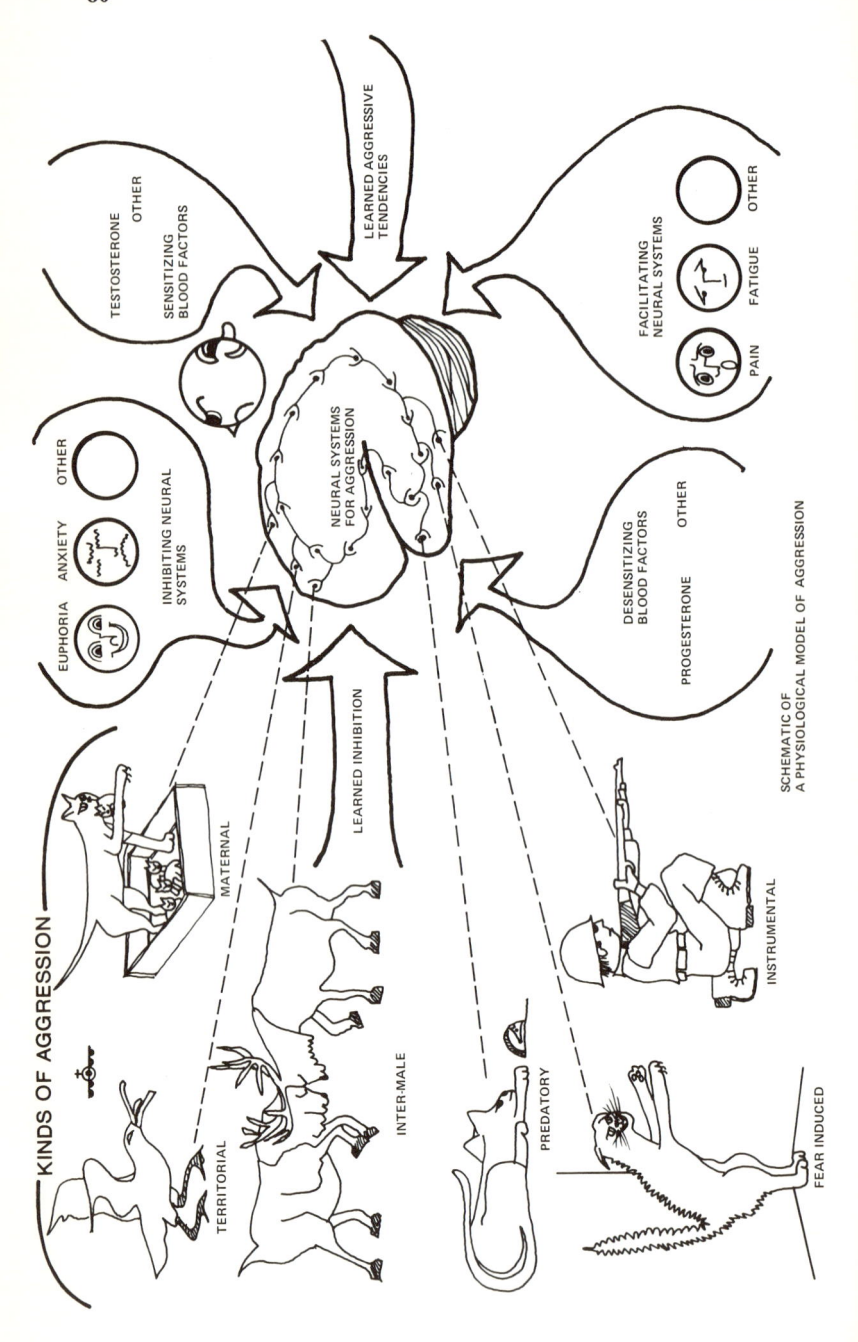

SCHEMATIC OF
A PHYSIOLOGICAL MODEL OF AGGRESSION

5

The Physiology of Aggression and the Implications for Aggression Control

K. E. MOYER

Daily newspaper reports make it obvious that there is a need for aggression control. Violence is all around us and is on the increase. According to the final report of the national commission on the causes and prevention of violence,

> Violence in the United States has risen to alarmingly high levels. Whether one considers assassination, group violence or individual acts of violence, the decade of the 1960's was considerably more violent than the several decades preceding it and ranks among the most violent in our history. The United States is the clear leader among modern, stable democratic nations in its rates of homicide, assault, rape and robbery, and it is at least among the highest in incidence of group violence and assassination. This high level of violence is dangerous to our society. It is disfiguring our society—making fortresses of portions of our cities and dividing our people into armed camps. It is jeopardizing some of our most precious institutions, among them our schools and universities—poisoning the spirit of trust and cooperation that is

essential to their proper functioning. It is corroding the central political processes of our democratic society—substituting force and fear for argument and accommodation (289: XV).

If we are to survive, both as individuals and as a nation, methods must be devised to reduce the levels of aggression and hostility.

The next paper deals with the physiological methods of reducing aggressive behavior. These are powerful methods and, as such, have considerable potential for abuse. However, it should be recognized that all methods of control, for all time, have had the potential for abuse. Violence can be controlled by the extensive use of punishment and other aversive methods. The lowest levels of civil strife in France occurred during the years between 1850–1860 and 1940–1950. This was achieved by the use of excessive repressive techniques after the sudden rise to power of Louis Napoleon in 1851 and by the overwhelming suppression of civil rights under the German occupation of the 1940's (383). This exemplifies the misuse of methods of control that have existed as long as men have interacted. These are familiar methods; we are aware of their potential for abuse and an informed public can take measures to guard against them.

Newer methods of control, such as those discussed in this paper, are being devised constantly. In this case too, an informed body politic can take measures to insure that these techniques are used wisely and not to excess.

This paper was originally presented at a symposium entitled Cognitive and Physiological Factors in Violence and Aggression and held at the City University of New York, June 6, 1969. It is to appear in a volume composed of the papers presented at the symposium under the editorship of Dr. Jerome Singer.

The paper has been little changed for this volume except that the introductory pages that consisted of a brief presentation of the physiological model for aggressive behavior have been eliminated. Since this paper is an extension of the ideas presented in the aggression control section of the "Internal Impulses to Aggression" paper, there is some overlap. In all cases, however, the information is more extensive and complete.

I am grateful to Dr. Singer for the invitation to participate in this symposium.

Now that the physiological model of aggressive behavior has been developed in some detail, we can look at the kinds of aggression controls that are available now, and what the potential might be for further controls. Although the emphasis in this paper is on the physiological methods useful in the control of hostile behavior, this should not be construed to imply that other control methods are either ineffective or unimportant. There are, in fact, a number of nonphysiological methods which can be briefly mentioned.

Since the sensitivity of the neural substrate for certain types of aggressive behavior appears to be sensitized by frustration, it should be possible, at least in part, to reduce aggressive behavior by changing the environment to reduce excessive frustration and deprivation.

Just as it is possible for some obese persons to learn to eat less, some individuals can learn to inhibit aggressive tendencies. This can be accomplished by the positive reinforcement of non-aggressive responses in the presence of aggression-eliciting stimuli or through the negative reinforcement of expressed aggression. Since negative reinforcement constitutes a stressor, the total effect of that approach must be carefully evaluated. It should also be possible to assist the individual to restructure his cognitive patterns as they relate to the objects of his hostility through the device of role playing (388). Finally, the expression of aggression can be reduced by removing some of the cues which instigate aggressive behaviors. Berkowitz (43) summarizes an outstanding series of studies that demonstrate that individuals react with greater hostility in the presence of objects such as guns, which have been previously associated with aggressive incidents.

If the model outlined above has any validity, it should also be possible to control aggressive tendencies through the direct physiological manipulation of the internal environment.

INHIBITION OF AGGRESSION IN ANIMALS BY BRAIN LESIONS

If there are neural systems that are active during, and responsible for, aggressive behavior, it should be possible to reduce or eliminate aggressive tendencies by interrupting or interfering with these neural systems. There is now abundant evidence that such a procedure is possible. As might be suspected when dealing with neural systems rather than neural centers, there are a number of different brain areas that may be lesioned to delimit aggressive tendencies. Further, it should be emphasized that there are different kinds of aggressive behavior and although there must obviously be some overlap in the neurological substrates, particularly at the final common path, they are reasonably independent centrally and can be experimentally delineated (275). This, then, is another reason to expect that lesions in a number of brain areas would produce a decrease in aggressive tendencies.

Because it has only recently been recognized that there are different kinds of aggressive behavior, it is frequently difficult to determine in any given experiment which type of aggression is being used as a dependent variable. However, it is not the purpose of this paper to deal with the physiology of the different kinds of aggression, but to emphasize those control measures that may be common to many types.

As early as 1937, it was shown that brain lesions could result in the physiological reduction of aggression. Using the very radical surgery of complete bilateral temporal lobe ablation, including the uncus and the greater part of the hippocampus, Kluver and Bucy (222; 223; 224) produced tameness in vicious rhesus monkeys. They report that the loss of both fear and anger reactions was complete. It is important to note that the lesioned animals, although quite docile, were not in any sense sedated, but were in a generally more aroused state. The animals never resented any form of handling and were always eager to engage in playful activities with the experimenter. The normal, extreme hostility was replaced by a state of "hypomania." This change to extreme tameness was especially remarkable because these investigators took particular care to use only wild and aggressive monkeys.

Since 1937, many investigators have supported the work of

Kluver and Bucy by showing that extensive damage to the temporal lobe results in an increase in docility in a variety of animals (4; 380). The evidence seems to indicate that aggressive behaviors are not completely eliminated from the animal's repertoire, but the threshold for such behavior is heightened. Monkeys and baboons with extensive lesions in the temporal region generally did not retaliate when attacked by other animals, but would sit and wince and grimace. However, if the lesioned animal were cornered, it would manifest enough aggression to extricate itself from that situation (298). Similar findings have been reported for the dog. The operated animals are less dominant and more docile toward the handler, but were quite able to defend themselves when attacked (134).

Social dominance, which involves aggressive components, can be directly manipulated by anterior temporal lobectomy. Plotnik (295) assessed the dominance hierarchy in a group of squirrel monkeys in three different group competitive situations which involved both positive and negative reinforcement. He then operated on each dominant animal in succession, with testing between operations, and showed that the lesioned animal fell from the top of the hierarchy postoperatively. Behavior changes resulting from extensive temporal lesions (uncus and amygdala) are so deviate that the animal in the natural state is rejected by the social group and may eventually die. Free ranging rhesus monkeys, observed on Cayo Santiago Island, which were subjected to this operation, failed to show either appropriate aggressive or submissive gestures (106).

Much of the more recent work on the diminution of hostile reactions through the interruption of the neural systems which underlie those reactions has been concentrated on attempts to delineate more clearly the specific relevant brain areas. The temporal lobectomy studies did, in fact, demonstrate that brain lesions could reduce hostility. However, such massive damage produced many other changes as well, including: hypersexuality, "psychic blindness," excessive orality, and a hyperreactivity to all visual stimuli.

A number of contradictory studies clearly indicated that damage to the amygdala resulted in changes in the subject's aggressive potential. Although some investigators have found that bilateral amygdalectomy resulted in increases in irritability (27; 28; 330), it has generally been found that aggressiveness is reduced by that operation. Bilateral amygdalectomy raises the threshold for at least three different kinds of aggressive behavior. Irritable aggression is dramatically reduced. Amygdalectomized cats do not become aggressive even when suspended by their tails or when they are generally roughed up (330). Amygdalectomy also eliminates predatory aggression in the cat (373) and in the rat (426). Fear reactions (escape tendencies) are also reduced by amygdalectomy in a variety of animals with consequent reduction in fear-induced aggressive behavior. This is true of the monkey (320; 330; 331; 348) the cat (399) the wild Norway rat (136; 203; 426) as well as the lynx and agouti (331).

Even amygdalectomy, which involves a relatively small, histologically separable structure, turns out to be a rather gross operation as far as aggressive behavior is concerned. The amygdala includes at least eight identifiable nuclei (147). Some of these nuclei function to facilitate certain kinds of aggressive behavior while others are inhibitory. Recent research indicates that some of the contradictory results in the studies involving total amygdalectomy were probably due to subtotal ablation. Thus, it seems likely that in those studies where increased aggressiveness occurred, one of the aggression-facilitating nuclei was missed (351).

While the exact relationships between the various nuclei in the amygdala and aggressive behavior remain to be worked out in detail (see Moyer, 275, for a recent attempt) it is clear from the results of a number of studies (130; 207; 351; 399) that aggressive behaviors of different kinds, in a variety of species, can be blocked by the removal of very tiny amounts of precisely the right brain tissue. In the cat, for example, this may involve as little as ½ cu. cm.

Lesions in a number of brain structures other than the amygdala also result in a reduction of hostile behavior. Bilateral removal of 50 percent to 90 percent of the hippocampus in the monkey, baboon or cat without damage to the overlying cortex or adjacent structures results in an increase in docility (153). Delgado and Kitahata (101) offer support for the role of the hippocampus in aggressive tendencies. They were able to produce functional reversible lesions in the hippocampus of monkeys by injecting anesthetics through permanently implanted cannulae. The injection of dibucaine, phenobarbital, and xylocaine produced a decrease in aggressiveness. The monkeys did not show their teeth or attempt to bite a glove even when struck lightly in the face with it. The above findings are contrary to a study by Green, Clemente and de Groot (156), which showed an increase in aggression after hippocampectomy, but it seems likely, as they suggest, that the aggression increase resulted from "tissue irritation."

Studies on the effects of lesions of the cingulum emphasize the need for caution in generalizing results of studies on one species of animal to another. Anand and Dua (13) and Kennard (211; 212) have reported an increase in irritability in cats after cingulectomy, although a recent study by Ursin (400) found no effect of that operation on cats. Brutkowski, Fonberg and Mempel (58) also found hyperirritability in dogs after lesions in the cingulum. However, cingulectomy in monkeys reduces fear and makes them more docile (146; 211; 408).

Lesions in the posteromedial hypothalamus (326), anterior thalamic nuclei (330), dorsomedial thalamus (362), midbrain (57), and lateral hypothalamus (208) have been shown to cause a reduction of one or another kind of aggressive behavior.

INHIBITION OF AGGRESSION IN HUMANS BY BRAIN LESIONS

There are men who have so much spontaneous activity in the neural systems which underlie aggressive behavior that they are a constant threat to themselves and to those around them. These are individuals who are confined to the back wards of mental hospitals under either constant sedation or constant restraint. The homicidal hostility of these persons can be reduced if appropriate brain lesions are made to interrupt the functioning of these systems for irascibility. In some cases, they have gone from the back wards out into society to lead useful lives.

There is now abundant evidence that pathological hyperirritability and aggressive behavior in humans is associated with several types of brain dysfunction. Tumors with an irritative focus frequently result in increased irritability and rage attacks. Cases manifesting this syndrome have been described with tumors in the temporal lobe (227; 281; 407), the frontal lobe (371), the hypothalamus (9), and the septal region (437). More recently, Sano (325) has reported on 1800 cases of brain tumor and found the irritability syndrome in those involving the temporal lobe and the anterior hypothalamus.

Gibbs (140) has estimated that approximately half of the patients with epilepsy who have an anterior temporal lobe focus have some psychiatric disorder. These non-ictal psychiatric symptoms are not directly related to electroencephalographic abnormalities (also see Gibbs, 141). Gloor (147) has suggested that there is a "propensity for these patients to be provoked into explosive and violent anger, often for causes of the most trifling nature."

EEG abnormalities in the temporal lobe have been correlated with behavioral aberrations in individuals diagnosed as having episodic behavior disorders (311). In 36 out of 100 consecutive temporal lobe epileptic patients selected for temporal lobectomy, Serafetinides (346) found overt physical aggressiveness as a part of the behavior pattern. (See Wilder, 419, for a further discussion of epilepsy and aggressive behavior.)

In some individuals manifesting the dyscontrol syndrome, the EEG appears to be normal. However, there is evidence that the patient's disturbed behavior is accompanied by hypersynchronous activity recorded from depth electrodes placed in rhinencephalic structures (119; 173; 268). It has been repeatedly shown that the surgical excision of the epileptogenic focus may result in an alleviation of the pathology.

This indicates that the cause was due to abnormal discharges and not to lesions in the brain (147). It is important to note that many of these inter-ictal, aggressive, dyscontrol symptoms are episodic just as epilepsy is episodic. Between episodes, the individual may behave in a completely normal manner. It should also be recognized that individuals manifesting inter-ictal or sub-ictal dyscontrol syndromes are on a continuum which varies from homicidal behavior to occasional "normal" irritability. As Jonas (196) points out so succinctly,

> Biological laws would demand the existence of a continuum extending from the intense focal and generalized electrical discharges in grand mal down to the normally firing brain. It is also probable that the brain, in its

complexity, could not function unceasingly without the occurrence of abnormal discharges resulting from occasionally overburdened circuits. Such manifestations, however, may escape detection because of the innocuous and inconsequential aspects of the symptoms.

Jonas goes on to make the important point that spontaneous firing in the motor system may result in the twitching eyelid or the activation of whole muscle groups such as in nocturnal jactitations during light sleep. Thus, it is most reasonable to expect that spontaneous firing in the temporal lobe might result in feelings of irritation, anger or rage. If this activity is sufficiently intense, the hostile impulses may be acted out. When J. P. Scott (339) says, "There is no known physiological mechanism by which spontaneous internal stimulation for fighting arises," he chooses to ignore all of the data presented here.

The experimental work of Kluver and Bucy, which involved bilateral temporal lobe ablation and resulted in surgically induced docility, inspired some surgeons to attempt the same operation on man in an attempt to modify aggressive behavior and agitation in schizophrenic patients (378). As might be suspected from the results of Kluver and Bucy, this radical operation resulted in a variety of dysfunctions. In one case report presented in detail by Terzian and Ore (378), bilateral removal of the temporal lobes, including most of the uncus and hippocampus, exactly reproduced the Kluver and Bucy syndrome, including rage and fear reduction, loss of recognition of people, increased sex activity, bulimia, and serious memory deficiencies. Prior to the operation, the patient had frequent attacks of aggressive and violent behavior during which he had attempted to strangle his mother and to crush his younger brother under his feet. After unilateral temporal lobectomy, he attacked the nurses and doctors and threatened some with death. After the second temporal lobe was removed, he became extremely meek with everyone and was "absolutely resistant to any attempt to arouse aggressiveness and violent reactions in him."

Temporal lobe lesions, both unilateral and bilateral, have been extensively used in man to control epilepsy which is not susceptible to drug therapy. A frequent side effect of the operation, in addition to seizure control, has been a general reduction in hostility compared to the individual's reactions prior to the operation (157; 297; 344; 377). Although cases have been reported in which aggressive behavior has been increased by the operation (328; 428), the increase is generally temporary. Some authors report no change in psychiatric symptoms (142). Bailey (19) indicates that temporal lesions do not generally reduce the psychiatric problems of the patient except that in certain subjects, the attacks of aggressive behavior were reduced or completely eliminated. He believes that the aggressive attacks were in fact psychomotor seizures. Falconer, Hill, Meyer and Wilson (121) report definite personality changes for the better after temporal lobe lesions and conclude that the most striking improvement was in the reduction of aggressiveness. "Whereas, previously, the relatives of the patient might be very careful as to what they said to the patient for fear of provoking an aggressive outbreak, they can now talk freely and joke with him" (120).

It is clear that radical ablation of the temporal lobes can reduce pathological hostility in man. However, as with animals, the production of surgical docility in man is not limited to temporal lobe lesions. Following Ward's demonstration of the calming effects of cingulectomy on monkeys, Le Beau (233) did cingulum ablations on humans in an attempt to control agitated behavior, obsessive compulsive states, and epilepsy. He concluded that "Cingulectomy is specially indicated in intractable cases of anger, violence, aggressiveness, and permanent agitation." Other investigators have found that lesions in the anterior cingular gyrus, while not eliminating outbursts of anger, have reduced the intensity and duration of such outbursts (325; 390; 418).

Operating on the theory that pathological aggression is due to an imbalance in the ergotropic circuits and the tropotropic circuits with a dominance of the ergotropic, Sano (325; 327) has performed what he calls "sedative surgery." This involves lesioning the ergotropic zone (posterior hypothalamus) in order to normalize the balance. He reports remarkable success with patients showing intractable violent behavior. They became markedly calm, passive and tractable, showing decreased spontaneity. Although they showed a recovery of the spontaneity within a month, the other changes persisted for up to three years and seven months, as long as the patients were followed up. Of course, one need not accept Sano's theory in order to accept his results. He may very well be getting the right results for the wrong reasons. Sano's theory implies that aggressive behavior is the result of excessive arousal and can thus be eliminated by sedation. Sedation can, of course, reduce hostile behavior as it does all other behavior. Sedation, however, is not essential to the limiting of aggression. It is quite possible to be hyperactive without being aggressive. For example, the Kluver-Bucy monkeys were extremely friendly but at the same time, they were hypomanic and always ready to engage in play.

Lesions in a number of other brain areas have resulted in reductions in aggressive behavior in humans. Bilateral lesions of the dorsomedial nuclei of the thalamus result in a reduction in tension, anxiety states, agitation and aggressiveness (362). Other areas resulting in calming effects after lesioning are the fornix, the upper mesencephalon (326) and the frontal lobes (242).

The most precise control of aggressive behavior through brain lesions, and the one which involves the greatest promise, has been more recently developed and involves stereotaxic lesions in the amygdala. Lesions 8 to 10 mm. in diameter have been produced by an injection of 0.6 to 0.8 ml. of oil to which lipiodol had been added (287; 288). These authors report that 85 percent of 51 patients showed a marked reduction in emotional excitability and a normalization of their social behavior. It should be emphasized that except for the reduction in hostility, none of the signs of the Kluver-Bucy syndrome resulted from the bilateral destruction of the amygdaloid nuclei.

Heimburger, et al. (179) have also reported success using partial amygdalectomy. They have lesioned approximately half of the amygdala using cryosurgery. The lesions were 8 to 10 mm. in diameter. This operation has resulted in dramatic improvement in some patients and an overall improvement in 23 of 25 patients. Destructiveness, hostility and aggression toward others were the behavior symptoms most frequently improved by the operation. The improvement in two of the patients was so great that they were released from mental institutions. Others were moved from solitary confinement to open wards. Some of them were observed to smile and laugh for the first time in their lives after the operation. Heimburger, et al. (179) conclude "Stereotaxic amygdalotomy is a safe and relatively easy procedure for treatment of a select group of patients who have previously been considered untreatable."

Similar results have been reported by Schwab, et al. (332). They use a very promising technique of implanting 48 pairs of recording electrodes bilaterally through the limbic system. Then they carry out a program of recording and stimulation over a period of several weeks in order to localize and limit as much as possible the precise area which, when destroyed, will relieve the symptoms. A radiofrequency lesion is then made through the indwelling electrodes. Ervin indicates that there is good reason to believe from their observations that the neural and neurochemical substrate for the motor seizure and for the interseizure assaultive and aggressive behavior are different. It is possible to eliminate the one without affecting the other (Ervin, personal communication).

AGGRESSION CONTROL BY BRAIN STIMULATION

The control of aggressive behavior can also be achieved by the activation of those neural systems which send inhibitory fibers to the aggression systems. Delgado has repeatedly shown that vicious rhesus monkeys can be tamed by the stimulation of aggression suppressor areas. A normally aggressive female monkey that had to be handled with gloves and would bite anything that came within range was implanted with an electrode in the caudate nucleus. As soon as the electrode was activated, the animal became docile. She closed her normally open and threatening mouth and if objects or the experimenter's hands were placed near her mouth, she either pushed them away or turned her head. Delgado emphasizes that this reaction was not one of "general arrest" in which the animal was immobilized by a generalized motor inhibition. She showed good coordination and no loss of mobility. She responded well to sensory stimulation and gave the impression that she was well "aware of her surroundings" (91). In another case, it was possible for the experimenter to put his finger in the monkey's mouth during the period when its aggressive behavior was blocked by caudate stimulation (97). As soon as the current was turned off, the animal was as dangerous as ever.

In order to eliminate the need for restraint and the necessity for connecting wires to the head, a technique was developed by which the brain of the subject could be stimulated by remote, radio control. The monkey wore a small stimulating device on its back which was connected by subcutaneous leads to the electrodes that were implanted in various locations in the brain. The leads were connected through a very small switching relay that could be closed by an impulse from a miniature radio receiver bolted to the animal's skull. The radio receiver could then be activated by a transmitter that was effective up to several hundred feet away. With this system, it was possible to study the monkeys while permitting them free range in the colony. The experimenter could control the brain stimulation by activating the radio transmitter from outside the cage. With this experimental setup, it was possible to change the normal social hierarchy in the colony. Stimulation of the caudate nucleus of the boss monkey blocked his spontaneous aggressive tendencies. His territoriality diminished and the other monkeys in the colony reacted to him differently. They made fewer submissive gestures and showed less fear of the boss. When the caudate n. was being stimulated, it was possible for the experimenter to enter the cage and catch the monkey with bare hands (93; 95). Reduction in aggressive behavior by caudate stimulation has also been demonstrated in the chimpanzee (100).

During one phase of the experiment described above, the button for the transmitter was placed inside the cage near the feeding tray and thus made available to all of the monkeys in the colony. One of the submissive monkeys learned to press the button during periods when the boss monkey showed aggressive tendencies. When the boss would make threatening gestures, the smaller monkey would frequently look him straight in the eye and press the button, thus directly calming him down and reducing his hostile tendencies (93; 95).

Man also has neural systems in the brain that, when activated, function to block ongoing aggressive behavior. Sem-Jacobsen and Torkildsen (345) report that stimulation in the ventromedial frontal lobes had a calming effect on a violent manic patient. A similar effect resulted from stimulating the central area of the temporal lobe. When both points were stimulated in rapid succession, the calming antihostility effect was greater and of some duration. Peterson, in a discussion of the above paper, also reports that actively disturbed and antagonistic patients become quite placid and talk well after about 15 minutes of stimulation in the frontal medial area of the brain. This period of calmness might last for a day or even longer.

Stimulation in the septal region of animals can function as a reinforcer.

In man, septal stimulation results in a variety of subjective positive feelings, not infrequently linked with sexual ideation (176). Septal stimulation can also block intractable pain. One 15-minute session may control the pain for several days (178). Stimulation in the same general brain area can also dramatically inhibit the rage response.

> Patient No. B-10, the psychomotor epileptic, was stimulated in the septal region during a period when he was exhibiting agitated violent psychotic behavior. The stimulus was introduced without his knowledge. Almost instantly, his behavioral state changed from one of disorganization, rage, and persecution to one of happiness and mild euphoria. He described the beginning of a sexual motive state. He was unable, when questioned directly, to explain the sudden shift in his feelings and thoughts (174).

Heath goes on to point out that the case described above is not unique, but has been repeated in a large number of patients in his laboratory. The same kind of dramatic change can also be produced by direct application of acetylcholine to the septal area through permanently implanted cannulae. In one patient described by Heath, the electrical recording characterized by spike and slow wave activity in the septal area was normalized by the application of acetylcholine at the same time that the rage responses associated with it were reduced (176).

Direct brain stimulation as a means of aggression control has some obvious problems connected with it, but a number of developments may resolve these difficulties and make this technique practicable in certain cases. It is already technically feasible to avoid the necessity of bringing the patient into the laboratory, plugging him in and stimulating at periodic intervals. Heath (171) has developed a transistorized self-contained unit which the patient can wear on his belt. The unit generates a preset train of stimulus pulses each time it is activated. This stimulator could be connected to an electrode implanted in an area of the brain which reduces aggressive tendencies. The patient would then have his own "antihostility button" which he could press to calm himself down whenever his irrational feelings of hostility occurred. The fact that septal stimulation also produces pleasurable sensations would be a bonus. (This device has already been used with a narcoleptic patient who, whenever he felt himself drifting off to sleep, could reach down and press his "on button" and once again become alert. His friends soon learned that they could press the button to get him back into the conversation if he fell asleep too rapidly to press it himself (174).)

Remote radio control of intracerebral stimulation is also possible in the completely free patient just as it is in the free-ranging monkey. The surgical team at Massachusetts General Hospital has already implanted electrodes in the brains of four patients and brought the leads out to a radio receiver which was attached to the patient's head and covered by the head bandages (102). It is thus possible to stimulate these patients from a considerable distance by activating the radio transmitter. Various effects have been reported to result from radio stimulation with this device including, "pleasant sensations, elation, deep thoughtful concentration, odd feelings, super relaxation, and colored vision." In one patient, outbursts of rage and assaultive behavior, similar to her spontaneous episodic anger responses, resulted from stimulation in the right amygdala. It is also possible to record from the electrodes because the unit on the head includes a very small RF transmitter. If the electrodes were implanted in an aggression inhibitory area, it would be quite possible to permit the patient to engage in his normal activities as long as he was within the range of the transmitter. Periodically then, the stimulator could be activated, thus keeping the patient in a nonaggressive state of mind.

Even though the unit described above weighs only about 70 grams, there are still some obvious difficulties with it. It must be worn under bandages on the head (although one patient was able to hide the device completely with a wig) and it is necessary for the leads to the electrodes to penetrate the skin, thus producing a constant source of irritation as well as the ever present possibility of infection. However, even these difficulties have been resolved by the recent developments in microminiaturization. At a recent symposium, Delgado (98) reported that an entire stimulation unit had been reduced in size and shaped so that it could be implanted under the skin. It is therefore possible for an individual to have an electrode implant in an aggression-inhibiting area attached to one of these devices. As soon as his hair grows back, he will look no different than any other individual. He could then return to all normal activities as long as he stayed within the range of the transmitter. Obviously, the range would depend on the transmitter's power.

One further development would also contribute to the use of brain stimulation as a means of aggression control. Devices are now in the process of development which will, in time, permit the stimulation of precise brain locations without the necessity of opening the skull. One of these devices involves the use of two parabolic reflectors to focus sound energy in such a way that only at the point of intersection of the two sources will there be an effect. This device is currently successfully used as a stereotaxic lesioning instrument (Baltimore Instrument Co., Baltimore, Md.). However, according to one of the developers, there is the distinct possibility that it could be modified to be used as a stimulator (C. Dickey, personal communication). If the effects of brain stimulation in reducing aggressive potential are reasonably long lasting, as they are for the inhibition of pain (178), it would be possible for the patient with intractable hostility to stop in for brain stimulation every few days and have his intractable hostility controlled without the necessity of surgery. It should be emphasized that this device and technique have not yet been developed. However, they are clearly within the range of possibility.

AGGRESSION CONTROL BY HORMONE THERAPY

Our physiological model of aggressive behavior indicates that the neurological systems for aggression are sensitized by chemical factors in the bloodstream, which are primarily but not exclusively hormones. An understanding of the endocrinology and blood chemistry influences on aggression should ultimately lead to a rational therapy for certain kinds of hostility in man.

The importance of androgens in the bloodstream for intermale and irritable aggression has already been mentioned and is well documented. Thus, any manipulation of the blood chemistry which results in reduction in the androgen level should raise the threshold for those aggressive tendencies. Castration as a means of accomplishing androgen reduction has been repeatedly reported to reduce fighting in animals (38; 347; 352; 397). The same procedure, although certainly a drastic one, has been found useful in the control of certain violent sex crimes in man (170; 234).

There are now several substances available that have demonstrated antiandrogenic activity (236). A-Norprogesterone (237), chlormadinone acetate (312), and cyproterone acetate (291) have been shown to be potent antagonists of androgens. In intact animals, the administration of these substances works in a manner similar to castration (291). Although there have not yet been extensive clinical trials, it certainly seems reasonable to suggest, as Neumann, Elger and Berswordt-Wallrabe (290) do, that these substances may be of particular value for the control of males with disturbed sex drive, particularly those who are unable to discontinue committing violent sexual offenses.

There is some evidence from animals that estrogenic substances may function to inhibit aggressive behavior. Clark and Birch (74), working with castrated chimpanzees, found that aggressivity was reduced by estrogen. The animal given the estrogen became subordinate to its cage mate. Suchowsky, et al. (372), have recently reported that the fighting behavior usually found in isolated mice was completely inhibited by injections of estradiol. He concluded "that an androgenic effect may be masked or inhibited by an impeded estrogenic side-effect or by estrogens themselves. . . . The strongest inhibitors of aggressiveness are represented by estrogens and followed by pregnane derivatives which seem to be longer lasting." The aggressive behavior of the female, golden hamster toward the male can be drastically reduced by the administration of six daily injections of estrogen followed by a single injection of progesterone (219).

So far, there are a limited number of studies which indicate that female hormones may be used in the control of aggressive tendencies in man. Golla (quoted in Sands, 323) suggested that estrogenic substances could be used as a form of chemical castration in man. This approach, he suggested, would be more efficient than an actual castration because the estrogens would block the effects of the adrenal androgens which would not be affected by the operation. Sands (323) reports a series of cases in which the aggressive tendencies of adolescents and young adults were controlled by the use of stilboestrol. Another case in which irritable aggression and excessive libido were controlled by the administration of stilboestrol is described in some detail by Dunn (111). This patient was a 27-year-old male under maximum sentence for sexual offenses against female minors. He was a persistent troublemaker in prison and was frequently placed in solitary confinement for insubordination. The prisoner had abnormal amounts of male hormone and gonadotropic hormone in the urine before therapy and was preoccupied with his sex life. After four weeks of daily treatment with stilboestrol, he reported that his sexual responses, both physical and mental, were reduced. He had also adapted much better to prison discipline and was no longer considered a troublemaker. He continued relatively symptom free for more than three months after discontinuance of therapy. Subsequently, however, he had a return of his symptoms and requested a resumption of therapy.

Although the above case reports can hardly be considered as definitive, they certainly indicate that further work should be done in this area and they present another possibility for the direct physiological manipulation of hostile behavior.

A significant number of women show a premenstrual syndrome which includes an increase in irritability and feelings of hostility (85; 158; 164). In individuals with inadequate controls, these feelings are acted upon with resulting aggressive behavior. In a study of female prison inmates, it was shown that 51 percent of the adult population, mean age of 32.4 years, showed premenstrual tension. Thirty-three percent of the reformatory population, mean age 21.4 years, manifested premenstrual tension. A study of the prison records revealed that 62 percent of the crimes of violence were committed during the premenstrual week and only 2 percent at the end of the period (273). A similar finding is reported by Dalton (84). He found that 49 percent of all crimes were committed by women during menstruation or in the premenstrum. Thus, the association between menstruation and crime is highly significant. One would expect only 29 percent of all crimes to be committed during the eight-day period if they were normally distributed. The probability of the obtained distribution occurring by chance is less than one in a thousand. Dalton (84) reports further that women prisoners were more frequently reported for "bad behavior" during the menstrual or premenstrual period.

Feelings of irritability and hostility during the premenstrum are not confined to a few asocial individuals who get into difficulties with the law. Moderate or severe degrees of the premenstrual syndrome occur in about a quarter of all women (82; 165). Janowsky, Gorney and Mandell (194) estimate that up to 90 percent of women claim to undergo some irritability, hopelessness, or depression prior to or during menstruation.

The underlying physiology of the irritability associated with premenstrual tension is obscure. It seems clear that the syndrome is associated with a fall in the progesterone level in the blood (165). Several studies have also shown that the symptoms can be alleviated by the administration of this hormone (85; 158). It has also been shown that women who take oral contraceptives that contain progestagenic agents show significantly less irritability than do women who are not taking the pill (165). It may be that the irritability-reducing effects of the progestogens are a function of their direct effect in the neural systems in the brain which relate to hostility. However, the explanation may be much less direct. Janowsky, et al. (194) hypothesize that the irritability results from the cyclic increase in aldosterone inasmuch as weight changes, behavioral changes and aldosterone changes seem to parallel each other. The resulting increase in sodium and water retention caused by the aldosterone results in a secondary neuronal irritability and consequent psychic symptoms. The therapeutic effects of lithium and diuretics in treating premenstrual tension may then be due to their tendency to reverse the aldosterone effect on sodium metabolism.

Another possible explanation relates to the tendency for a cyclic hypoglycemic reaction. Morton, et al. (273) reported that a sugar tolerance test during the premenstrual period resulted in a typical hypoglycemic type curve in the female prisoners they studied. A reduction in premenstrual symptoms occurred under treatment, including improvement in behavior and attitude and less punishment for infraction of rules. Their therapeutic regimen consisted of placebo, high-protein diet alone and with ammonium chloride. Although the greatest improvement occurred with the combined therapy, 39 percent improved with the high-protein diet which is a recommended therapy for hypoglycemia (247).

Hypoglycemia, from what ever cause, is, in many cases, associated with tendencies to hostility and is another dysfunction in the blood chemistry which evidently sensitizes the neural substrates for aggression. There has, unfortunately, been relatively little systematic study of this relationship. However, Gyland (quoted in Frederichs and Goodman, 132) studied six-hundred patients with hypoglycemia and indicates that 89 percent of them showed hyper-irritability and 45 percent manifested "unsocial, asocial, or antisocial behavior." A study of Salzer (quoted in Frederichs and Goodman, 132) indicated that irritability was found in 45 percent and unsocial or antisocial behavior in 22 percent of patients with low blood sugar. Gloor (148) suggests that some of the most aggressive patients are those with Islet cell tumors during the periods when they are hypoglycemic. When their blood sugar is raised, they again become "quite civilized."

A much neglected paper by Wilder (420) compiles a remarkable amount of evidence that implicates low blood sugar as a causal factor in hostility and crime. He indicates that the aggressive tendency associated with hypoglycemic states is manifest in matrimonial relationships, homicidal threats and acts, destructiveness, and cruelty towards children. Wilder suggests that the hypoglycemic state may represent a temporary state of "moral insanity." Although there is a clear-cut need for further work on this problem, particularly experimental studies with control groups, there appears to be reasonable evidence of this relationship.

Hypoglycemia and the psychological effects related to it are readily treated by altering the blood chemistry through diet or through the use of adrenocortical steroids (247).

Low blood sugar tends to intensify allergic reactions and although the physiological mechanism has not yet been found, a frequent component of allergic reactions is an increase in aggressive tendencies. These reactions may vary from slight irritability through argumentativeness to obviously abnormal aggressive behavior (302). Some highly allergic individuals respond to specific foods with a full-blown rage reaction within half an hour after ingestion. Observations by a mother of a child so affected rather dramatically illustrate this point.

> You wouldn't believe bananas. Within twenty minutes of eating a banana this child would be in the worst temper tantrum—no, seizures—you have ever seen. I tried this five times because I couldn't believe my own eyes. He reacted with behavior to all sugars except maple sugar. We went to California the Christmas of 1962 to be with my parents. Robbie's Christmas treats were all made from maple sugar. He was asking for some other candy. My mother wanted him to have it and I told her alright if she wanted to take care of the tantrum. Of course she didn't believe me—but predictably, within thirty minutes she had her hands full with Robbie in a tantrum. It made a believer of her. These discussions did not take place in front of the child if you're wondering about the power of suggestion.
>
> If you go into this food reaction thing, it will make you feel so sorry for people you can't stand it. After bad behavior from food, Robbie would cry and say he couldn't help it and feel so badly about it. You won't be able to read of a crime of violence without wondering if a chemical reaction controlled the aggressor—in fact you'll be unable to condemn anyone for anything—or maybe you're less impressionable.

Allergies can, of course, be treated by the direct or indirect manipulation of the blood chemistry.

AGGRESSION CONTROL BY DRUGS

The activity of the neural systems responsible for aggressive behavior and feelings of hostility can also be reduced by the use of drugs. Although there is currently no drug that is a completely specific antihostility agent, there are available a significant number of preparations that do reduce aggressive tendencies as one component of their action. The current state of the art is summarized nicely by Resnick (305) when he says, "There is ample evidence to indicate that psychotropic drugs now available may help individuals who are aggressive, irritable, unstable, egocentric, easily offended, obsessive, compulsive and dependent, who demonstrate such symptoms as anxiety, depression, hysteria, agony, unexplainable and motiveless behavior, recurrent violent emotional upsets, including temper tantrums and violent rages."

Some kind of a measure for aggressiveness is a part of the battery of screening tests used in the initial evaluation of psychotropic drugs on animals and many standard drugs are being evaluated for antiaggression effects. A review article by Valzelli (402) provides some notion of the extent of these investigations. He reported two hundred four animal studies which dealt with the drug-aggression interaction. Eight of these studies reported drugs which produced an increase in aggressiveness; twenty-four reported no effect on the particular behavior studied. Of the eighty drugs covered in the studies reported by Valzelli, seventy-four of them inhibited some form of aggression in some animal studied. Thus, the potential for the development of aggression-inhibiting drugs for humans is very great. It is important, however, to recognize that drug effects may be both species specific and situation specific. Valzelli is one of the few authors who makes an attempt to discriminate among the different kinds of aggressive behavior. His table of drug effects shows that some drugs tend to block one kind of aggression and facilitate another within the same species and that a given drug may block aggression in one species but facilitate it in another. In addition, there are wide individual differences in the susceptibility to the taming effects of various drugs.

All of the above factors are significant in the treatment of hostile tendencies in humans. Aggressive behavior has many causes and can result from an overactivity or dysfunction in a number of different neural systems. It is therefore not surprising that a specific drug may be effective in reducing the hostility of some individuals and have no effect on others with similar symptoms. Nevertheless, a large number of cases in which hostility is a major disturbing factor can be successfully treated with pharmacotherapy.

The advent of the widespread use of phenothiazines less than fifteen years ago led to a significant reduction in psychotic hostility.

Kline (220) suggests that "wards formerly filled with screaming denudative, assaultive patients now have window curtains and flowers on the table." Quantitative estimates of the reduction of destructive, assaultive behavior are difficult to find, but Kline (220) offers one that is dramatic in its simplicity. In 1955, prior to the use of the major tranquilizers in the Rockland State Hospital, there were 8,000 window panes broken and three full-time glaziers were needed to keep the windows in repair. By 1960, when full use was being made of the psychotropic drugs, the window pane breakage was down to 1,900 panes a year. It has been suggested that the sedative action of the phenothiazines alone could account for the improved picture in the mental hospitals. However, it must be recognized that potent sedative hypnotics such as chloral hydrate and paraldehyde have been known and used for three-quarters of a century.

The phenothiazines, or major tranquilizers, all appear to have a taming effect over and above their sedative action (21; 154). However, some tend to exacerbate hostility symptoms in some patients, while others appear to be particularly effective in the reduction of those symptoms. Perphenazine alone or in combination with the antidepressant amitriptyline has been useful in reducing the aggressive tendencies of depressed patients (294), aggressive mental defectives (266), sex deviated criminals (59), and aggressive alcoholics (34). The hostile tendencies of a wide variety of patients from epileptic psychotics (424) to disturbed adolescents (315) and hyperactive children (6) have been successfully controlled with thioridazine. A survey of the studies on thioridazine is given by Cohen (78).

Dilantin® (sodium diphenylhydantoin) is a drug which has been used with considerable success in the control of seizures. It has recently come into popular prominence because of its apparent tendency to control hyperexcitability and hostility in nonepileptic patients (317). Zimmerman (438), as early as 1956, studied 200 children with severe behavior disorders and reported that 70 percent improved under sodium diphenylhydrantoin therapy showing less excitability, as well as less frequent and less severe temper tantrums.

® Registered trademark for diphenylhydantoin, Parke, Davis & Co., Detroit, Mich.

Turner (394), in a study of 72 subjects seen in psychiatric practice, found that 86 percent showed drug-related improvement, particularly in relation to anger, irritability and tension. The drug is effective with individuals having both abnormal and normal EEG records (149; 319).

There seems to be little question that dilantin is useful in a wide variety of disorders, including neurosis, psychosis, psychopathology, and emotionally disturbed children. The behavioral syndrome that seems to be common in such a diverse group of patients includes explosiveness, low frustration tolerance, irritability, impulsive behavior, compulsive behavior, aggressive behavior, erratic behavior, inability to delay gratification, mood swings, short attention span, undirected activity and similar symptoms (304). The general findings above were supported in an excellent double-blind study of behavior modification in selected prisoners and juvenile delinquents (304). Resnick (304) gives excerpts from tape recordings of interviews with the prisoners during the study which reveal the potency of the drug in manipulating negative affect. Certainly, a great many more studies must be done, but there is every reason to believe that drug administration to selected prisoners would not only make them feel better, but would also facilitate prison management.

Hyperkinetic children present a behavior disorder syndrome that includes overactivity, restlessness, aggressiveness, temper tantrums, disobedience, impulsivity and poor concentration. There are now a variety of drugs that dramatically reduce these symptoms without appreciable sedation. One of the earliest and most effective drugs that is still being used is the stimulant, amphetamine (52). Although there is no adequate explanation for the effect, it is clear that aggressively noisy children and those inclined toward antisocial acting out behavior are "normalized" by amphetamines (177). The same class of drugs also seems to be useful with adult patients who have immature personalities with outbursts of spontaneous aggression (21). A variety of other drugs quell the outbursts of hostility in children with behavior disorders. Benadryl is useful in children below the age of ten years, but is considerably less effective in older children (125). Several studies have shown that haloperidol is particularly effective in the treatment of children with severe behavior disorders. Barker and Fraser (29), in a double-blind crossover study, showed that children with the hyperactive aggressive syndrome were significantly improved on haloperidol. Similar findings have been reported by Cunningham, Pillai, and Rogers (83). They suggest that the reduction in overactivity, destructiveness, teasing and bullying should provide greater opportunity to positively reinforce more desirable forms of behavior.

Two more classes of drugs that effectively reduce irritability should be mentioned because of their extensive use and their potential for even greater use. These are the so-called minor tranquilizers, which include the propanediols (meprobamate and tybamate) at the benzodiazepines (including chlordiazepoxide, diazepam, and oxazepam). Although the propanediols have a taming effect on vicious monkeys and aggressive cats (40; 182), the benzodiazepines seem to be effective at a dose level that produces neither sedation nor ataxia (329). (See Cook and Kelleher, 81, for an extensive review of these findings.) Meprobamate effectively controls tension and anxiety symptoms which are associated with irritability in humans (21) and is effective in the reduction of premenstrual tension. A large number of studies have shown that the benzodiazepines can effectively reduce aggressive excitability, hostility and irritability. (References 33; 90; and 103 are a few.) Diazepam has been used with "remarkable success" in eliminating the destructive rampages of psychotic criminals (202). Kalina indicates that schizophrenia is unaffected by the drug, but the aggressive and destructive elements which make the patient difficult and dangerous to manage are eliminated.

FURTHER IMPLICATIONS

There can be little doubt that when certain physiological conditions occur, both men and animals will react with hostility toward any appropriate stimulus object. If the organism is manipulated physiologically so as to alter or prevent those internal conditions, aggressive behavior will not occur. In light of the studies presented above, it is naive to suggest, as does Montagu (269), that "all of man's natural inclinations are toward the development of goodness" or that "there is not a shred of evidence that man is born with 'hostile' or 'evil' impulses which must be watched and disciplined" (269:44). Whether man is born good or evil is a value judgment and depends on who is making the judgment and at what point in history the judgment is being made. However, there is abundant evidence that man has innate, neural and endocrine organizations which when activated result in hostile thoughts and behaviors. To ignore these data is to forfeit means of control which are valuable to both the victims and the aggressors.

Although there is still much to learn about the physiological control of aggression, there can be little doubt that such control is now possible through brain lesion and brain stimulation or manipulation of the internal environment with hormones or drugs. The control is here now. How it is to be used remains to be determined. I suggested in the initial paper in this volume that there is reason to be concerned about the potential misuse of such powerful controls. The in-depth survey of the means of aggression control presented here will not provide peace of mind for those who are concerned about the potential absolute control of man by man.

I also suggested, in the initial paper in this volume, that it was not inconceivable that specific anti-hostility agents could be placed in the water supply.

In my laboratory at Carnegie-Mellon, we have squirrel monkeys who are vicious and untameable. A hand put into the cage to touch or pet them will be savagely and repeatedly bitten. They can only be handled with heavy gauntlet gloves. Judy Parkman and I have recently shown that it is possible to put a few thousandths of a gram of diazepam in the milk that we give them. They evidently cannot taste it, nor could I. When the drug begins to take effect, they lose their hostility and can be handled with bare hands. As others have reported, the drug does not sedate them, it simply makes them more friendly. Most of the milk available today is pasturized and homogenized and has vitamin D added. Will the milk available tomorrow have an antihostility drug added or will it indeed be added to the water supply? Resnick (305) has suggested that by the year 2000, we will have a drug-controlled society or a society that will self-destruct. But, who will make the controlling decisions?

The absolute physiological control of some kinds of aggression in individuals is a realization. The control of hostility in masses of people is so near attainment that we should be concerned about it. We should begin to seriously ask the question, "Who will control the controllers of the mind?"

EPILOGUE

I have had the opportunity to present this paper to several audiences since the original presentation in June of 1969. The question period frequently reveals that some members of the audience assume that I am advocating immediately dispensing anti-hostility drugs into the water supply. It should be made clear that I am not. When an epidemiologist warns that the conditions are conducive to an outbreak of typhoid fever, it does not mean that he is in favor of, or advocates, a typhoid epidemic.

It should also be mentioned that aggression is not the only type of behavior that can be subjected to physiological manipulation and, thereby, controlled. The potential for the control of other kinds of behavior will be briefly considered in the next paper in this volume.

The potential for the absolute control of man by man is well documented in the book *Behavior Control* by Perry London (New York: Harper & Row, 1969).

> The number of activities connected to specific places and processes in the brain and aroused, excited, augmented, inhibited, or suppressed at will by stimulation of the proper site is simply huge. Animals and men can be oriented toward each other with emotions ranging from stark terror or morbidity to passionate affection and sexual desire. Docility, fearful withdrawal, and panicked efforts at escape can be made to alternate with fury and ferocity of such degree that its subject can as readily destroy himself by exhaustion from his consuming rage as he can the object of it, whom he attacks, heedless of both danger and opportunity. Eating, drinking, sleeping, moving of bowels or limbs or organs of sensation, gracefully or in spastic comedy, can all be managed on electrical demand by puppeteers whose flawless strings are pulled from miles away by the unseen call of radio and whose puppets, made of flesh and blood, look "like electronic toys," so little self-direction

do they seem to have. Memory can be aroused with an immediacy that, in ordinary life, it almost never has; speech can be speeded up from halting phrases to relative chatter; laughter and tears, anger and friendliness, and fatigue and curiosity—all these and more can be aroused, reduced, shifted, and maneuvered by stimulations of the brain. Developments in the isolation of distinct brain structures, in mapping the anatomy of the brain, in neurosurgical techniques and instruments, and in electronics, especially the miniaturization of equipment, make all these things realities right now. Improvements in all these areas can only increase ability to control behavior by intervention in the brain (p. 137).

6

The Physiology of Affiliation and Hostility

K. E. MOYER

The evidence in the preceding papers makes it abundantly clear that there are internal impulses to various kinds of aggressive behavior. A judicious search of the literature seems to indicate that there are also internal impulses to a variety of affiliative responses and that there are interactions at the physiological level between the tendencies to hostility and the tendencies to affiliation. It is the purpose of this paper to explore the physiology of affiliative processes and to comment on the implications of these findings.

This paper is an outgrowth of discussions during the University of Virginia Sesquicentennial Symposium on "Allegiance and Hostility, Man's Mammalian Heritage" held October 8–11, 1969. It is to be published with papers presented at the symposium in a book to be edited by Dr. Frederick Richardson.

The original paper systematically presented information on the physiology of hostility and on the physiology of affiliative tendencies and then contrasted them. Since the material on the physiology of aggression has already been elaborated earlier in this volume, the paper has been substantially altered to avoid repetition by simply referring to the relevant sections in the previous papers.

I am grateful to Dr. Richardson for the invitation to participate in this symposium and for his kind hospitality while I was there. This series of conferences was held in the relaxed environment of the Boars Head Inn in the beautiful hills of Virginia.

The tendencies to affiliation function to make a given society more cohesive and increase the probabilities that the group members will interact. Tendencies to hostility, however, have the opposite effect in that they disrupt the society and increase the probabilities that the group members will avoid close relationships. The tendencies to hostility also provide for the dispersal of the species and limit the size of the social groups.

There are selective advantages to the dispersal of the members of a given species, such as the better distribution of available food (see Wynne-Edwards, 430). There are also selective advantages to social interactions and to group living, such as protection against predators (209). As a result of these selection pressures, various species have developed mechanisms that result in dispersal of the species as well as mechanisms that result in the formation of societies. As Barnett (31: 36) puts it, "A species with a system of threats and responses which cause dispersion must also have ways of bringing individuals together, if only for mating. Colonial species further require means by which conflict within groups is prevented or controlled."

There is no doubt that, particularly in higher mammals, many of the tendencies to affiliation and hostility are learned and many of the behavioral patterns for affiliation and hostility are culturally determined. However, it is the contention of this paper that there are innate physiological mechanisms which are the substrates of both affiliation and hostility. The purpose of this paper is to examine some of those physiological mechanisms.

It is important to recognize that there are no single unitary mechanisms for either hostility or affiliation. There are groups of behavior patterns that serve these two functions.

The various kinds of aggressive behavior and their physiological bases have been presented in detail in the third paper in this volume (275).

KINDS OF AFFILIATIVE RESPONSES

It is generally recognized that there is not a single affiliative motive that results in an increase in grouping tendencies. The following behavior proclivities increase the probability of proximal interactions and group formation. *Sexual behavior tendencies* obviously perform that function and are well enough known and documented not to require further comment here.

Body contact tendencies are very strong in a number of animal species. The stimulus object that is readily available and provides that type of stimulation is most frequently a conspecific. Wild rats, for example, manifest a strong tendency to crawl under another conspecific. Barnett (31: 36) indicates that "This is a quite distinctive taxon-specific act: it may be performed by an adult male in a strange area on meeting a resident (territory-holder), but also by a peaceful resident on meeting a stranger (juvenile rats at play crawl under any other rat that happens to be near)." The tendency of the juvenile monkey to approach the warm, resilient, supportive type of stimulus object is well documented. Tinklepaugh and Hartman (386) suggest that contact-seeking behavior is one of the strongest motivational factors in the infant monkey. Harlow (167) has shown that the infant monkey has a stronger tendency to approach a surrogate mother made of a comfortable contact material such as terry-cloth than it has to approach a mother surrogate made of wire. This is true even though the infant is fed at the wire mother surrogate. Rosenblum and Harlow (316) have shown further that infant monkeys are not deterred from clinging to their terry-cloth mother surrogates by aversive air blasts. If the mother and the infant monkey are separated, depriving them of the opportunity for close contact, both the mother and the infant manifest considerable emotionality (261) and the infant will ultimately show severe behavioral disturbances similar to the depression syndrome in man (209; 210). In fact, McKinney and Bunney (261) have suggested that this may be a reasonable animal model for the study of depression.

A third behavioral tendency that increases group interaction and cohesiveness is grooming. *Mutual grooming* is an activity engaged in by a number of animal species. Marler (255) gives an excellent account of the signals that constitute an invitation to groom in primates and discusses the importance of this activity in decreasing the distances between animals. Barnett (30) discusses similar material for the rat.

Parental behavior, either paternal or maternal, also tends to increase the proximity of at least the parents and the young. In some primate species, an infant tends to be the center of attention and other members of the troop are attracted to it. (See Marler, 255 for a more detailed discussion of this point; also, Mitchell, 267.)

In some animal species, grouping tendencies are facilitated by the *imprinting* process. The young, during a certain critical period, tend to fixate on and to follow the first moving objects in their environment (183; 184). Since the first moving object encountered by the organism is generally a member of its own species, intragroup attraction is increased.

Finally, although little is known about the mechanism, many organisms tend to conduct their behavior so that they can remain in visual and auditory contact with members of their species.

PHYSIOLOGICAL MECHANISMS

Since there are a number of different kinds of aggression and a variety of affiliative tendencies, it is not within the scope of this paper to survey all that is known about the physiology of all of these different kinds of behavior. The types of physiological mechanisms that are common to a number of different types of aggression have already been covered. An attempt will be made here to determine whether similar types of mechanisms are also common to the affiliative tendencies.

It has been shown (278) that the brains of animals and men contain innately organized neural systems which, when active in the presence of particular complexes of stimuli, result in a tendency for the organisms to behave destructively toward that stimulus complex. The hostile behavior is, in effect, stimulus bound.

Although there is less data for neural-system-activated affiliative responses, it too appears to be stimulus bound. In an experiment by Caggiula and Hoebel (67), male rats were induced to copulate with an estrus female by electrical stimulation of the posterior hypothalamus. When the males were stimulated in the absence of the female, they would perform learned responses to get to the female but they did not engage in inappropriate mounting responses to thin air.

Thus, it is clear that behavior results from an interaction between the activation of the neural system for that behavior and appropriate external stimulation.

NEURAL SYSTEMS FOR AFFILIATION

Brain stimulation studies also offer evidence concerning the neural mechanisms underlying affiliative responses. On the whole, these responses are less dramatic than aggressive responses and are more likely to be overlooked during brain stimulation studies that are not specifically designed for their study. Nonetheless, there is evidence. In addition to the study by Caggiula and Hoebel (67), cited above, Vaughan and Fisher (403) have shown that it is possible to elicit sexual behavior in the male rat by direct electrical stimulation of the brain. In this case, the anterior hypothalamus in the region of the preoptic nucleus was stimulated. Fisher (128) suggests that this behavior is highly dramatic and that during a 7-hour satiation test in which the current was on for 5 minutes and off for 5 minutes, one subject achieved 45 ejaculations (this is a record that will not be found in *Guinness Book of World Records* (262)).

Delgado (95) has shown that it is possible to induce a female monkey to repeatedly present herself for copulation if the nucleus medialis dorsalis of the thalamus is electrically stimulated. This presentation response has all of the characteristics of the normal presentation and is followed by the mounting of a male. Delgado says, "The entire behavioral sequence was repeated once every minute following each stimulation, and a total of 81 mountings was recorded in a 90-minute period, while no other mountings were recorded on the same day" (another record for Guinness).

Chemical stimulation of the brain has produced more information on the neural systems involved in affiliative responses than has electrical stimulation. Fisher (126; 127) injected the male hormone testosterone into the medial preoptic nucleus of a male rat in an attempt to induce mating behavior. When an anestrus female was placed in the cage with this subject, he repeatedly dragged the resisting female over to a corner of the cage. Fisher decided that this apparently baffling behavior was the manifestation of a maternal response. This hypothesis was confirmed when he found that the male, thus stimulated, would respond to paper strips by building a nest and to rat pups by retrieving them and bringing them to the nest. If the paper and pups were again scattered around the cage, the male responded by rebuilding the nest and again retrieving the young. After about 30 minutes, when the hormone injection had worn off, the rat abandoned the maternal behavior and again showed the usual male response of ignoring the pups. However, the maternal behavior was immediately reactivated by another injection to the same area of the brain. In addition to the maternal response, this animal also manifested another of the categories of affiliative response, that of grooming the young. The same pattern of response has also been induced in female rats by testosterone injection.

When the testosterone was injected into a more lateral portion of the preoptic region, both male and female rats showed the male sexual response of mounting any available partner, male or female. When the injection was made between these two anatomical points, the rat became a maternally activated satyr. It attempted to engage in both activities at the same time. If it encountered a female while it was in the process of retrieving a pup, it would stop and copulate while continuing to hold the pup in its mouth. The fact that these various affiliative neural systems are all activated by the same male hormone is probably due to the lack of complete specificity found in steroid hormones. Testosterone may very well be the hormone which naturally activates male sex behavior whereas some other steroid hormone, not yet tested, would be the normal one to activate the neural systems for maternal behavior.

Ovariectomized cats that are completely unreceptive sexually have been brought into continuous estrus by the implantation of very tiny pellets of stilbestrol in the anterior hypothalamus. Stilbestrol implants in other portions of the brain were not, however, effective (168). Similar findings have also been reported for the rat (243).

BRAIN STIMULATION AND AFFILIATION IN MAN

Considerable evidence has been cited above to demonstrate that it is possible to produce irritability and hostility in man by direct brain stimulation. Stimulation of the brain of man has also resulted in the activation of neural systems associated with affiliative tendencies. Although these data are frequently difficult to interpret, some examples are presented. It is not uncommon, as in the case presented by King (217), for the individual to report negative affect associated with the arousal of feelings of hostility. There are also several different areas in the brain of man that result in clear positive affect when stimulated. Although some of these areas appear to be associated with one of the affiliative behavior tendencies, it is quite possible to have pleasurable sensations not necessarily associated with affiliative responses. For example, stimulation in the medial forebrain bundle in the anterior hypothalamus resulted in a report by the patient of relaxation and mild euphoria. The patient attempted to quantify the euphoric reaction by suggesting that it was, "like two martinis." This patient also became more communicative, which implies an affiliative tendency (119). However, it is quite possible that the subject could feel euphoric without any inclination to associate with other people.

Erotic tendencies that clearly imply affiliative responses have been produced in humans by electrical stimulation in the septal region. One patient, for example, was on the verge of tears while discussing the illness of his father. At that point, the electrode implanted in the septal region was activated, and within a 15-second period, the patient grinned and shifted the conversation to a discussion of his plans to seduce a particular girl friend. The patient was not aware that he had received stimulation and could not account for the sudden change in his train of thought. Another patient in a severe depressive state expressing feelings of hopelessness smiled and began to talk about a youthful sexual experience within one minute after septal stimulation (175).

Erotic ideation has also been produced by stimulation in the area of the fornix (396) and in the temporal lobe (95). In the latter case, one of the woman patients who was normally quite reserved became flirtatious, held the therapist's hands, and expressed a fondness for him. Another patient, on stimulation of the superior part of the temporal lobe, became communicative, flirtatious and openly expressed her wish to marry the interviewer. During non-stimulation control periods she did not manifest excessive friendliness or improper behavior (99).

It also appears that an increase in the tendency to communicate and a general increase in friendliness without necessarily involving sexual tendencies can be induced by direct, electrical stimulation of points in the temporal lobe. A statistical analysis of interview data in which control periods and post stimulation periods were compared revealed that there was a significant increase in the number of friendly comments following temporal lobe stimulation (186).

BRAIN LESIONS AND INHIBITION OF AFFILIATIVE TENDENCIES

Lesions in the appropriate areas of the brain in both man and animal can reduce or eliminate several kinds of aggressive behavior (277). The interruption of the neural systems for affiliative responses results in a reduction of those tendencies also. Ward (408), for example, describes such a loss of affiliative behavior after lesions in the anterior cingular gyrus:

> The monkey's mimetic activity decreased and it lost its preoperative shyness and fear of man. . . . In a large cage with other monkeys of the same size it showed no grooming or acts of affection toward its companions. In fact, it behaved as though they were inanimate. It would walk over them, walk on them if they happened to be in the way, and would even sit on them. It would openly take food from its companions and appeared surprised when they retaliated, yet this never led to a fight for it was neither pugnacious nor even

aggressive, seeming merely to have lost its "social conscience." There was no change in motor control, deep reflexes, muscle tone or resistance to manipulation.

This lack of affiliative tendencies appears to be specific to social types of stimuli and is not the result of a generalized apathy or indifference to the surroundings. The monkeys were more inquisitive than normal monkeys of the same age and one of the animals in this series was distinctly hyperactive.

Cingulate lesions have also been shown to seriously impair maternal behavior in the rat whereas control lesions of comparable size in other areas of the brain have no significant effect (367).

Bunnell (60) studied social interactions in hooded rats before and after amygdaloid lesions. He showed that there was a significant decrease in the number of inter-animal interactions. He concluded that "The effects of the lesions appeared to result from a raised threshold to social stimuli." Similar effects were found as a result of amygdaloid lesions in the hamster and were accompanied by increased activity and hoarding (64).

Lesions in the temporal lobe of the rhesus monkey can be highly disruptive of affiliative tendencies. Dicks, Myers and Kling (106) studied the social behavior of free-ranging monkeys in naturalistic conditions of Cayo Santiago Island. They found that uncinectomy resulted in social indifference. These subjects failed to display either appropriate aggressive or submissive gestures. As a result, they were expelled from their social group and eventually died.

There are a large number of studies which show that ablation of various neural systems in the brain lead to a reduction in both male and female sexual behavior. These are adequately summarized in standard textbooks of physiological psychology and need not be detailed here (105; 160). It should be mentioned, however, that sexual behavior reduction by brain lesions can be either direct, leaving the hormonal balance intact (lesions in the preoptic area for example) or indirect, in which there is an atrophy of the gonads and a reduction in hormonal output (359). The role of the endocrines in aggressive and affiliative behavior will be discussed further below.

Little is known about the effects of brain lesions on affiliative behavior in man, except that lesions which reduce hostile tendencies generally facilitate affiliative tendencies.

FACTORS INFLUENCING NEURAL SYSTEM SENSITIVITY

The strength of the tendencies to hostile or affiliative behavior wax and wane over time in both animals and man. The fluctuations of these tendencies are frequently unrelated to changes in the environment and appear to be due to changes in the sensitivity of the controlling neural systems. There are a variety of physiological factors which produce variations in the ease with which neural systems for the various kinds of affiliation and aggression can be fired. It is proposed here that the stages of sensitivity of the neural mechanisms for affiliative tendencies are essentially the same as those outlined for the tendencies to hostility in "The Preliminary Physiological Model of Aggressive Behavior" (278).

The neural substrate for the prepuberal rat, for example, is neither active nor sensitized. Thus, it does not respond to the stimulus of a female with the mating response. In this case, the sensitivity for both the male mating response and the inter-male aggression neural systems are controlled in part by the gonadal hormones.

If gonadal hormones are administered to the immature male rat, the neural substrates for both mating behavior and for inter-male aggression are sensitized with the result that mating or aggressive behavior occurs to the appropriate stimuli. Fisher (127) suggests that the direct application of hormones to the hypothalamus does not cause those neurones to fire, but simply makes them more sensitive to activation by the relevant stimuli.

Finally, it is suggested that it is possible for the neural substrates for the various kinds of affiliative behavior to fire spontaneously. As with the spontaneous activity of the neural substrates for aggression, the organism becomes restless and moves about the environment. If, in its explorations, it encounters the appropriate stimulus complex, it reacts accordingly. In humans, it seems likely that activity in the affiliative neural systems is accompanied by subjective feelings appropriate to that particular system. Thus, the individual feels love or engages in extensive sexual or maternal fantasies.

BLOOD CHEMISTRY INFLUENCES ON NEURAL SENSITIVITY

A considerable body of evidence has been cited to indicate that the tendency to various kinds of aggression is influenced by changes in the organism's blood chemistry. It is suggested here that certain blood constituents also act on the neural systems for affiliative tendencies to either increase or decrease their sensitivity with the result that they are more or less easily fired by the relevant stimuli.

Ovariectomized female guinea pigs manifest considerable hostility toward the male. However, if they are given a series of estrogen injections followed by an injection of progesterone, the females' hostility is reduced and they are made receptive to sexual advances (219). The influence of hormones on sexual behavior in general is well-documented and is summarized in most textbooks of physiological psychology (160).

Maternal behavior is also influenced by the blood level of hormones. Prolactin injected into both males and virgin females causes active retrieval of the young whereas estrogens will block maternal behavior (105).

There is considerable evidence that the hostile tendencies of man are, in part, influenced by various chemical constituents in the blood. However, the influences of blood chemistry on affiliative behavior in humans is somewhat less understood.

In regard to sexual tendencies in humans, for example, it has been common to deemphasize the hormonal role in the determination of sexual motivation (166). However, Whalen (415) has compiled impressive data that emphasize the biological basis of sexual motivation in man.

Bremer (56: 67), after a study of 215 legally castrated males from Norway, concludes, "It can be stated at the beginning that in all cases without exception the amount of sexual activity has been altered. It has been reduced or abolished irrespective of the (precastrational) direction or the form of the sexual urge."

Whalen (415) also cites evidence to show that sexual arousability in women is related to androgen level in the blood. Sexual arousability in ovariectomized female cancer patients appears to be reduced. In female patients who had both an ovariectomy and an adrenalectomy (which would reduce the major source of androgens in the female), there was a report of 100 percent decline in activity, a 92 percent decline in responsiveness and an 82 percent decline in desire (411). The administration of androgens to women tends to increase sexual desire (131; 322). A dysfunction of the adrenal cortex in children which results in the adrenogenital syndrome with excess production of certain adrenal corticosteroids produces a remarkable personality change in some individuals. Boys of prepuberal age lose interest in the usual childhood activities and their playmates and prefer the company of adult females (86).

Although there is relatively little data available on the blood chemistry influences in other affiliative responses in the human, research on animals suggests that they may be revealed by further studies.

NEURAL INHIBITION INFLUENCES ON NEURAL SENSITIVITY

There can be little doubt that the brains of both animals and man are equipped with suppressor systems that, when activated, tend to inhibit the functioning of hostility systems (277).

Affiliative behavior can also be blocked by the activation of inhibitory neural systems. However, there is relatively little experimental data on this particular problem as yet. Delgado (99) cites an experiment in which he was able to eliminate maternal behavior in the rhesus monkey by stimulation of the mesencephalon for ten seconds. For the following 8 to 10 minutes, this previously very attentive mother left her baby, lost interest in it, and rejected any attempts by the baby to approach. After the 10-minute period, the mother reverted to maternal behavior and behaved in a normal motherly fashion toward her infant. This experiment was replicated several times on different days and mesencephalic stimulation always disrupted the mother-infant relationship. Simple motor effects, such as head turning or arm flexion, induced by stimulation had no effect on the mother's maternal tendencies.

RECIPROCAL INHIBITION OF AFFECTIVE STATES

The concept of reciprocal inhibition in antagonistic muscle groups is well established and there is abundant evidence to demonstrate that a similar reciprocal relationship exists between the anterior and the posterior hypothalamus as well as other brain areas (51; 137; 138). It is suggested here that there exists a reciprocal inhibition in some of the neural systems that underlie certain of the hostile and affiliative tendencies. It is, of course, common experience that one does not have both affiliative and hostile tendencies toward the same stimulus object *at the same time*. Activity in one neural system results in the active suppression of incompatible neural systems.

Aggressive behavior and escape behavior are an example of incompatible, reciprocally inhibitory, affective states. Stimulation and lesion studies indicate that the neural systems for these two states are controlled by separate but overlapping anatomical areas within the amygdala (as well as other places in the brain) (198; 275).

A similar type of relationship seems to hold for the interactions between affiliative and hostile neural systems. Lesions in the temporal lobes of rhesus monkeys (222; 223; 224) completely eliminated both fear and hostile behavior. These monkeys, however, were not apathetic. They were actively friendly, seeking the experimenter. When aggressive behavior in the monkey is blocked by drugs of the benzodiazepine class, it is replaced by friendly approach tendencies toward the experimenter and a general increase in sociability (329). Similar findings have been reported on cats (21).

The data on man are, of course, still limited, but they certainly suggest similar neural mechanisms for reciprocal inhibition of neural systems. As indicated above, septal stimulation in man that results in a sexual motive state inhibits or suppresses feelings of sadness, hopelessness, and depression (175). It can also block intractable pain (178). Stimulation of the same area dramatically inhibits the rage response. The individual can be in a state of violent agitated behavior and when the septal region is stimulated without his knowledge, feelings of happiness and mild euphoria with sexual ideation replace the disorganized rage and feelings of persecution (174).

Thus, we are lead to a complex neural model in which there are a number of neural systems that underlie a variety of affective states (total number not yet determined). These various systems are anatomically linked and constantly interact functionally. One system may send inhibitory fibers to several other systems. As a result, the organism is protected from the experience of incompatible affective states under normal circumstances. (For the sake of completeness, there is also evidence that some of the neural systems send facilitating fibers to other neural systems. For example, activation of the substrate for pain facilitates activity in the neural system for irritable aggression.)

THE ROLE OF LEARNING

The emphasis in this paper on the physiology of affiliation should not be construed to imply that learning is unimportant. It is *obviously* important. All of the points that have been made about the role of learning in aggressive behavior could equally well have been made about affiliative behavior (278).

It is also important to recognize that a given behavior may or may not be accompanied by the affective state implied by that behavior. In hostility, for example, learned aggressive behaviors may occur without the activation of any of the neural substrates which result in feelings of anger or rage. Evidence makes it clear that it is possible to eliminate certain destructive behaviors by lesioning portions of the neural substrates for feelings of hostility. However, it should also be clear that a "trigger man" for "Murder Inc." could not be "cured" by the same technique. The "trigger man" kills, not because he is angry, but because he is paid (rewarded) for that behavior. That behavior, as well as much of the aggressive behavior manifest during war, is learned or instrumental aggression. At this point in the development of the biological sciences, learned behavior cannot be directly manipulated by physiological means.

SOME THEORETICAL IMPLICATIONS

Absolute behaviorism, long dying, is dead. Man is not infinitely malleable. The innate physiological constraints on both intellect and temperament are much more potent than Watson realized when he made his famous statement about his ability to take a child at random and make it doctor, lawyer, beggar or thief (410).

The beautiful, optimistic, Pollyana theorizing of Ashley Montagu (269; 270; 271) is, alas, not supported by the data. As he so eloquently argues in *On Being Human* (269), man does indeed have innate tendencies to cooperation, parental behavior, social behavior and other affiliative responses. However, it appears to me that the evidence presented in the series of papers in this volume demonstrates conclusively that man also has innate physiological mechanisms that, when activated, lead him to the expression of hostile responses that are on a continuum from sarcasm to murder. The fact that they are (usually) subject to modification by learning does not mean that they do not exist. Affiliative responses are also modifiable by learning but Montagu is quite willing to accept their existence. The same general arguments apply to J. P. Scott's theorizing on aggression (337; 341). Montagu attacks a straw man (271) when he indicates that those who suggest that man has innate tendencies to hostility are advocating a "New Litany of 'Innate Depravity,' " "or that man is "evil" (269: 44). From a moral standpoint, when man is born, he is nothing. He is born with the physiological tendencies for both affiliation and hostility. Whether these are evil or good, depraved or enlightened, depends, of course, on the frame of reference of the evaluator.

Lorenz's (245) hydrolic model of aggressive tendencies has some basis in physiological fact. If, as suggested above, the neural systems for aggressive behavior are sensitized by changes in the blood chemistry with the result that they are more likely to fire, the "pressure" to behave aggressively can gradually increase. The result is that the individiual becomes more and more likely to display hostility. However, the view that this "pressure" to become aggressive can only be relieved by the expression of that aggression is too simple. The same mechanisms that make the tendency to aggression wax also make it wane. For example, a woman who has intense feelings of irritability during her premenstrual period, because of her particular hormone balance, may very well be able to keep her behavior under control and not display hostility. As the endocrine cycle continues and her hormone balance returns to normal, the neural system for irritability is desensitized and she loses her aggressive tendencies whether she has expressed her hostility or not. Further, whereas in certain circumstances, the expression of some aggressive behaviors results in a reduction of the tendency to aggress further (228), there is considerable doubt that this is generally true (44; 252).

Lorenz also suggests that there is an inextricable link between hostility and affiliation, "Thus intra-specific aggression can certainly exist without its counterpart, love, but conversely there is no love without aggression" (245: 217). This argument and others leads him to the conclusion that the elimination of aggressive tendencies would be a disastrous step, eliminating or severely limiting ambition, artistic and scientific endeavors and "countless other equally indispensible behavior patterns," including, among other things, laughter.

At the moment, insufficient information to adequately evaluate this interesting conjecture is available. However, the data that is available does not support the conjecture. Lorenz's line of reasoning implies that an energy source is available to man, that it rests in some way in a repository of hostility, and that the positive, creative, and affiliative tendencies are a result of redirection of that *hostile* energy. There is no physiological support for such a point of view. When certain of the neural systems for hostility are activated, there is also increased activity in the arousal system which results in a release of sugar into the bloodstream and consequent available energy. It is not true, however, that the arousal system can be activated only through the neural substrates for hostility. The living brain is constantly active and the living organism has continuous sources of energy available. What behavior results from the expenditure of this energy depends upon the particular neural system activated.

The evidence presented above shows conclusively that it is quite possible to activate affiliative tendencies without activating tendencies to hostility. It seems highly likely, in fact, that the neural substrates for hostility and affiliation are reciprocally inhibiting. When the tendencies to one are physiologically blocked, the result is an *increase* in the display of its counterpart.

As for laughter, it will be recalled that some of Heimberger's patients were seen to smile and laugh for the first time in their lives after their intractable aggressiveness was controlled by brain surgery (179). A number of cases have shown that the physiological elimination of hostility enables the patient to lead a productive life. The evidence available so far seems to indicate that man would lose little but unhappiness if he found a reliable method for the physiological control of hostility. It is true, however, that evidence is incomplete.

SOME PRACTICAL IMPLICATIONS

There is little doubt that one of the most serious problems facing man today is the control of aggressive behavior. If the evidence from animal populations has any validity, there is every reason to believe that an aggression explosion will accompany the population explosion. Man needs every available method for controlling both.

Aggression can, of course, be controlled by manipulating the environment to eliminate frustration and stress, as well as by various training procedures. It can also be controlled by the direct manipulation of the internal environment to deactivate or desensitize the hostility systems and thus reduce or eliminate the tendency for the individual to respond to the external stimuli with hostility. As indicated above, this can be accomplished through the use of drugs which selectively suppress aggressive tendencies; through hormone therapy; by the stimulation of brain systems that inhibit aggressive tendencies; and by the surgical lesioning of portions of the aggressive systems. All of these methods have been successfully used on man (277).

Since it is quite likely that there are several neural systems for different kinds of aggressive behavior in man as in animals, it is unlikely that the application of any of these methods will provide for the control of all hostile behaviors. However, if further experimental work substantiates the concept that there is, indeed, a reciprocal inhibition between the neural systems for the various affiliative and aggressive tendencies, aggression control through a single physiological manipulation may be possible. It seems quite plausible that there are affiliative systems (socially acceptable in themselves) that send inhibitory fibers to most of the systems for aggression as well as to other systems involving negative affect. If this is substantiated, it is at least theoretically possible to develop a physiological method (drug, hormone balance, direct stimulation) which will activate that system and thus, by a single manipulation, indirectly deactivate most of the neurology governing feelings of hostility.

If further research makes this approach feasible, all men can be slow to anger, and

> He that is slow to anger is better than the mighty; and he that ruleth his spirit than he that taketh a city.
> Proverbs 16:32

7

Maternal Aggression: A Failure to Replicate

RUSSELL REVLIS and K. E. MOYER

In earlier papers in this volume, and elsewhere, I have frequently referred to the study of Endroczi, et al. (118) as an excellent illustration of the direct manipulation of maternal aggression through the use of hormones. The following study indicates that the aggressive behavior studied by those investigators was probably not maternal and that there is a general tendency for rats to attack frogs. The latter finding has more recently been substantiated in other studies (24; 25; 104). The study is included in this volume because it illustrates the importance of attempting to replicate or extend particularly significant experiments.

This paper was originally published in *Psychonomic Science*, 1969, 16: 135–136 and is reprinted here with the permission of the publisher and the senior author, Russell Revlis.

The tendency for females of many species to behave aggressively toward any intruder during the period that they are nursing is a well recognized but little investigated phenomenon (32; 37; 99). It has been suggested by Moyer (275) that maternal aggression is one of several kinds of aggressive behavior and that it has a physiological basis distinct from other types of aggression. Some support for the unique physiological basis of this particular kind of aggression is provided by the experimental work of Endroczi, Lissak, and Telegdy (118). They indicate that frog-killing behavior in the albino rat is specific to the lactating mother who is in her home cage with her litter present. This behavior showed a gradual suppression with the weaning period of the litter (Endroczi, personal communication). According to these authors, neither male rats nor nonlactating female rats will attack a frog placed in its cage. It was further demonstrated (118) that the maternal aggression of the rat was dependent on a particular hormone balance. Oestrone treatment for 10 days eliminated frog killing without interfering with the care of the young, and the suppressive effects of the oestrone on frog killing could be reversed by injections of hydrocortisone. The descriptive nature of these data preclude a more quantitative analysis of the treatment effects.

This study is an attempt to replicate the above findings with more precise measurements of aggressive behavior.

EXPERIMENT 1

Subjects

Eleven female albino rats (Sprague-Dawley) between 95 and 110 days of age were used. Stimulus animals were a frog (*Rana pipiens*, female, 76 mm. long) and a female albino mouse.

Apparatus

Subjects lived in standard Hoeltge cages ($7'' \times 7'' \times 9.5''$) with a plexiglas top through which E could make observations. Latencies and response durations were recorded on a multipen event recorder which was activated by a panel of switches controlled by E.

Procedure

Subjects were adapted to the cages for 48 hours and then given a 7-minute pretest with the stimulus animals. Each S was presented with a frog and a mouse. The order of presentation was counterbalanced across the S population but remained constant for each rat for both the pre- and post-test conditions. The interval between presentations was 3–5 minutes. The following behavioral measures were made during test periods: (a) duration of sniffing of the stimulus animal (S faced the stimulus animal at a distance of less than 2 inches and simultaneously moved its whiskers up and down), (b) latency of first bite of the stimulus animal, (c) duration of biting behavior, (d) latency of kill (defined as permanent immobilization of stimulus animal), and (e) whether S attempted to eat a stimulus animal that it had killed. Ss that killed frogs in the pretest were assigned to Experiment 2. No mice were killed during either experiment.

After the pretest, 11 nonkillers were placed in the colony room and subjected to the standard laboratory conditions to induce pregnancy. On the 14th day of their gestation period, these pregnant animals who had remained in their home cages, were returned to the experimental room. They were kept there for 10 days prior to the posttest conditions, which were the same as those used in the pretest. Each rat was tested with her litter present 48 hours after parturition.

Results

No rat in this experiment killed either a frog or a mouse. Analyses of variance (subjects by sessions by stimuli) for each measure revealed that there was a significant change in all measures between the sessions. There were no significant interactions. Results are given in Table 7-1 and will be discussed below.

TABLE 7-1

Entries are in seconds except for investigation which was calculated in terms of percent of time investigating prior to kill because Ss could have killed with different latencies.

| | Measures taken prior to pregnancy and after parturition ||||||
| | *Frog Means* ||| *Mouse Means* |||
	F	Pre	Post	t	Pre	Post	t
Latency 1st Bite	46.0*	377.7	183.6	3.18*	402.7	75.0	10.61*
Biting Duration	9.4**	.3	28.0	2.68**	.6	5.3	2.49**
Investigation	5.0**	4.5%	8.3%	2.04	17.5%	29.4%	1.77

* $p < .01$
** $p < .05$

EXPERIMENT 2

Contrary to the findings of Endroczi et al. (118), preliminary experiments in our laboratory indicated that a significant number of naive virgin female rats killed frogs. Experiment 1 showed that lactating rats in the presence of their young did not kill frogs. It was therefore considered possible that the killing observed by Endroczi, et al. was a form of predatory aggression, and the oestrone injections blocked this tendency to predation.

Experiment 2 tested this hypothesis by determining the effects of oestrone injections on the frog-killing response of virgin female rats, using the same oestrone dosage as used by the previous investigators.

Procedure

Twenty female albino rats (Sprague-Dawley), between 95 and 110 days of age, were used as Ss. All of these Ss killed a frog during the 7-minute pretest. The procedures for this experiment were exactly the same as those for Experiment 1 with the following exceptions: 24 hours following the pretest procedure, the oestrone group was given a subcutaneous injection of 500 I.U./100 gm. body weight of oestrone (aqueous suspension) and the control group received a comparable volume of distilled water. Each S's injection was given at the same hour each day for a period of 10 days. The animals remained in the experimental room during the treatment period. The posttest observations were made 4 hours following the 10th injection and the O did not know which injections the animals had received.

Results

Analyses of variance (groups by sessions by stimuli) for each measure revealed significant main effects for stimulus animal for latency to first bite ($F = 53.0, p < .01$) and duration of biting ($F = 13.0, p < .01$). This indicates that the rats had a significantly greater tendency to attack frogs than mice. (Relevant results are presented in Table 7-2.)

TABLE 7-2

Entries are in seconds except for investigation which was calculated in terms of percent of time investigating prior to kill because Ss killed with different latencies.

	\multicolumn{6}{c}{Measures taken before and after oestrone injection}
	\multicolumn{6}{c}{*Oestrone*}
	\multicolumn{3}{c}{*Frog Means*}	\multicolumn{3}{c}{*Mouse Means*}
	Pre	Post	t	Pre	Post	t
Latency 1st Bite	158.4	20.8	3.03*	307.8	305.8	.04
Biting Duration	29.1	45.3	.68	.8	2.3	.75
Investigation	13.5%	18.7%	.86	25.0%	24.2%	.08
	\multicolumn{6}{c}{Measures taken before and after water injection}
	\multicolumn{6}{c}{*Water*}
	\multicolumn{3}{c}{*Frog Means*}	\multicolumn{3}{c}{*Mouse Means*}
	Pre	Post	t	Pre	Post	t
Latency 1st Bite	90.4	56.4	.69	323.5	248.2	1.19
Biting Duration	17.8	14.5	.78	.4	2.2	2.04
Investigation	16.2%	30.0%	1.23	24.2%	19.2%	1.21

*$p < .05$

In the posttest, only one S did not kill the frog. That S was in the control group. An analysis of variance of latency to kill revealed a significant main effect for treatment ($F = 5.7$) and for sessions ($F = 43.7$). However, the absence of a significant session by drug interaction ($F = 1.5$) indicates that the difference between the two groups was not due to the oestrone treatment, but to the fact that the groups were unmatched on kill latency on pretesting. The mean latencies for pretest were: oestrone group, 282.1 seconds; water group, 172.8 seconds. Posttest means were: oestrone group, 90.0 seconds; water group, 40.7 seconds.

On the pretest, 60 percent of the oestrone group and 70 percent of the water group attempted to eat the killed frog. On the posttest, 100 percent of the oestrone group and 80 percent of the water group did so.

DISCUSSION

The results of these two experiments do not in any respect confirm the findings of Endroczi, et al. (118). Lactation and presence of the young did not increase the frog-killing tendency in any of the rats. Further, a significant number of naive virgin female rats kill frogs. More recent experiments in this laboratory have shown that the rat is a highly predatory animal and that the frog is a favored prey. If the Ss are adapted to the situation, almost 100 percent of hooded and albino male and female rats will kill frogs placed in their cages (25).

The decrease in latency to first bite and the increase in duration of biting produced during the posttest in Experiment 1 cannot be construed as an increase in hostility. The rat made no attempt to kill the stimulus animals and did not behave in a manner which would keep the stimulus animals away from the nest. The rats repeatedly attempted to pick up the stimulus animals and bring them to the nest. If the stimulus animal left the nest after having been placed there by the mother rat, she would immediately attempt to retrieve it, just as she did her pups. This reaction of mother rats toward mice is well described by Karli (203). The increased biting, then, represents maternal care rather than maternal aggression.

The reasons for the differences in findings in these experiments and the previous ones by Endroczi and his colleagues are obscure. It appears clear, however, that a different technique must be found for investigating maternal aggression.

8

Aggressive Behavior in the Rat: Effects of Isolation and Olfactory Bulb Lesions

HENRY BERNSTEIN and K. E. MOYER

This paper is an experimental study. It illustrates the importance of providing the subject with a number of aggression-eliciting situations in order to arrive at a valid interpretation of a given physiological manipulation. It is presented in this volume without modification.

It was originally published in *Brain Research,* 1970, and is reprinted here with the permission of the Elsevier Publishing Company, Amsterdam, The Netherlands, as well as with the permission of the senior author, Henry Bernstein.

This study was initiated to investigate the effects of isolation and olfactory lesions on aggressive behaviors in the rat. Olfactory lesions may inhibit, facilitate, or have no effect on aggression, depending on the species and the kind of aggressive behavior studied (for a discussion of the various kinds of aggression, see 275). Inter-male aggression among mice is completely eliminated by bulbectomy and the latency for fighting is tripled if the odor of the mice is masked by French perfume (314). In the cat, olfactory bulb lesions have no effect on the "rage" reaction (199; 361) or on predatory aggression induced by hypothalamic stimulation (250). In the rat, the results appear to be contradictory. Rats that killed mice but not rat pups killed pups if the scent was altered by oil of lavender. Rats made anosmic by bulbectomy did not differentiate between mice and rat pups as they had prior to the operation. However, some of the olfactory lesioned animals showed a general waning of the killing after the lesions (282).

It has also been shown that total, bilateral, olfactory bulbectomy will convert 50 percent to 100 percent of non-mouse killing rats into killers (109; 208; 404; 406).

Isolation increases the probability of certain kinds of aggressive behavior in rats (169; 226). Some studies, however, report either no change in aggressive behavior after prolonged isolation (aggression toward the handler, 284; 318) or a decrease in aggressive behavior (shock-induced aggression, 191).

There is some evidence of an interaction between isolation and olfactory lesions in the facilitation of aggressive behavior. If rats are isolated after bulbectomy, they will kill mice. However, if they are kept in group cages for a two-month period postoperatively, they do not kill mice. If these grouped bulbectomized animals are then isolated for several weeks, they will again kill mice (107).

The experiments to date seem to indicate that different kinds of aggressive behavior may be affected differently by olfactory lesions and isolation. Thus, in the experiment presented here, several dependent measures were included in an attempt to determine more precisely the type of aggression affected by these two aggression facilitators—olfactory lesions and isolation.

The three independent variables used were preoperative isolation, the operation (real or sham), and postoperative isolation. The seven dependent variables were mouse killing and frog killing (predatory aggression), reaction to a mechanical grasping hand (squeaks, escape and bites), a measure of inter-male aggression, and shock-induced aggression.

METHOD

Subjects

Forty-nine naive male hooded rats obtained from Simonsen Laboratories (Gilroy, California) were used. All Ss were between 84 and 94 days of age at the beginning of the experiment.

Apparatus

The test cage was 10″ × 10″ × 18″, of clear plastic with a grid floor of ⅛″ brass rods spaced ¾″ apart on center, and wired for scrambled shock. An applegate stimulator, Model 228, was used to charge the grids. An opaque guillotine door could be lowered to divide the test cage into two compartments 5½″ and 13½″ long, with the smaller compartment to the front of the cage. Thus, a stimulus object could be placed in the smaller compartment and presented to the S by raising the opaque door.

Procedure

A table of random numbers was used to divide the Ss into eight groups that were housed in cages 9½″ × 7″ × 24″. After a two-week adjustment period, each group was either placed in a new group cage or the Ss in the group were placed in individual cages (7″ × 7″ × 9½″). At the end of 30 or 31 days, each S was given either an olfactory ablation or a sham operation. The operation was accomplished by removing a circle of skull nine mm. anterior to bregma on the midline by means of a five mm. trephine. The exposed olfactory bulbs were removed by aspiration. The sham operation was identical, except that the olfactory bulbs were not aspirated. Ss were housed in single cages for 48 hours postoperatively. Then, those Ss assigned to the postoperative group condition were placed in group cages.

Thirty or thirty-one days after the postoperative formation of the groups, the Ss were tested. On a test day, the S was transported to the test room in a single cage. The isolated rats were transported in their home cages. They were placed in the test cage and given 15 minutes to acclimate to it.

The procedures for the specific tests were as follows:

Mouse kill—The opaque door was lowered and an albino mouse was placed in the forward compartment. One minute later, the door was raised. The latency of the kill was recorded. If a kill did not occur within 30 minutes, the mouse was removed.

Frog kill—The procedure was the same as for the mouse kill except that the frog was removed after 15 minutes. Pilot work had shown that a frog kill rarely occurred after 15 minutes.

Grasping hand procedures—A stuffed leather glove on a metal rod was covered with a disposable plastic glove and used to simulate a hand grasping the rat. The glove was moved around the cage until the rat could be pinned against the back wall. Vocalization and escape behavior were rated on a scale from 1 (little) to 4 (vigorous). The number of bites on the glove was measured by counting the holes in the plastic glove. This test lasted 5 minutes.

Inter-male aggression—The opportunity for inter-male aggression was provided by placing an albino rat (a different one for each S) in the test cage with the S for 15 minutes prior to the procedure for shock-induced aggression. Aggression was measured as indicated for shock-induced aggression.

Shock-induced aggression—At the end of the 15-minute period for inter-male aggression, a 2.5 ma. shock was delivered through the grid floor for .5 seconds every ten seconds for ten minutes. The number of aggressive responses was counted. The aggressive response was defined as a striking movement by either animal while standing on its hind legs in the stereotyped "boxing" posture or a wrestling response which involved attack responses in which the S jumped at the opponent and rolled around the cage. The observer recorded these responses by pressing a switch that activated an event-recorder pen. Only one response was recorded for each assumption of the "boxing" position or each wrestling response.

At the end of testing, all rats were placed in single cages and a mouse was left in the cage overnight. Kills were noted on the next morning.

Because of the disrupting effect of shock, this test was always given last. The other three tests were given in counterbalanced order. The sequence of orders for each test day was determined randomly.

Results

The means and standard deviations of all measures are given in Table 8-1.

Table 8-2 shows the significant results derived from a multivariate analysis of variance. Tests of significance were obtained using Wilks Lambda Criterion and Canonical Correlations (Jones, 197: 197).

The rats isolated for one month immediately before testing showed a greater tendency to kill mice ($p < .05$); showed more intense escape responses ($p < .001$); and bit the stuffed glove more frequently ($p < .019$).

The only dependent variable significantly affected by the olfactory ablation was the number of bites on the gloved hand ($p < .002$). There was also an interaction between the operation and postoperation isolation ($p < .034$), indicating that the operated animals had a significantly greater tendency to bite the hand if they were isolated after the operation. Isolation for two months significantly increased the tendency to frog kill ($p < .016$). There was also a triple interaction among pre- and post-operation isolation and the operation in regard to shock-induced aggression.

A within-cells correlation of criteria was computed (Table 8-3). The two measures of predatory aggression, mouse and frog killing, correlated highly ($r = .527$, $p < .001$). The two measures of fear, escape and vocalization, also correlated significantly ($r = .404$, $p < .005$).

TABLE 8-1
Means and Standard Deviations for All Conditions

A	Factor* S	B	N		Mouse Kill	Frog Kill	Variable Escape	Squeek	Bites	Shock Induced
1	1	1	6	M SD	0.167 0.408	0.333 0.516	2.167 0.983	2.333 1.506	0.0 0.0	32.333 12.549
1	1	2	5	M SD	0.200 0.447	0.200 0.447	1.400 0.894	2.200 1.643	0.0 0.0	39.000 10.932
1	2	1	5	M SD	0.600 0.548	1.000 0.000	3.600 0.548	2.400 0.894	2.400 1.817	43.200 14.990
1	2	2	6	M SD	0.0 0.0	0.0 0.0	1.500 0.837	1.667 0.816	0.0 0.0	29.500 1.871
2	1	1	6	M SD	0.167 0.408	0.333 0.516	2.833 1.169	2.667 1.211	0.0 0.0	32.167 19.549
2	1	2	6	M SD	0.0 0.0	0.500 0.548	2.167 0.753	2.333 0.816	0.0 0.0	25.500 11.397
2	2	1	9	M SD	0.333 0.500	0.444 0.527	3.111 1.269	1.889 0.601	4.222 4.658	35.556 24.275
2	2	2	6	M SD	0.167 0.408	0.500 0.548	1.833 1.169	2.333 1.366	1.000 2.000	46.667 10.405

Factors. A1 = pre-op isolation
S1 = sham operation
B1 = post-op isolation
A2 = pre-op group living
S2 = olfactory ablation
B2 = post-op group living

TABLE 8-2

Significant results derived from a Multivariate Analysis of Variance*

Treatment	Variable	p <
Postoperative Isolation	Mouse Kill	.059
	Escape	.001
	Bites	.019
Operation	Bites	.002
Operation × Postoperation Isolation	Bites	.034
Preoperation × Postoperation Isolation	Frog Kill	.016
Preoperation Isolation × Operation × Postoperation Isolation	Shock-Induced Aggression	.041

* Summary tables of the complete analysis are available from K. E. Moyer, Carnegie-Mellon University, Pittsburgh, Pa.

In addition, the measure of irritability, biting, was found to correlate significantly with mouse killing ($r = .304$, $p < .05$) and escape behavior ($r = .306$, $p < .05$).

The extent of the lesions was measured by Dr. L. E. Jarrard without knowledge of experimental results. A rank-order correlation between extra olfactory bulb damage and biting aggression was computed and was not significant ($r = .01$). In all operations, the olfactory bulbs were completely destroyed.

TABLE 8-3

Within-Cells Correlation of Dependent Measures

Variable	Mouse Kill	Frog Kill	Escape	Squeek	Bites	Im Shock
Mouse Kill						
Frog Kill	0.572*					
Escape	−0.143	−0.149				
Squeek	−0.022	−0.177	0.404*			
Bites	0.304*	0.191	0.306*	−0.112		
Im Shock	0.226	0.069	−0.208	0.033	0.061	

* if $r > .288$ $p < .05$
  $r > .338$ $p < .02$
  $r > .372$ $p < .01$ $r > .403$ $p < .005$
  $r > .465$ $p < .001$

DISCUSSION

Previous research (3; 144; 159; 169; 280; 307) has indicated that isolated animals are more emotional in a variety of test situations. This study, in general, confirms those results. The disorganized vigorous escape reactions to the gloved hand ($p < .001$) and the significantly greater amount of biting of the hand ($p < .019$) reflect an increase in emotionality in that test situation. These reactions were quite similar to the descriptions given by Korn and Moyer (226).

It has been reported that isolated rats learn an escape response less readily than grouped subjects (159; 307). However, those reports referred to escape from shock in which the disorganization produced by high emotionality would result in increased latencies. That situation was quite different from the escape from a grasping hand reported here.

The effects of postoperative isolation on mouse killing approach significance ($p < .059$). Neither Korn and Moyer (226) nor Myer (284) found differences in mouse killing between grouped rats and those isolated for 96 days or 100 days, respectively. However, Myer did find that the tendency to kill mice was significantly reduced if the rats were repeatedly exposed to mice until they were five months old. Presumably, the rats exposed to mice habituated to some of the stimuli presented by the mice with the result that those stimuli no longer elicited the attack tendency. It may be, in the current study, that the stimuli of the social situation were sufficiently similar to the stimuli presented by the mouse that there was a generalization of the habituation to the mouse-killing situation, with the result that the grouped Ss had less of a tendency to kill than the isolated ones that were not exposed to the social stimulation.

The increased tendency in mouse killing found in this experiment might also be accounted for by differences in strain since it has been shown that there are large strain differences in mouse killing and that these differences tend to interact with other variables (see below).

Olfactory lesions did not significantly increase the mouse-killing tendency of the animals in this experiment ($p < .22$). This does not confirm the results of Karli and his collaborators. Strain differences could very well account for this lack of confirmation. Karli, et al. (208) have indicated that 100 percent of one stock of rats from his laboratory became mouse killers after olfactory ablation, whereas only 50 percent of another stock became killers after the operation. Both stocks were bred from the same original Wistar strain, but the first group has been exclusively bred from mouse killers for a two-year period.

Mouse killing was used as a dependent variable in the experiments by Karli, et al. (208). However, the mouse killing in that situation may not be a measure of predatory aggression. A number of authors have differentiated between predatory aggression and other aggressive responses. In predatory aggression, the consumption of the prey is the common terminal behavior of the response (71; 96; 275). The topography of the response is important in discriminating predation and other aggression types (113; 275; 409). The predatory response is generally quiet, quick and efficient with little or no affective display. The rat kills the mouse in a matter of seconds by biting through the spinal cord in the cervical region. The eliciting stimuli for this type of attack are limited to the natural prey of the animal. In irritable aggression, however, a wider variety of objects may be attacked. If the predatory response in the cat is activated by electrical stimulation of the lateral hypothalamus, it will attack a rat but not the experimenter. However, if the irritable or affective aggressive response is activated by medial hypothalamic stimulation, the cat will attack the experimenter in preference to a rat, but if the experimenter is not available, a rat will be attacked with a response that is topographically quite different from the predatory attack (409).

There is evidence from this experiment, as well as from Karli's experiments, that olfactory ablation produces affective or irritable aggressive behavior. Although the lesioned animals in this study did not show a greater incidence of either mouse killing or frog killing ($p < .222$, $p < .411$) they did show a significant increase in the tendency to bite the gloved hand ($p < .002$). Further, there was a small (.304) but significant (.05) correlation between mouse killing and number of bites on the gloved hand. Although Karli, et al. (208) did not systematically measure any type of aggression except mouse killing, there are a number of indications that the lesioned animals in his studies reacted with considerable emotionality. The topography of the killing response is not the typical, quiet, quick kill of predation. The kill, "Usually has the aspect of a compulsory 'disinhibited' reaction, the rat biting the mouse all over the body and covering it with blood from head to tail" (208). The lesioned rats placed in group cages show violent intraspecific aggression for a few days after the operation (107). It has also been reported that the lesioned Ss which became killers were generally more vicious and emotional than those that did not (109). None of the above behaviors is characteristic of the precise, well-organized, non-emotional response of predation.

There is also indirect evidence from the work of Karli that olfactory lesions affect a kind of aggression that is not predatory. He has shown that androgens appear to have no effect on natural predatory behavior. Castration does not block mouse killing in a natural killer, nor do exogenous androgens induce killing in a non-killer (204). There is considerable evidence, however, that the androgens do play a role in inter-male aggression (38; 240; 389). There is also some experimental and clinical evidence that supports the importance of androgenic hormones in irritable aggression (275). Thus, the findings of Didiergeorges and Karli (108) to the effect that castration and unilateral adrenalectomy reduce the percentage of non-killing rats that are converted into killers by olfactory lesions and that these castrated non-killers can be induced to kill after testosterone injections may reflect the effect of the androgens on what appears to be irritable aggression. In the experiment reported here, olfactory lesions made the Ss irritable but did not increase mouse killing. If the above hypothesis is correct, it would be expected that castration would reduce that irritability.

There is an interaction between postoperation isolation and bulbectomy in the number of bites on the grasping hand ($p < .034$). Thus, the amount of irritability shown after the operation was enhanced by postoperative isolation. The finding is similar to that of Didiergeorges and Karli (107), who found that grouping rats for two months after bulbectomy prevented the highly irritable attack on mice.

The only dependent variable differentially affected by the prolonged isolation (preoperation isolation by postoperation isolation interaction ($p < .016$) was frog killing. The lack of effect on the other measures is somewhat surprising in that other investigators have reported that the longer the isolation, the stronger the effect on the behaviors measured (169; 226; 321). However, interruption of the isolation period by the traumatic event of the operation may have had a mitigating effect.

The signification triple interaction (preoperation isolation × operation × postoperation isolation) for shock-induced aggression ($p < .041$) can be understood if the role of learned inhibition is considered. Rats living in a group learn to inhibit aggressive responses to the stimulus complex of other rats during the development of a dominance hierarchy. Other rats are the stimulus complex toward which attack is directed in the shock induced aggression situation. It is plausible that olfactory ablation enhances the irritability of the S and increases the tendency for it to attack. However, that tendency to attack may be blocked by the inhibitions which were learned through group living either during the pre- or post-operative period. Thus, the facilitation of the aggressive tendencies of one rat toward another in the shock-induced aggression situation would only be manifest in those Ss that were isolated both before and after the operation.

It is clear from the results that the Ss in this experiment were not made "generally more aggressive." (In the inter-male aggression situation, for example, aggressive behavior was notably absent with only an occasional response recorded in any condition.) It is, in fact, meaningless to talk about "general aggressiveness." The physiological substrates of aggressive behaviors will be understood when the various kinds of aggression are treated separately (275).

The results of the within-cell correlation of criteria also contribute to the interpretation of the results. In predatory behavior, for example, all mouse killers are frog killers although the reverse is not true. As would be expected, the correlation between these two measures is quite significant ($r = .572$, $p < .001$). The two measures of fear, escape and vocalization, also correlate significantly ($r = .404$, $p < .005$). The significant correlation between bites and escape behavior ($r = .306$, $p < .05$) may indicate that under certain circumstances, there is a fear component in the aggressive behavior indicated by the biting response, i.e. the S only bit when it was cornered and thus unable to escape. However, the size of the correlation as well as the frequent observation of the "bull dog" tenacity of the biting response indicate that much of the biting aggression was, in fact, unrelated to fear and might best be interpreted as irritable (275).

Since septal lesions have been shown to result in a general increase in emotionality and irritability, it should be pointed out that septal lesions would not account for the results of this study because: (a) the correlation between the extent of damage beyond olfactory ablation and biting aggression was .01; (b) only two animals had damage as far back as the septal region; and (c) the animals were tested 30 to 31 days after the operation and most studies have shown that the irritability of septal lesions abates before this period (75; 435).

SUMMARY

Forty-nine male hooded rats 84 or 94 days of age were housed individually or in groups for one month and were then subjected to an olfactory bulbectomy or a sham operation. They were again housed either individually or in a group cage for one month. *S*s were then tested for mouse killing, frog killing, reactions to a gloved hand, including squealing, escape and biting, inter-male aggression and shock-induced aggression.

Results indicate that biting the glove was the only type of aggressive behavior significantly affected by olfactory bulb lesions. Postoperative isolation increased mouse killing and escape from the gloved hand and the number of bites on the hand. There was also a significant operation by postoperation isolation interaction for a number of bites on the glove. Mouse killing and frog killing were significantly correlated, as were escape and squealing; escape and bites; and bites and mouse killing. Inter-male aggressive behavior was notably absent and was unaffected by any condition.

It was concluded that this study adds further evidence that aggression is not a unitary phenomenon and that different manipulations differentially affect different kinds of aggression.

References

1. Adams, D. B. Cells related to fighting behavior recorded from midbrain central gray neuropil of cat. *Science,* 1968, **159,** 894–896.
2. Adams, D., & Flynn, J. P. Transfer of an escape response from tail shock to brain stimulated attack behavior. *Journal of the Experimental Analysis of Behavior,* 1966, **9,** 401–408.
3. Ader, R. Effects of early experience and differential housing and susceptibility to gastric erosions in the rat. *Journal of Comparative and Physiological Psychology,* 1965, **60,** 233–238.
4. Adey, W. R., Merrilless, N. C. R., & Sunderland, S. The entorhinal area: Behavioral, evoked potential, and histological studies of its inter-relationships with brain stem regions. *Brain,* 1956, **79,** 414–438.
5. Akert, K. Diencephalon. In D. E. Sheer (Ed.) *Electrical stimulation of the brain.* Austin: University of Texas Press, 1961. Pp. 288–310.
6. Alderton, H., & Hoddinott, B. A. A controlled study of the use of thioridazine in the treatment of hyperactive and aggressive children in a children's psychiatric hospital. *Canadian Psychiatric Association Journal,* 1964, **9,** 239–247.
7. Allikmets, L. Kh. Behavioral reactions to electrical stimulation of amygdala in cats. *Zhurnal Vysshei Nervnoi Deyatel 'nosti imeni* I. P. Paulova, 1966, **16,** 119–127.
8. Alonso-de Florida, F., & Delgado, J. M. R. Lasting behavioral and EEG changes in cats induced by prolonged stimulation of amygdala. *American Journal of Physiology,* 1958, **193,** 223–229.
9. Alpers, B. J. Personality and emotional disorders associated with hypothalamic lesions. *Association for Research in Nervous & Mental Diseases.* Baltimore: Williams & Wilkins, 1940, **20,** 725–748.
10. Altman, J. *Organic foundations of animal behavior.* New York: Holt, Rinehart, & Winston, 1966.
11. Anand, B. K., & Brobeck, J. R. Hypothalamic control of food intake in rats and cats. *Yale Journal of Biology and Medicine,* 1951, **24,** 123–140.

12. Anand, B. K., & Dua, S. Stimulation of limbic system of brain in waking animals. *Science,* 1955, **122,** 1139.
13. Anand, B. K., & Dua, S. Electrical stimulation of the limbic system of the brain ("visceral brain") in the waking animal. *Indian Journal of Medicinal Research,* 1966, **44,** 107–119.
14. Ardery, R. *The territorial imperative.* New York: Atheneum, 1966.
15. Azrin, N. H. Aggression. Paper presented at the meeting of the American Psychological Association, Los Angeles, September, 1964.
16. Azrin, N. H., Hutchinson, R. R., & Hake, D. F. Extinction induced aggression. *Journal of the Experimental Analysis of Behavior,* 1966, **9,** 191–204.
17. Azrin, N. H., Hutchinson, R. R., & McLaughlin, R. The opportunity for aggression as an operant reinforcer during aversive stimulation. *Journal of the Experimental Analysis of Behavior,* 1965, **8,** 171–180.
18. Baenninger, R. Contrasting effects of fear and pain on mouse killing by rats. *Journal of Comparative and Physiological Psychology,* 1967, **63,** 298–303.
19. Bailey, P. Discussion. In M. Baldwin and P. Bailey (Eds.), *Temporal lobe epilepsy.* Springfield, Ill.: Charles C. Thomas, 1958. Pp. 551.
20. Ball, J. The effect of testosterone on the sex behavior of female rats. *Journal of Comparative Psychology,* 1940, **29,** 151–165.
21. Ban, T. A. *Psychopharmacology.* Baltimore: Williams & Wilkins, 1969.
22. Bandler, R. J., Jr. Facilitation of aggressive behavior in the rat by direct cholinergic stimulation of the hypothalamus. *Nature,* 1969, **224,** 1035–1036.
23. Bandler, R. J., Jr. Cholinergic synapses in the lateral hypothalamus for the control of predatory aggression in the rat. *Brain Research,* 1970, **20.**
24. Bandler, R. J., Jr. Direct chemical stimulation of hypothalamus, thalamus and midbrain: Effects on aggressive behavior in the rat. PhD dissertation, Carnegie-Mellon University, 1970.
25. Bandler, R. J., Jr., & Moyer, K. E. The animals spontaneously attacked by the rat. *Communications in Behavioral Biology,* 1970, **5,** 177–182.
26. Barclay, A. M., & Haber, R. N. The relation of aggressive to sexual motivation. *Journal of Personality,* 1965, **3,** 462–475.
27. Bard, P. Central nervous mechanisms for the expression of anger in animals. In M. L. Reymert (Ed.), *Feelings and emotions: The Mooseheart symposium.* New York: McGraw-Hill, 1950. Pp. 211–237.
28. Bard, P., & Mountcastle, V. B. Some forebrain mechanisms involved in expression of rage with special reference to suppression

of angry behavior. *Research Publications of the Association of Nervous and Mental Disease,* 1948, **27,** 262–404.
29. Barker, P., & Fraser, I. A. A controlled trial of haloperidol in children. *British Journal of Psychiatry,* 1968, **114,** 855–857.
30. Barnett, S. A. *A Study in Behavior.* London: Metheun & Company, 1963.
31. Barnett, S. A. Attack and defense in animal societies. In C. D. Clemente and D. B. Lindsley (Eds.), *Aggression and defense: Neural mechanisms and social patterns.* Vol. 5. *Brain function.* Los Angeles: University of California Press, 1967. Pp. 35–56.
32. Barnett, S. A. Grouping and dispersive behaviour among wild rats. In S. Garattini and E. B. Sigg (Eds.), *Aggressive behaviour.* New York: Wiley, 1969. Pp. 3–14.
33. Barsa, J., & Saunder, J. C. Comparative study of chlordiazepoxide and diazepam. *Diseases of the Nervous System,* 1964, **25,** 244–246.
34. Bartholomew, A. A. Perphenazine (Trilafon) in the immediate management of acutely disturbed chronic alcoholics. *Medical Journal of Australia,* 1963, **1,** 812–814.
35. Beach, F. A. Male and female mating behavior in prepuberally castrated female rats treated with androgens. *Endocrinology,* 1942, **31,** 673–678.
36. Beach, F. A. Bisexual mating behavior in the male rat: Effects of castration and hormone administration. *Physiological Zoology,* 1945, **18,** 195–221.
37. Beach, F. A. *Hormones and behavior.* New York: Hoeber, 1948.
38. Beeman, E. A. The effect of male hormone on aggressive behavior in mice. *Physiological Zoology,* 1947, **20,** 373–405.
39. Bennett, M. A. Social hierarchy in ring doves II: The effects of treatment with testosterone propionate. *Ecology,* 1940, **21,** 148–165.
40. Berger, F. M. The pharmacological properties of 2-methyl-2N*propyl-1,3 propanediol dicaramate (Miltown): A new interneuronal blocking agent. *Journal of Pharmacology and Experimental Therapeutics,* 1954, **112,** 412.
41. Berkowitz, L. *Aggression: A social psychological analysis.* New York: McGraw-Hill, 1962.
42. Berkowitz, L. The concept of aggressive drive: Some additional considerations. In L. Berkowitz (Ed.), *Advances in experimental social psychology.* Vol. 2. New York: Academic Press, 1965.
43. Berkowitz, L. Experiments on automatism and intent in human aggression. In C. D. Clemente and D. B. Lindsley (Eds.), *Aggression and defense: Neural mechanisms and social patterns.* Vol. 5. *Brain function.* Los Angeles: University of California Press, 1967. Pp. 243–266.
44. Berkowitz, L. The study of urban violence: Some implications

of laboratory studies of frustration and aggression. In L. H. Masotti and D. R. Bowen (Eds.), *Riots and rebellion.* Beverly Hills, Calif.: Sage Publications, 1968. Pp. 39–49.
45. Bernstein, H., & Moyer, K. E. Aggressive behavior in the rat: Effect of isolation and olfactory bulb lesions. *Brain Research,* 1970, **20,** 75–84.
46. Bevan, J. M., Bevan, W., & Williams, B. F. Spontaneous aggressiveness in young castrate C_3H male mice treated with three dose levels of testosterone. *Physiological Zoology,* 1958, **31,** 284–288.
47. Bevan, W., Daves, W. F., & Levy, G. W. The relation of castration, androgen therapy and pre-test fighting experience to competitive aggression in male C57 BL/10 mice. *Animal Behavior,* 1960, **8,** 6–12.
48. Bevan, W., Levy, G. W., Whitehouse, J. M., & Bevan, J. M. Spontaneous aggressiveness in two strains of mice castrated and treated with one of three androgens. *Physiological Zoology,* 1958, **30,** 341–349.
49. Bolles, R. C. The usefulness of the drive concept. In M. R. Jones (Ed.), *Nebraska Symposium on Motivation.* Lincoln: University of Nebraska Press, 1958.
50. Boshka, S. C., Weisman, H. M., & Thor, D. H. A technique for inducing aggression in rats utilizing morphine withdrawal. *Psychological Record,* 1966, **16,** 541–543.
51. Bovard, E. W. A concept of hypothalamic functioning. *Perspectives in Biology and Medicine,* 1961, 52–61.
52. Bradley, C. The behavior of children receiving benzedrine. *American Journal of Psychiatry,* 1937, **94,** 577.
53. Brady, J. V. Emotional behavior. In J. Field, H. W. Magoun, and V. E. Hall (Eds.), *Handbook of physiology.* Vol. 3. Washington, D.C.: American Physiological Society, 1960. Pp. 316–318.
54. Brady, J. V., & Nauta, W. J. H. Subcortical mechanisms in emotional behavior: Affective changes following septal forebrain lesions in the albino rat. *Journal of Comparative and Physiological Psychology,* 1953, **46,** 339–346.
55. Brady, J. V., & Nauta, W. J. H. Subcortical mechanisms in emotional behavior: The duration of affective changes following septal forebrain lesions in the albino rat. *Journal of Comparative and Physiological Psychology,* 1955, **48,** 412–420.
56. Bremer, J. *Asexualization.* New York: Macmillan, 1959.
57. Brown, J. L., & Hunsperger, R. W. Neuroethology and the motivation of agnostic behaviour. *Animal Behavior,* 1963, **11,** 439–448.
58. Brutkowski, S., Fonberg, E., & Mempel, E. Angry behavior in dogs following bilateral lesions in the genual portion of the rostral cingulate gyrus. *Acta Biologiae Experimentalis,* 1961, **21,** 199–205.

59. Buki, R. A. The use of psychotropic drugs in the rehabilitation of sex-deviated criminals. *American Journal of Psychiatry,* 1964, **120,** 1170–1175.
60. Bunnell, B. N. Amygdaloid lesions and social dominance in the hooded rat. *Psychonomic Science,* 1966, **6,** 93–94.
61. Bunnell, B. N., Bemporad, J. R., & Flesher, C. K. Septal forebrain lesions and social dominance behavior in the hooded rat. *Psychonomic Science,* 1966, **6,** 207–208.
62. Bunnell, B. N., Burkett, E. E., & Jarrard, L. E. Hippocampal lesions and social behavior in the golden hamster. Paper presented at the meeting of the Midwestern Psychological Association, Chicago, May, 1967.
63. Bunnell, B. N., & Smith, M. H. Septal lesions and aggressiveness in the cotton rat, sigmodon hispidus. *Psychonomic Science,* 1966, **6,** 443–444.
64. Bunnell, B. N., Sodetz, F. J., & Shalloway, D. M. The effects of septal and amygdaloid lesions on aggressiveness and social dominance in the hamster. Paper presented at the meeting of the Psychonomic Society, Chicago, October, 1965.
65. Burnand, G., Hunter, H., & Hoggart, K. Some psychological test characteristics of Klinefelter's syndrome. *British Journal of Psychiatry,* 1967, **113,** 1091–1096.
66. Buss, A. *The Psychology of aggression.* New York: Wiley, 1961.
67. Caggiula, A. R., & Hoebel, B. G. "Copulation-reward site" in the posterior hypothalamus. *Science,* 1966, **153,** 1284–1285.
68. Carpenter, C. R. Effects of complete and partial gonadectomy on fighting behavior in domestic pigeons. Unpublished doctoral dissertation, Stanford University, 1930.
69. Carpenter, C. R. Territoriality: A review of concepts and problems. In A. Rowe and G. G. Simpson (Eds.), *Behavior and evolution.* New Haven, Conn.: Yale University Press, 1958.
70. Carpenter, C. R. *Naturalistic behavior of nonhuman primates.* University Park, Pa.: Pennsylvania State University Press, 1964.
71. Carthy, J. D., & Ebling, F. J. *The natural history of aggression.* New York: Academic Press, 1964.
72. Christian, J. J., & Davis, D. E. Endocrines, behavior and population. *Science,* 1964, **146,** 1550–1560.
73. Clark, L. D. Experimental studies of the behavior of an aggressive predatory mouse, onychomys leucogaster. In E. L. Bliss (Ed.), *Roots of behavior.* New York: Hoeber, 1962. Pp. 179–186.
74. Clark, G., & Birch, H. G. Hormonal modifications of social behavior; The effect of sex-hormone administration on the social status of a male-castrate chimpanzee. *Psychosomatic Medicine,* 1945, **7,** 321–329.
75. Clark, S. M., Meyer, P. M., Meyer, D. R., & Yutzey, D. A.

Emotionality changes following septal and neocortical ablations in the albino rat. *Psychonomic Science,* 1967, **8,** 125–127.
76. Cleghorn, R. A. Steroid hormones in relation to neuropsychiatric disorders. In H. Hoagland (Ed.), *Hormones, brain function and behavior.* New York: Academic Press, 1957.
77. Cofer, C. N., & Appley, M. H. *Motivation theory and research.* New York: Wiley, 1964.
78. Cohen, S. Thioridazine (Mellaril): Recent deveiopments. *Journal of Psychopharmacology,* 1966, **1,** 1–15.
79. Collias, N. E. Aggressive behavior among vertebrate animals. *Physiological Zoology,* 1944, **17,** 83–123.
80. Conner, R. L., & Levine, S. Hormonal influences on aggressive behaviour. In S. Garattini and E. B. Sigg (Eds.), *Aggressive behaviour.* New York: Wiley, 1969. Pp. 150–163.
81. Cook, L., & Kelleher, R. T. Effects of drugs on behavior. *Annual Review of Pharmacology,* 1963, **3,** 205–222.
82. Coppen, A., & Kessel, N. Menstruation and personality. *British Journal of Psychiatry,* 1963, **109,** 711–721.
83. Cunningham, M. A., Pillai, V., & Rogers, W. J. B. Haloperidol in the treatment of children with severe behaviour disorders. *British Journal of Psychiatry,* 1968, **114,** 512.
84. Dalton, K. Menstruation and crime. *British Medical Journal,* 1961, 1752–1753.
85. Dalton, K. *The premenstrual syndrome.* Springfield, Illinois: Charles C. Thomas, 1964.
86. Danowski, T. S. *Clinical endocrinology.* Vol. 4. *Adrenal cortex and medulla.* Baltimore: Williams & Wilkins, 1962.
87. Darwin, C. *The expression of emotions in man and animals.* New York: D. Appleton, 1896 (authorized edition).
88. DaVanzo, J. P., Daugherty, M., Ruckert, R., & Kang, L. Pharmacological and biochemical studies in isolation induced fighting mice. *Psychopharmacologia,* 1966, **9,** 210–219.
89. Davis, F. C. The measurement of aggressive behavior in laboratory rats. *Journal of Genetic Psychology,* 1933, **43,** 213–217.
90. De Craene, O. Nervoses et therapeutique tranquillisante. *Scalpel,* 1964, **117,** 1044–1050.
91. Delgado, J. M. R. Emotional behavior in animals and humans. *Psychiatric Research Reports,* 1960, **12,** 259–271.
92. Delgado, J. M. R. Pharmacological modifications of social behavior. In First International Pharmacological Meeting. *Pharmacological Analysis of Central Nervous Action,* 1962, **8,** 265–292.
93. Delgado, J. M. R. Cerebral heterostimulation in a monkey colony. *Science,* 1963, **141,** 161–163.
94. Delgado, J. M. R. Pharmacology of spontaneous and conditioned behavior in the monkey. Pharmacology of conditioning, learning and retention. *Proceedings of the Second International Pharmacological Meeting.* Prague, 20–23 August, 1965. Pp. 133–156.

95. Delgado, J. M. R. *Evolution of physical control of the brain.* New York: The American Museum of Natural History, 1965.
96. Delgado, J. M. R. Aggressive behavior evoked by radio stimulation in monkey colonies. *American Zoologist,* 1966, **6,** 669–681.
97. Delgado, J. M. R. Brain research and behavioral activity. *Endeavour,* 1967, **26,** 149–154.
98. Delgado, J. M. R. Aggression in free monkeys modified by electrical and chemical stimulation of the brain. Paper presented at The Symposium on Aggression, Interdepartmental Institute for Training in Research in the Behavioral and Neurologic Sciences, Albert Einstein College of Medicine, New York, June 5, 1969.
99. Delgado, J. M. R. *Physical control of the mind.* New York: Harper & Row, 1969.
100. Delgado, J. M. R., Bradley, R. J., Johnston, V. S., Weiss, G., & Wallace, J. D. Implantation of multilead electrode assemblies and radio stimulation of the brain in chimpanzees. *Technical Report, ARL-TR-69-2,* 6571st Aeromedical Research Laboratory. Aerospace Medical Division, Air Force Systems Command, Holloman Air Force Base, New Mexico.
101. Delgado, J. M. R., & Kitahata, L. M. Reversible depression of hippocampus by local injections of anesthetics in monkeys. *Electroencephalography and Clinical Neurophysiology,* 1967, **22,** 453–464.
102. Delgado, J. M. R., Mark, V., Sweet, W., Ervin, F., Weiss, G., Bach-Y-Rita, & Hagiwara, R. Intracerebral radio stimulation and recording in completely free patients. *Journal of Nervous and Mental Diseases,* 1968, **147,** 329–340.
103. Denhan, J. Psychotherapy of obsessional neurosis assisted by Librium. Topical problems of psychotherapy. *Supplementum ad Acta Psychotherapeutica et Psychosomatica,* 1963, **4,** 195–198.
104. DeSisto, M. J., & Huston, J. P. Facilitation of interspecific aggression by subreinforcing electrical stimulation in the posterior lateral hypothalamus. Paper presented at the meeting of the Eastern Psychological Association, Atlantic City, N.J., April, 1970.
105. Deutsch, J. A., & Deutsch, D. *Physiological psychology.* Homewood, Ill.: Dorsey Press, 1966.
106. Dicks, D., Myers, R. D., & Kling, A. Uncus and amygdala lesions: Effects on social behavior in the free-ranging rhesus monkey. *Science,* 1969, **165,** 69–71.
107. Didiergeorges, F., & Karli, P. Stimulations sociales et inhibition de l'aggressivité interspécifiques chez le rat privé de ses afférances olfactives. *Comptes Rendus des Séances de la Société de Biologie,* 1966, **160,** 2445.
108. Didiergeorges, F., & Karli, P. Hormones stéroides et maturation

d'un comportement d'agression interspécifique du rat. *Comptes Rendus des Séances de la Société de Biologie,* 1967, **161,** 179.
109. Didiergeorges, F., Vergnes, M., & Karli, P. Privation des afférences olfactives et agressivité interspécifique du rat. *Comptes Rendus des Séances de la Société de Biologie,* 1966, **160,** 866.
110. Dollard, J., Miller, N. E., Doob, L. W., Mowrer, O. H., & Sears, R. R. *Frustration and aggression.* New Haven, Conn.: Yale University Press, 1939.
111. Dunn, G. W. Stilbesterol induced testicular degeneration in hypersexual males. *Journal of Clinical Endocrinology,* 1941, **1,** 643–648.
112. Edwards, D. A. Mice: Fighting by neonatally androgenized females. *Science,* 1968, **161,** 1027–1028.
113. Egger, M. D., & Flynn, J. P. Effect of electrical stimulation of the amygdala on hypothalamically elicited attack behavior in cats. *Journal of Neurophysiology,* 1963, **26,** 705–720.
114. Egger, M. D., & Flynn, J. P. Further studies on the effects of amygdaloid stimulation and ablation on hypothalamically elicited attack behavior in cats. In W. R. Adey and T. Tokizane (Eds.), *Progress in Brain Research.* Vol. 27. Amsterdam: Elsevier, 1967.
115. Ehrlich, A. Neural control of feeding behavior. *Psychological Bulletin,* 1964, **61,** 100–114.
116. Eibl-Eibesfeldt, I. The fighting behavior of animals. *Scientific American,* 1961, **205,** 112–122.
117. Eisenberg, J. The behavior of heteromyid rodents. *University of California Publication in Zoology,* 1963, **69,** 1–114.
118. Endroczi, E., Lissak, K., & Telegdy, G. Influence of sexual and adrenocortical hormones on the maternal aggressivity. *Acta Physiologica Academiae Scientiarum Hungaricae,* 1958, **14,** 353–357.
119. Ervin, F. R., Mark, V. H., & Stevens, J. Behavioral and affective responses to brain stimulation in man. In J. Zubin and C. Shagass (Eds.), *Neurobiological aspects of psychopathology.* New York: Grune & Stratton, 1969. Pp. 54–65.
120. Falconer, M. A. Discussion. In M. Baldwin and P. Bailey (Eds.), *Temporal lobe epilepsy.* Springfield, Ill.: Charles C. Thomas, 1958.
121. Falconer, M. A., Hill, D., Meyer, A., & Wilson, J. L. Clinical, radiological, and EEG correlations with pathological changes in temporal lobe epilepsy and their significance in surgical treatment. In M. Baldwin and P. Bailey (Eds.), *Temporal lobe epilepsy.* Springfield, Ill.: Charles C. Thomas, 1958. Pp. 396–410.
122. Fernandez de Molina, A., & Hunsperger, R. W. Central representation of affective reaction in forebrain and brain stem: Electrical stimulation of amygdala, stria terminalis, and adjacent structures. *Journal of Physiology,* 1959, **145,** 251–265.

123. Fernandez de Molina, A., & Hunsperger, R. W. Organization of the subcortical system governing defense and flight reactions in the cat. *Journal of Physiology,* 1962, **160,** 200–213.
124. Feshbach, S. The function of aggression and the regulation of aggressive drive. *Psychological Review,* 1964, **71,** 257–272.
125. Fish, B. Drug therapy in child psychiatry: Pharmacological aspects. *Comparative Psychiatry,* 1960, **1,** 212–227.
126. Fisher, A. E. Maternal and sexual behavior induced by intracranial chemical stimulation. *Science,* 1956, **124,** 228–229.
127. Fisher, A. E. Chemical stimulation of the brain. *Scientific American,* 1964, **210,** 60–68.
128. Fisher, A. E. Chemical and electrical stimulation of the brain in the male rat. In R. A. Gorski and R. E. Whalen (Eds.), *Brain and behavior.* Vol. 3. *The brain and gonadal function.* Los Angeles: University of California Press, 1966. Pp. 117–130.
129. Flynn, J., Vanegas, H., Foote, W., & Edwards, S. Neural mechanisms involved in a cat's attack on a rat. In R. Whalen, R. F. Thompson, M. Verzeano, and N. Weinberger (Eds.), *The neural control of behavior.* New York: Academic Press, 1970.
130. Fonberg, E. Effect of partial destruction of the amygdaloid complex on the emotional-defensive behavior of dogs. *Bulletin de L'Academie Polonaise des Sciences* Cl. II. 1965, **13,** 429–431.
131. Foss, G. L. The influence of androgens on sexuality in women. *Lancet,* 1951, **1,** 667–669.
132. Frederichs, C., & Goodman, H. *Low blood sugar and you.* New York: Constellation International, 1969.
133. Fredericson, E. The effects of food deprivation upon competitive and spontaneous combat in C57 black mice. *Journal of Psychology,* 1950, **29,** 89–100.
134. Fuller, J. L., Rosvold, H. E., & Pribram, K. H. The effect on affective and cognitive behavior in the dog of lesions of the pyriform-amygdala-hippocampal complex. *Journal of Comparative and Physiological Psychology,* 1957, **50,** 89–96.
135. Funkenstein, D. H., King, S. H., & Drolette, M. E. *Mastery of stress.* Cambridge, Mass.: Harvard University Press, 1957.
136. Galef, B. G. Aggression and timidity: Response to novelty in feral Norway rats. *Journal of Comparative and Physiological Psychology,* 1970, **70,** 370–375.
137. Gellhorn, E. *Principles of autonomic-somatic integrations.* Minneapolis: University of Minnesota Press, 1967.
138. Gellhorn, E. *Biological foundation of emotion.* Glenview, Ill.: Scott, Foresman, 1968.
139. Giacalone, E., Tansella, M., Valzelli, L., & Garattini, S. Brain serotonin metabolism in isolated aggressive mice. *Biochemical Pharmacology,* 1968, **17,** 1315–1327.
140. Gibbs, F. A. Ictal and non-ictal psychiatric disorders in temporal

lobe epilepsy. *Journal of Nervous and Mental Diseases,* 1951, **113,** 522–528.
141. Gibbs, F. A. Abnormal electrical activity in the temporal regions and its relationship to abnormalities of behavior. *Research Publication of the Association for Research in Nervous and Mental Disease,* 1956, **36,** 278–294.
142. Gibbs, F. A., Amader, L., & Rich, C. Electroencephalographic findings and therapeutic results in surgical treatment of psychomotor epilepsy. In M. Baldwin, and P. Bailey (Eds.), *Temporal lobe epilepsy.* Springfield, Ill.: Charles C. Thomas, 1958. Pp. 358–367.
143. Gibson, J. G. Emotions and the thyroid gland. *Journal of Psychosomatic Research,* 1962, **6,** 93–116.
144. Gill, J. H., Reid, L. D., & Porter, P. S. Effects of restricted rearing on Lashley Stand performance. *Psychological Reports,* 1966, **14,** 239–242.
145. Ginsburg, B., & Allee, W. C. Some effects of conditioning on social dominance and subordination in inbred strains of mice. *Physiological Zoology,* 1942, **15,** 485–596.
146. Glees, P., Cole, J., Whitty, C., & Cairns, H. The effects of lesions in the cingular gyrus and adjacent areas in monkeys. *Journal of Neurology, Neurosurgery and Psychiatry,* 1950, **13,** 178–190.
147. Gloor, P. Amygdala. In J. Field, H. W. Magoun, and V. E. Hall (Eds.), *American physiological society handbook of physiology, section I; Neurophysiology.* Vol. 2. Baltimore: Williams & Wilkins, 1960. Pp. 1395–1416.
148. Gloor, P. Discussion of brain mechanisms related to aggressive behavior by B. Kaada. In C. D. Clemente and D. B. Lindsley (Eds.), *Aggression and defense: Neural mechanisms and social patterns.* Vol. 5. *Brain Function.* Los Angeles: University of California Press, 1967.
149. Glueck & Boelhouwer. Paper presented at the American Psychiatric Association, May, 1967.
150. Glusman, M., & Roisin, L. Role of the hypothalamus in the organization of agonistic behavior in the cat. *Transactions of American Neurology Association,* 1960, 177–179.
151. Glusman, M., Won, W., Burdock, E. I., & Ransohoff, J. Effects of midbrain lesions on "savage' behavior induced by hypothalamic lesions in the cat. *Transactions of the American Neurological Association,* 1961, 216–218.
152. Goddard, G. V. Functions of the amygdala. *Psychological Bultin,* 1964, **62,** 89–109.
153. Gol, A., Kellaway, P., Shapiro, M., & Hurst, C. M. Studies of hippocampectomy in the monkey, baboon, and cat. *Neurology,* 1963, **13,** 1031.

154. Goodman, L. S., & Gilman, A. *The pharmacological basis of therapeutics.* New York: Macmillan, 1966.
155. Graff, H., & Stellar, E. Hyperphagia, obesity and finickiness. *Journal of Comparative and Physiological Psychology,* 1962, **55,** 418–424.
156. Green, J. D., Clemente, C. D., & de Groot, J. Rhinencephalic lesions and behavior in cats. *Journal of Comparative Neurology,* 1957, **108,** 505–536.
157. Green, J. R., Duisberg, R. E. H., & McGrath, W. B. Focal epilepsy of psychomotor type, a preliminary report of observations on effects of surgical therapy. *Journal of Neurosurgery,* 1951, **8,** 157–172.
158. Greene, R., & Dalton, K. The premenstrual syndrome. *British Medical Journal,* 1953, **1,** 1007–1014.
159. Griffiths, W. J., Jr. Effects of isolation and stress on escape thresholds in albino rats. *Psychological Reports,* 1960, **6,** 23–29.
160. Grossman, S. P. *A textbook of physiological psychology.* New York: Wiley, 1967.
161. Guhl, A. M. Gonadal hormones and social behavior in infrahuman vertebrates. In W. C. Young and G. W. Corner (Eds.), *Sex and internal secretions.* Baltimore: Williams & Wilkins, 1961. Pp. 1240–1267.
162. Hafez, E. S. *The behaviour of domestic animals.* Baltimore: Williams & Wilkins, 1962.
163. Hall, C. S., & Klein, S. J. Individual differences in aggressiveness in rats. *Journal of Comparative Psychology,* 1942, **33,** 371–383.
164. Hamburg, D. A. Effects of progesterone on behavior. In R. Levine (Ed.), *Endocrines and the central nervous system.* Baltimore: Williams & Wilkins, 1966.
165. Hamburg, D. A., Moos, R. H., & Yalom, I. D. Studies of distress in the menstrual cycle and the postpartum period. In R. P. Michael (Ed.), *Endocrinology and human behavior.* London: Oxford University Press, 1968.
166. Hardy, K. R. An appetitional theory of sexual motivation. *Psychological Review,* 1964, **71,** 1–18.
167. Harlow, H. F. The nature of love. *American Psychologist,* 1958, **12,** 673–685.
168. Harris, G. W., Michael, R. P., & Scott, P. P. Neurological site of action of stilboestrol in eliciting sexual behavior. In G. E. W. Wolstenholme and C. M. O'Connor (Eds.), *Neurological basis of behavior.* London: Churchill, 1958. Pp. 236–254.
169. Hatch, A., Wiberg, G. S., Balzas, T., & Grice, H. C. Long-term isolation stress in rats. *Science,* 1963, **142,** 507.
170. Hawke, C. C. Castration and sex crimes. *American Journal of Mental Deficiency,* 1950, **55,** 220–226.
171. Heath, R. G. Behavioral changes following destructive lesions

in the subcortical structure of the forebrain in cats. In R. G. Heath, et al., *Studies in schizophrenia*. Cambridge: Harvard University Press, 1954. Pp. 83–84.
172. Heath, R. G. *First Hahnemann symposium on psychosomatic medicine*. Philadelphia: Lea and Febiger, 1962. Pp. 228–240.
173. Heath, R. G. Common characteristics of epilepsy and schizophrenia—Clinical observation and depth electrode studies. *American Journal of Psychiatry*, 1962, **118,** 1013–1026.
174. Heath, R. G. Electrical self-stimulation of the brain in man. *American Journal of Psychiatry*, 1963, **120,** 571–577.
175. Heath, R. G. Pleasure response of human subjects to direct stimulation of the brain: Physiologic and psychodynamic considerations. In R. G. Heath (Ed.), *The role of pleasure in behavior*. New York: Hoeber, 1964.
176. Heath, R. G. Developments toward new physiologic treatments in psychiatry. *Journal of Neuropsychiatry*, 1964, **5,** 318–331.
177. Heath, R. G., & Buddington, W. Drugs for stimulation of mental and physical activity. In W. Modell (Ed.), *Drugs of Choice, 1968–1969*. St. Louis, Mo.: Mosby, 1967.
178. Heath, R. G., & Mickle, W. A. Evaluation of seven years' experience with depth electrode studies in human patients. In E. R. Ramey and D. S. O'Doherty (Eds.), *Electrical studies on the unanesthetized brain*. New York: Hoeber, 1960. Pp. 214–247.
179. Heimburger, R. F., Whitlock, C. C., & Kalsbeck, J. E. Stereotaxic amygdalotomy for epilepsy with aggressive behavior. *Journal of the American Medical Association*, 1966, **198,** 165–169.
180. Heimstra, N. W. A further investigation of the development of mouse killing in rats. *Psychonomic Science*, 1965, **2,** 179–180.
181. Heimstra, N. W., & Newton, G. Effects of prior food competition on the rat's killing response to the white mouse. *Behaviour*, 1961, **17,** 95–102.
182. Hendley, C. D., et al. Effect of 2-methyl-2-N-propyl-1-3-propanediol dicarbamate (Miltown) on central nervous system. *Proceedings of the Society for Experimental Biology and Medicine*, 1954, **87,** 608.
183. Hess, E. H. Imprinting. *Science*, 1959, **130,** 133–141.
184. Hess, E. H. Imprinting in birds. *Science*, 1964, **146,** 1128–1139.
185. Hess, W. R. *The biology of mind*. Chicago: University of Chicago Press, 1964.
186. Higgins, J. W., Mahl, G. F., Delgado, J. M. R., & Hamlin, H. Behavioral changes during intracerebral electrical stimulation. *Archives of Neurology and Psychiatry*, 1956, **76,** 309–419.
187. Hill, D., & Watterson, D. Electro-encephalographic studies of psychopathic personalities. *Journal of Neurology and Psychiatry*, 1942, **5,** 47–65.
188. Hinde, R. A. The nature of aggression. *New Society*, 1967, **9,** 302–304.

189. Huffman, J. W. Effect of testosterone propionate upon reproduction in the female. *Endocrinology,* 1941, **29,** 77–79.
190. Hutchinson, R. R., & Renfrew, J. W. Stalking attack and eating behavior elicited from the same sites in the hypothalamus. *Journal of Comparative and Physiological Psychology,* 1966, **61,** 300–367.
191. Hutchinson, R. R., Ulrich, R. E., & Azrin, N. H. Effects of age and related factors on the pain aggression reaction. *Journal of Comparative and Physiological Psychology,* 1965, **59,** 365–369.
192. Ingram, W. R. The hypothalamus: A review of the experimental data. *Psychosomatic Medicine,* 1939, **1,** 48–91.
193. Jacobsen, E. The clinical effect of drugs and their influence on animal behavior. *Revue de Psychologie Appliquée,* 1961, **11,** 421–532.
194. Janowsky, E. S., Gorney, R., & Mandell, A. J. The menstrual cycle: Psychiatric and ovarian-adrenocortical hormone correlates: Case study and literature review. *Archives of General Psychiatry,* 1967, **17,** 459–469.
195. Jenkins, R. L., & Pacella, B. L. Electroencephalographic studies of delinquent boys. *American Journal of Orthopsychiatry,* 1943, **13,** 107–120.
196. Jonas, A. D. *Ictal and subictal neurosis: Diagnosis and treatment.* Springfield, Ill.: Charles C. Thomas, 1965.
197. Jones, L. U. Analysis of variance in its multivariate developments. In R. Cattell (Ed.), *Handbook of Multivariate Experimental Psychology.* Chicago: Rand McNally, 1966.
198. Kaada, B. Brain mechanisms related to aggressive behavior. In C. D. Clemente and D. B. Lindsley (Eds.), *Aggression and defense; Neural mechanisms and social patterns.* Vol. 5. *Brain Function.* Los Angeles: University of California Press, 1967. Pp. 95–134.
199. Kaada, B. R., Andersen, P., & Jansen, J. Stimulation of the amygdaloid nuclear complex in unanesthetized cats. *Neurology,* 1954, **4,** 48–64.
200. Kaelber, W. W., Mitchell, C. L., & Way, J. S. Some sensory influences on savage (affective) behavior in cats. *American Journal of Physiology,* 1965, **209,** 866–870.
201. Kahn, M. W. The effect of severe defeat at various age levels on the aggressive behavior of mice. *Journal of Genetic Psychology,* 1951, **79,** 117–130.
202. Kalina, R. K. Use of dizaepam in the violent psychotic patient: A preliminary report. *Colorado General Practitioner,* 1962, **4,** 11–14.
203. Karli, P. The Norway rat's killing response to the white mouse. *Behavior,* 1956, **10,** 81–103.
204. Karli, P. Hormones stéroides et comportement d'aggression inter-

spécifique rat-souris. *Journal de Physiologie et de Pathologie Generale,* 1958, **50,** 346–357.
205. Karli, P., & Vergnes, M. Role du rhinencephale dans le controle du comportement d'aggression inter-spécifique rat-souris. *Journal de Physiologie,* 1963, **55,** 272–273.
206. Karli, P., & Vergnes, M. Nouvelles données sur les bases neurophysiologiques du comportement d'agression interspécifique rat-souris. *Journal de Physiologie,* 1964, **56,** 384.
207. Karli, P., & Vergnes, M. Role des différentes composantes du complexe nucléaire amygdalien dans la facilitation de l'agressivité interspécifique du rat. *Comptes Rendus des Séances de la Société de Biologie,* 1965, **159,** 754.
208. Karli, P., Vergnes, M., & Didiergeorges, F. Rat-mouse interspecific aggressive behavior and its manipulation by brain ablation and brain stimulation. In S. Garattini and E. B. Sigg (Eds.), *Aggressive behaviour.* Amsterdam: Wiley, 1969. Pp. 47–55.
209. Kaufman, C. Affiliation and aggression—Some bases, patterns, uses and limitations. Paper presented at the University of Virginia Symposium on "Allegiance and Hostility, Man's Mammalian Heritage," October 8–11, 1969.
210. Kaufman, I. C., & Rosenblum, L. A. The reaction to separation in infant monkeys: Anaclitic depression and conservation-withdrawal. *Psychosomatic Medicine,* 1967, **29,** 648–675.
211. Kennard, M. A. The cingulate gyrus in relation to consciousness. *Journal of Nervous and Mental Disease,* 1955, **121,** 34–39.
212. Kennard, M. A. Effect of bilateral ablation of cingulate area on behaviour of cats. *Journal of Neurophysiology,* 1955, **18,** 159–169.
213. Kennedy, G. C. The role of depot fat in the hypothalamic control of food intake in the rat. *Proceedings of the Royal Society,* Ser. B., 1953, **140,** 578–592.
214. Kessler, S., & Moos, R. H. The XYY karyotype and criminality: A review. *Journal of Psychiatric Research,* 1970, **7,** 153–170.
215. King, F. A. Effects of septal and amygdaloid lesions on emotional behavior and conditioned avoidance responses in the rat. *Journal of Nervous and mental Disease,* 1958, **126,** 57–63.
216. King, F. A., & Meyer, P. M. Effects of amygdaloid lesions upon septal hyperemotionality in the rat. *Science,* 1958, **128,** 655–656.
217. King, H. E. Psychological effects of excitation in the limbic system. In D. E. Sheer (Ed.), *Electrical stimulation of the brain.* Austin: University of Texas Press, 1961. Pp. 477–486.
218. King, M. B. & Hoebel, B. G. Killing elicited by brain stimulation in rat. *Communications in Behavioral Biology,* 1968, **2,** 173–177.
219. Kislak, J. W., & Beach, F. A. Inhibition of aggressiveness by ovarian hormones. *Endocrinology,* 1955, **56,** 684–692.

References

220. Kline, N. Drugs are the greatest practical advance in the history of psychiatry. *New Medical Materia,* 1962, 49.
221. Kling, A., & Hutt, P. J. Effect of hypothalamic lesions on the amygdala syndrome in the cat. *AMA Archives of Neurology and Psychiatry,* 1958, **79,** 511–517.
222. Kluver, H., & Bucy, P. C. "Psychic blindness" and other symptoms following bilateral temporal lobectomy in rhesus monkeys. *American Journal of Physiology,* 1937, **119,** 352–353.
223. Kluver, H., & Bucy, P. C. An analysis of certain effects of bilateral temporal lobectomy in the rhesus monkey, with special reference to "psychic blindness." *Journal of Psychology,* 1938, **5,** 33–54.
224. Kluver, H. & Bucy, P. C. Preliminary analysis of functions of the temporal lobes in monkeys. *Archives of Neurology and Psychiatry,* 1939, **42,** 979–1000.
225. Komisaruk, B. R., & Olds, J. Neuronal correlates of behavior in freely moving rats. *Science,* 1968, **161,** 810–813.
226. Korn, J. H., & Moyer, K. E. Behavioral effects of isolation in the rat: The role of sex and time of isolation. *Journal of Genetic Psychology,* 1968, **113,** 263–273.
227. Kreschner, M., Bender, M., & Strauss, I. Mental symptoms in cases of tumor of the temporal lobe. *Archives of Neurology and Psychiatry,* 1936, **35,** 572–596.
228. Kulkarni, A. S. Satiation of instinctive mouse killing by rats. *Psychological Record,* 1968, **18,** 385–388.
229. Kuo, Z. Y. Studies on the basic factors in animal fighting: Part I–IV. *Journal of Genetic Psychology,* 1960, **96,** 210–239.
230. Lagerspetz, K. Genetic and social causes of aggressive behavior in mice. *Scandanavian Journal of Psychology,* 1961, **2,** 167–173.
231. Lagerspetz, K. Studies on the aggressive behavior of mice. *Annales Academiae Scientiarum Fennicae,* 1964, Series B, **131,** 1–131.
232. Laties, V. G. Modification of affect, social behavior and performance by sleep deprivation and drugs. *Journal of Psychiatric Research,* 1961, **1,** 12–25.
233. Le Beau, J. The cingular and precingular areas in psychosurgery (agitated behaviour, obsessive compulsive states, epilepsy). *Acta Psychiatrica et Neuroligica.* Copenhagen, 1952, **27,** 305–316.
234. LeMaire, L. Danish experience regarding the castration of sexual offenders. *Journal of Criminal Law and Criminology,* 1956, **47,** 294–310.
235. Lennox, W. G. The genetics of epilepsy. *American Journal of Psychiatry,* 1947, **103,** 457–462.
236. Lerner, L. J. Hormone antagonists: Inhibitors of specific activities of estrogen and androgen. *Recent progress in hormone research.* Vol. 20. New York: Academic Press, 1964. Pp. 435–490.

237. Lerner, L. J., Bianchi, A., & Borman, A. A-Norprogesterone: An androgen antagonist. *Proceedings of the Society for Experimental Biology and Medicine,* 1960, **103**, 172–175.
238. Levison, P. K., & Flynn, J. P. The objects attacked by cats during stimulation of the hypothalamus. *Animal Behavior,* 1965, **13**, 217–220.
239. Levy, J. V. The effects of testosterone propionate on fighting behaviour in C57BL/10 young female mice. *Proceedings of the West Virginia Academy of Science,* 1954, **26**, 14. (Abstract.)
240. Levy, J., & King, J. A. The effects of testosterone propionate on fighting behaviour in young male C57BL/10 mice. *Anatomical Record,* 1953, **117**, 562–563. (Abstract.)
241. Lichtenstein, P. E. Studies of anxiety II: The effects of lobotomy on a feeding inhibition in dogs. *Journal of Comparative and Physiological Psychology,* 1950, **43**, 419–427.
242. Liddell, D. W. Observation on epileptic automatism in a mental hospital population. *Journal of Mental Science,* 1953, **99**, 731–748.
243. Lisk, R. D. Hormonal implants in the central nervous system and behavioral receptivity in the female rat. In R. A. Gorski and R. E. Whalen (Eds.), *Brain and behavior.* Vol. 3. *The brain and gonadal function.* Los Angeles: University of California Press, 1966. Pp. 82–98.
244. Lissak, K., & Endroczi, E. Neurohumoral factors in the control of animal behaviour. In A. Fessard, R. W. Girard and J. Konoski (Eds.), *Brain mechanisms and learning,* Oxford, England: Blackwell, 1961. Pp. 293–308.
245. Lorenz, K. *On aggression.* New York: Harcourt, Brace & World, 1966.
246. Lorenz, K. World figures sum up their aspirations. *Who's who in America.* Vol. 36, 1970–1971. Chicago: Marquis–Who's Who, 1970.
247. Lyght, C. E. (Ed.). *The Merck manual of diagnosis and therapy.* West Point, Pa.: Merck, 1966.
248. MacDonnell, M. F., & Flynn, J. P. Attack elicited by stimulation of the thalamus of cats. *Science,* 1964, **144**, 1249–1250.
249. MacDonnell, M. F., & Flynn, J. P. Control of sensory fields by stimulation of hypothalamus. *Science,* 1966, **152**, 1406–1408.
250. MacDonnell, M. F., & Flynn, J. P. Sensory control of hypothalamic attack. *Animal Behaviour,* 1966, **14**, 399–405.
251. MacLean, P. D., & Delgado, J. M. R. Electrical and chemical stimulation of frontotemporal portion of limbic system in the waking animal. *EEG, and Clinical Neurophysiology,* 1953, **5**, 91–100.
252. Mallick, S. K., & McCandless, B. R. A study of catharsis of aggression. In L. Berkowitz (Ed.), *Roots of aggression.* New York: Atherton, 1969. Pp. 92–105.

References

253. Mark, V. H., Ervin, F. R., Sweet, W. H., & Delgado, J. Remote telemeter stimulation and recording from implanted temporal lobe electrodes. *Confina Neurologica,* 1969, **31,** 86–93.
254. Mark, V. H., Sweet, W. H., & Ervin, R. R. Role of brain disease in riots and urban violence. *Journal of the American Medical Association,* 1967, **201,** 217.
255. Marler, P. Familiarity and strangeness as determinants of animal allegiance and hostility. Paper presented at the University of Virginia Symposium on "Allegiance and Hostility, Man's Mammalian Heritage," October 8–11, 1969.
256. Marler, P., & Hamilton, W. J. III. *Mechanisms of Animal Behavior.* New York: Wiley, 1966.
257. Marrone, R. L., Pray, S. L., & Bridges, C. C. Norepinepherine elicitation of aggressive display responses in Betta splendens. *Psychonomic Science,* 1966, **5,** 207–208.
258. Masserman, J. H. *Behavior and neuroses.* Chicago: University of Chicago Press, 1943.
259. Mayer, J. Glucostatic mechanism of regulation of food intake. *New England Medical Journal,* 1953, **249,** 13–16.
260. McAdam, D. W., & Kaelber, W. W. Differential impairment of avoidance learning in cats with ventromedial hypothalmic lesions. *Experimental Neurology,* 1966, **15,** 293–298.
261. McKinney, W. T., & Bunney, W. E. Animal model of depression. *Archives of General Psychiatry,* 1969, **21,** 240–248.
262. McWhirter, N. & McWhirter, R. *Guinness book of world records.* New York: Sterling, 1968.
263. Miller, N. E. Experiments on motivation. *Science,* 1957, **126,** 1271–1278.
264. Miller N. E. Learning and performance motivated by direct stimulation of the brain. In D. E. Sheer (Ed.), *Electrical stimulation of the brain.* Austin: University of Texas Press, 1961. Pp. 387–396.
265. Miller, R. E., Murphy, J. V., & Mirsky, I. A. The modification of social dominance in a group of monkeys by interanimal conditioning. *Journal of Comparative and Physiological Psychology,* 1955, 48, 392–396.
266. Mises, R., & Beauchesne, H. Essai de la perphenazine chez 1 enfant, et 1 adolescent. *Annales Medico Psychologiques,* 1963, 2, 89–92.
267. Mitchell, G. D. Paternalistic behavior in primates. *Psychological Bulletin,* 1969, **71,** 399–417.
268. Monroe, R. R. Episodic behavioral disorders—Schizophrenia or epilepsy. *Archives of General Psychiatry,* 1959, **1,** 205–214.
269. Montagu, M. F. A. *On being human.* New York: Hawthorn, 1966.
270. Montagu, M. F. A. *The human revolution.* New York: Bantam Books, 1967.

271. Montagu, M. F. A. *Man and aggression.* London: Oxford University Press, 1968.
272. Morrison, S. D., & Mayer, J. Adipsia and aphagia in rats after lateral subthalamic lesions. *American Journal of Physiology,* 1957, **191,** 248–254.
273. Morton, J. H., Addition, H., Addison, R. G., Hunt, L., & Sullivan, J. J. A clinical study of premenstrual tension. *American Journal of Obstetrics & Gynecology,* 1953, **65,** 1182–1191.
274. Moyer, K. E. Brain research must contribute to world peace. *Fiji School of Medicine Journal,* 1968, **11,** 2–5.
275. Moyer, K. E. Kinds of aggression and their physiological basis. *Communications in Behavioral Biology,* 1968, **2,** 65–87.
276. Moyer, K. E. Internal impulses to aggression. *Transactions of the New York Academy of Sciences,* 1969, **31,** 104–114.
277. Moyer, K. E. The physiology of aggression and the implications for aggression control. Paper presented at a Symposium on Aggressive Behavior at the City University of New York, June 6, 1969.
278. Moyer, K. E. A preliminary physiological model of aggressive behavior. In J. P. Scott and B. E. Eleftheriou (Eds.), *The physiology of fighting and defeat.* Chicago: University of Chicago Press, 1970.
279. Moyer, K. E. The physiology of affiliation and hostility. *Carnegie-Mellon Report No. 70–1,* 1970.
280. Moyer, K. E. & Korn, J. H. Behavioral effects of isolation in the rat. *Psychonomic Science,* 1965, **3,** 503–504.
281. Mulder, D., & Daly, D. Psychiatric symptoms associated with lesions of temporal lobe. *Journal of the American Medical Association,* 1952, **150,** 173–176.
282. Myer, J. S. Stimulus control of mouse killing rats. *Journal of Comparative and Physiological Psychology,* 1964, **58,** 112–117.
283. Myer, J. S. Associative and temporal determinants of facilitation and inhibition of attack by pain. *Journal of Comparative and Physiological Psychology,* 1968, **66,** 17–21.
284. Myer, J. S. Early experience and the development of mouse killing by rats. Mimeographed. Baltimore, Md.: Johns Hopkins, 1968.
285. Myer, J. S., & White, R. T. Aggressive motivation in the rat. *Animal Behaviour,* 1965, **13,** 430–433.
286. Nakao, H. Emotional behavior produced by hypothalamic stimulation. *American Journal of Physiology,* 1958, **194,** 411–418.
287. Narabayashi, H., Nagao, T., Saito, Y., Yoshida, M., & Nagahata, M. Stereotaxic amygdalotomy for behavior disorders. *Archives of Neurology,* 1963, **9,** 1–16.
288. Narabayashi, H., & Uno, M. Long range results of stereotaxic amygdalotomy for behavior disorders. *Second International Sym-*

posium Stereoencephalotomy, Confina Neurologica, 1966, **27,** 168–171.
289. National Commission on the Causes and Prevention of Violence. *To establish justice, to insure domestic tranquility, final report.* Washington, D.C.: U.S. Government Printing Office, 1969.
290. Neumann, F., Elger, W., & Von Berswordt-Wallrabe, R. Intersexuality of male foetuses and inhibition of androgenic functions in adult animals with a testosterone blocker. *German Medical Monthly,* 1967, **12,** 1–17.
291. Neumann, F., Von Berswordt-Wallrabe, R., Elger, W., & Steinbeck, H. Activities of antiandrogens: Experiments in prepuberal and puberal animals and in foetuses. In J. Tamm (Ed.), *Testosterone.* Proceedings of the Work Shop Conference, April, 1967, Tremsbuettel, Georg Thieme Verlag, Stuttgart, 1968, 134–143.
292. Pearson, O. P. Reproduction in the shrew (Blarina Brevicauda Say). *American Journal of Anatomy,* 1944, **75,** 39–93.
293. Penfield, W., & Jasper, H. *Epilepsy and the functional anatomy of the human brain.* Boston: Little, Brown, 1954.
294. Pennington, V. M. The phrenotropic action of perphenazine amytriptyline. *American Journal of Psychiatry,* 1964, **120,** 1115–1116.
295. Plotnik, R. Changes in social behavior of squirrel monkeys after anterior temporal lobectomy. *Journal of Comparative and Physiological Psychology,* 1968, **66,** 369–377.
296. Plotnik, R., & Delgado, J. M. R. Aggression and pain in unrestrained rhesus monkeys. In J. P. Scott and B. E. Eleftheriou (Eds.), *The physiology of fighting and defeat.* Chicago: University of Chicago Press, 1971.
297. Pool, J. L. The visceral brain of man. *Journal of Neurosurgery,* 1954, **11,** 45–63.
298. Pribram, K. H., & Bagshaw, M. Further analysis of the temporal lobe syndrome utilizing frontotemporal ablations. *Journal of Comparative Neurology,* 1953, **99,** 347–375.
299. Price, W. H., & Whatmore, P. B. Criminal behaviour and the XYY male. *Nature,* 1967, **213,** 815–816.
300. Price, W. H., & Whatmore, P. B. Behavior disorders and pattern of crime among XYY males identified at a maximum security hospital. *British Medical Journal,* 1967, **1,** 533–536.
301. Randall, L. O., Schallek, W., Heise, G. A., Keith, E. F., & Bagdon, R. E. The psychosedative properties of methaminodiazepoxide. *Journal of Pharmacology and Experimental Therapeutics,* 1960, **120,** 163–171.
302. Randolph, T. G. *Human ecology and susceptibility to the chemical environment.* Springfield, Ill.: Charles C. Thomas, 1962.
303. Reiss, M. Psychoendocrinology. *Journal of Mental Science,* 1954, **100,** 211–219.

304. Resnick, O. The psychoactive properties of diphenylhydantoin: Experiences with prisoners and juvenile delinquents. *International Journal of Neuropsychiatry*, 1967, supplement 2, S 20–S47.
305. Resnick, O. Use of psychotropic drugs with criminals. *Psychopharmacology Bulletin*, 1969, **5**, 17.
306. Revlis, R., & Moyer, K. E. Maternal aggression: A failure to replicate. *Psychonomic Science*, 1969, **16**, 135–136.
307. Reynolds, H. H. Effect of rearing and habituation in social isolation on performance of an escape task. *Journal of Comparative and Physiological Psychology*, 1963, **56**, 520–525.
308. Richter, C. P. Psychotic behavior produced in wild Norway and Alexandrine rats apparently by fear of food poisoning. In M. L. Reymert (Ed.), *Feelings and emotions: The Mooseheart symposium*. New York: McGraw-Hill, 1950. Pp. 189–202.
309. Roberts, W. W., & Kiess, H. O. Motivational properties of hypothalamic aggression in cats. *Journal of Comparative and Physiological Psychology*, 1964, **58**, 187–193.
310. Robinson, B. W., Alexander, M., & Bowne, G. Dominance reversal resulting from aggressive responses evoked by brain telestimulation. *Physiology and Behavior*, 1969, **4**, 749–752.
311. Robinson, W. G., & Guerrero-Figueroa, R. Electrophysiological studies during wakefulness and natural sleep in patients with episodic behavioral disorders. In R. Guerrero-Figueroa (Ed.), *Clinical and experimental research approaches to problems in mental illness*. Baton Rouge: Louisiana State University Press, 1971, in press.
312. Rocky, S. & Neri, R. O. Comparative biological properties of SCH 12600 (6-chloro 4,6 pregnadien 16-methylene 17-α-ol-3,20-dione-17-acetate) and chlormadinone acetate. *Federation Proceedings*, 1968, 27.
313. Romaniuk, A. Representation of aggression and flight reactions in the hypothalamus of the cat. *Acta Biologicae Experimentalis Sinica* (Warsaw), 1965, **25**, 177–186.
314. Ropartz, P. The relation between olfactory stimulation and aggressive behaviour in mice. *Animal Behaviour*, 1968, **16**, 97–100.
315. Rosenberg, P. H. Management of disturbed adolescents. *Diseases of the Nervous System*, 1966, **27**, 60–61.
316. Rosenblum, L. A., & Harlow, H. F. Approach-avoidance conflict in the mother-surrogate situation. *Psychological Reports*, 1963, **12**, 83–85.
317. Rosenfeld, A. 10,000-to-1 payoff. *Life Magazine*, 1967, **63**, 121–128.
318. Rosenzweig, M. R. Environmental complexity, cerebral change, and behavior. *American Psychologist*, 1966, **21**, 321–331.

319. Ross, A. T., & Jackson, V. A. B. Dilantin sodium: Its influence on conduct and on psychometric ratings of institutionalized epileptics. *Annals of International Medicine*, 1940, **14**, 770–773.
320. Rosvold, H. S., Mirsky, A. F., & Pribram, K. H. Influences of amygdalectomy on social behavior in monkeys. *Journal of Comparative and Physiological Psychology*, 1954, **47**, 173–178.
321. Salazar, J. M. Gregariousness in young rats. *Psychonomic Science*, 1968, **10**, 391–392.
322. Salmon, U. J., & Geist, S. H. Effect of androgens upon libido in women. *Journal of Clinical Endocrinology*, 1943, **3**, 235–238.
323. Sands, D. E. Further studies on endocrine treatment in adolescence and early adult life. *Journal of Mental Science*, 1954, **100**, 211–219.
324. Sands, D. E., & Chamberlain, G. H. A. Treatment of inadequate personality in juveniles by dehydroisoandrosterone. *British Medical Journal*, 1952, 66–68.
325. Sano, K. Sedative neurosurgery: With special reference to postero-medial hypothalamotomy. *Neurologia Medico Chirrurgica*, 1962, **4**, 112–142.
326. Sano, K. Sedative stereoencephalotomy; Fornicotomy, upper mesencephalic reticulotomy and posteromedial hypothalamotomy. *Progress in brain research*. Vol. 21B. *Correlative Neuroscience Part B: Clinical Studies*. Amsterdam: Elseiver, 1966. Pp. 350–372.
327. Sano, K., Yoshioka, M., Ogashiwa, M., Ishijima, B., & Ohye, C. Posterior-medial hypothalamotomy in the treatment of aggressive behaviors. *Second International Symposium on Stereoencephalotomy, Confina Neurologica*, 1966, **27**, 164–167.
328. Sawa, M., Ueki, Y., Arita, M., & Harada, T. Preliminary report on the amygdaloidectomy on the psychotic patients, with interpretation of oral-emotional manifestation in schizophrenics. *Folia Psychiatrican et Neurologica Japonica*, 1954, **7**, 309–329.
329. Scheckel, C. L., & Boff, E. Effects of drugs on aggressive behavior in monkeys. *Excerpta Medica International Congress Series No. 129, Proceedings of the Vth International Congress of the Collegium Internationale Neuropsychopharmacologicum*, 1966, 789–795.
330. Schreiner, L., & Kling, A. Behavioral changes following rhinencephalic injury in cat. *Journal of Neurophysiology*, 1953, **16**, 643–658.
331. Schreiner, L., & Kling, A. Rhinencephalon and behavior. *American Journal of Physiology*, 1956, **184**, 486–490.
332. Schwab, R. S., Sweet, W. H., Mark, V. H., Kjellberg, R. N., & Ervin, F. R. Treatment of intractable temporal lobe epilepsy by stereotactic amygdala lesions. *Transactions of the American Neurological Association*, 1965, 12–19.

333. Schwade, E. D., & Geiger, S. C. Abnormal EEG findings in severe behavior disorder. *Diseases of the Nervous System*, 1956, **17,** 307–317.
334. Schwade, E. D., & Gieger, S. C. Severe behavior disorders with abnormal electroencephalograms. *Diseases of the Nervous System*, 1960, **21,** 616–620.
335. Scott, J. P. Genetic differences in the social behavior of inbred strains of mice. *Journal of Heredity*, 1942, **33,** 11–15.
336. Scott, J. P. Dominance and the frustration-aggression hypothesis. *Physiological Zoology*, 1948, **21,** 31–39.
337. Scott, J. P. *Aggression.* Chicago: University of Chicago Press, 1958.
338. Scott, J. P. Hostility and aggression in animals. In E. L. Bliss (Ed.), *Roots of behavior.* New York: Harper & Row, 1962.
339. Scott, J. P. Review of J. D. Carthy and F. J. Ebling, The natural history of aggression. *Science*, 1965, **148,** 820–821.
340. Scott, J. P. Review of K. Lorenz, On aggression. *Science*, 1966, **154,** 636–637.
341. Scott, J. P. Agonistic behavior of mice and rats: A review. *American Zoologist*, 1966, **6,** 683–701.
342. Scott, J. P. The development of social motivation. In D. Levine (Ed.), *Nebraska Symposium on Motivation.* Lincoln: University of Nebraska Press, 1967.
343. Scott, J. P., & Fredericson, E. The causes of fighting in mice and rats. *Physiological Zoology*, 1951, **24,** 273–309.
344. Scoville, W. B., & Milner, B. Loss of recent memory after bilateral hippocampal lesions. *Journal of Neurology, Neurosurgery and Psychiatry*, 1957, **20,** 11–21.
345. Sem-Jacobsen, C. W., & Torkildesen, A. Depth recording and electrical stimulation in the human brain. In E. R. Ramey and D. S. O'Doherty (Eds.), *Electrical Studies on the Unanesthetized Brain.* New York: Hoeber, 1960. Pp. 275–290.
346. Serafetinides, E. A. Aggressiveness in temporal lobe epileptics and its relation to cerebral dysfunction and environmental factors. *Epilepsia*, 1965, **6,** 33–42.
347. Seward, J. P. Aggressive behavior in the rat: I. General characteristics; age and sex differences. *Journal of Comparative Psychology*, 1945, **38,** 175–197.
348. Shealy, C., & Peele, J. Studies on amygdaloid nucleus of cat. *Journal of Neurophysiology*, 1957, **20,** 125–139.
349. Sheard, M. H. The effects of amphetamine on attack behavior in the cat. *Brain Research*, 1967, **5,** 330–338.
350. Sheard, M. H., & Flynn, J. P. Facilitation of attack behavior by stimulation of the midbrain of cats. *Brain Research*, 1967, **4,** 324–333.
351. Siegel, A., & Flynn, J. P. Differential effects of electrical stimula-

tion and lesions of the hippocampus and adjacent regions upon attack behavior in cats. *Brain Research,* 1968, **7,** 252–267.
352. Sigg, E. B. Relationship of aggressive behaviour to adrenal and gonadal function in male mice. In S. Garattini and E. B. Sigg (Eds.), *Aggressive Behaviour,* Amsterdam: Wiley, 1969. Pp. 143–149.
353. Sigg, E. B., Day, C., & Colombo, C. Endocrine factors in isolation induced aggressiveness in rodents. *Endocrinology,* 1966, **78,** 679–684.
354. Skultety, F. M. Stimulation of periaqueductal gray and hypothalamus. *Archives of Neurology,* 1963, **8,** 608–620.
355. Smith, D. E., King, M. B., & Hoebel, B. G. Lateral hypothalamic control of killing: Evidence for a cholinoceptive mechanism. *Science,* 1970, **167,** 900–901.
356. Sodetz, F. J. The social behavior and aggressiveness of the hamster following the application of chemicals to the septal region of the forebrain. Unpublished doctoral dissertation, University of Florida, 1967.
357. Sodetz, F. J., & Bunnell, B. N. Interactive effects of septal lesions and social experience in the hamster. Paper presented at the meeting of the Eastern Psychological Association, 1967.
358. Sodetz, F. J., & Bunnell, B. N. Septal ablation and the social behavior of the golden hamster. Paper presented at the meeting of the Midwestern Psychological Association, Chicago, May, 1967.
359. Soulairac, A., & Soulairac, M. L. Effects de lesions hypothalamiques sour le comportement sexuel et le tractus genital du rat male. *Annales d'Endocrinologie,* 1956, **17,** 731–735.
360. Southwick, C. H. An experimental study of intragroup agonistic behavior in rhesus monkeys (macaca mulatta). *Behaviour,* 1967, **28,** 182–209.
361. Spiegal, E. A., Miller, H. R., & Oppenheimer, M. J. Forebrain and rage reactions. *Journal of Neurophysiology,* 1940, **3,** 538–548.
362. Spiegel, E. A., & Wycis, H. T. Physiological and psychological results of thalamotomy. *Proceedings of the Royal Society, Medical Supplement,* 1949, **42,** 84–93.
363. Spiegel, E. A., Wycis, H. T., Freed, H., & Orchinik, C. The central mechanism of the emotions. *American Journal of Psychiatry,* 1951, **108,** 426–432.
364. Sprague, J. M., Chamber, W. W., & Stellar, E. Attentive, effective, and adaptive behavior in the cat. *Science,* 1961, **133,** 165–173.
365. Stachnik, T. J., Ulrich, R., & Mabry, J. H. Reinforcement of intra- and inter-species aggression with intracranial stimulation. *American Zoologist,* 1966, **6,** 663–668.

366. Stachnik, T. J., Ulrich, R. E., & Mabry, J. H. Reinforcement of aggression through intracranial stimulation. *Psychonomic Science,* 1966, **5,** 101–102.
367. Stamm, J. S. The functions of the median cerebral cortex in maternal behavior of rats. *Journal of Comparative and Physiological Psychology,* 1955, **48,** 347–356.
368. Stone, C. P. Wildness and savageness in rats of different strains. In K. S. Lashley (Ed.), *Studies in Dynamics of Behavior.* Chicago: University of Chicago Press, 1932.
369. Storr, A. *Human aggression.* New York: Atheneum, 1968.
370. Strauss, E. B., Sands, D. E., Robinson, A. M., Tindall, W. J., & Stevenson, W. A. Use of dehydroisoandrosterone in psychiatric treatment. *British Medical Journal,* 1952, 64–66.
371. Strauss, I., & Keschner, M. Mental symptoms in cases of tumor of the frontal lobe. *Archives of Neurology and Psychiatry,* 1935, **33,** 986–1005.
372. Suchowsky, G. K., Pegrassi, L., & Bonsignori. The effect of steroids on aggressive behaviour in isolated male mice. In S. Garattini and E. B. Sigg (Eds.), *Aggressive behaviour.* New York: Wiley, 1969. Pp. 164–171.
373. Summers, T. B., & Kaelber, W. W. Amygdalectomy: Effects in cats and a survey of its present status. *American Journal of Physiology,* 1962, **203,** 1117–1119.
374. Sweet, W. H., Ervin, E., & Mark, V. H. The relationship of violent behaviour to focal cerebral disease. In S. Garattini and E. B. Sigg (Eds.), *Aggressive behaviour,* New York: Wiley, 1969. Pp. 336–352.
375. Teitelbaum, P., & Epstein, A. N. The lateral hypothalamic syndrome. *Psychological Review,* 1962, **69,** 74–90.
376. Telfer, M. A., Baker, D., Clark, G. R., & Richardson, C. E. Incidence of gross chromosomal errors among tall criminal American males. *Science,* 1968, **159,** 1249–1250.
377. Terzian, H. Observations on the clinical symptomatology of bilateral partial or total removal of the temporal lobes in man. In M. Baldwin and P. Bailey (Eds.), *Temporal lobe epilepsy.* Springfield, Ill.: Charles C. Thomas, 1958. Pp. 510–529.
378. Terzian, H., & Ore, G. D. Syndrome of Kluver and Bucy reproduced in man by bilateral removal of the temporal lobes. *Neurology,* 1955, **5,** 378–380.
379. Thiessen, D. D., & Rodgers, D. A. Population density and endocrine function. *Psychological Bulletin,* 1961, **58,** 441–451.
380. Thompson, A., & Walker, E. A. Behavioral alterations following lesions of the medial surface of the temporal lobe. *Folia Psychiatrica Neurologica et Neurochirurgicao Neerlandica,* 1950, **53,** 444–452.
381. Thompson, T., & Bloom, W. Aggressive behavior and extinction

induced response rate increase. *Psychonomic Science,* 1966, **5,** 335–336.
382. Tidwell, J., & Sutton, J. H. Fatigue: An introduction to a concept. Contract NONR-126801, San Diego State College, California, 1954.
383. Tilly, C. Collective violence in European perspective. In H. D. Graham, & T. R. Gurr (Eds.), *Violence in America: Historical and Comparative Perspectives.* Washington, D.C.: U.S. Government Printing Office, 1969. Pp. 5–34.
384. Tinbergen, N. Fighting and threat in animals. *New Biology,* 1953, **14,** 9–24.
385. Tinbergen, N. On war and peace in animals and man, *Science,* 1968, **160,** 1411–1418.
386. Tinklepaugh, O. L., & Hartman, C. G. Behavior and maternal care of the newborn monkey (Macaca mulatta—'M rhesus"). *Journal of Genetic Psychology,* 1932, **40,** 257–286.
387. Tobias, C. A. The use of accelerated heavy particles for production of radiolesions and stimulation in the central nervous system. In T. J. Haley and R. S. Snider (Eds.), *Responses of the nervous system to ionizing radiation.* New York: Academic Press, 1962.
388. Toch, Hans. H. *Violent men.* Chicago: Aldine, 1969.
389. Tolman, J., & King, J. A. The effects of testosterone propionate on aggression in male and female C57 BL/10 mice. *British Journal of Animal Behaviour,* 1956, **4,** 147–149.
390. Tow, P. M., & Whitty, C. W. Personality changes after operations on the cingulate gyrus in man. *Journal of Neurology, Neurosurgery and Psychiatry,* 1953, **16,** 186–193.
391. Treffert, D. A. The psychiatric patient with an EEG temporal lobe focus. *American Journal of Psychiatry,* 1964, **120,** 765–771.
392. Turner, E. A. Cerebral control of respiration. *Brain,* 1954, **77,** 448–486.
393. Turner, W. J. Therapeutic use of diphenylhydantoin in neuroses. *International Journal of Neuropsychiatry,* 1967, **3,** 94–105.
394. Turner, W. J. The usefulness of diphenylhydantoin in treatment of non-epileptic emotional disorders. *International Journal of Neuropsychiatry,* 1967, **3,** Supplement No. 2, S 8–S 20.
395. Ulrich, R. Pain as a cause of aggression. *American Zoologist,* 1966, **6,** 643–662.
396. Umbach, W. Electrophysiological and clinical observations in 1280 stereotactic operations in man. Second International Congress of Neurological Surgery, Abstracts and Descriptions of Contributions to the Scientific Program, 1961. *Excerpta Medica, International Congress Series,* #36, E152–E153.

397. Urich, J. The social hierarchy in albino mice. *Journal of Comparative Psychology*, 1938, **25**, 373–413.
398. Ursin, H. The temporal lobe substrate for fear and anger. *Acta Psychiatrica et Neurologica Scandinavica*. Kjøbenhavn, 1960, **38**, 278–396.
399. Ursin, H. The effect of amygdaloid lesions on flight and defense behavior in cats. *Experimental Neurology*, 1965, **11**, 61–79.
400. Ursin, H. The cingulate gyrus—A fear zone. *Journal of Comparative and Physiological Psychology*, 1969, **68**, 235–238.
401. Ursin, H., & Kaada, B. R. Functional localization within the amygdaloid complex in the cat. *Electroencephalography and Clinical Neurophysiology*, 1960, **12**, 1–20.
402. Valzelli, L. Drugs and aggressiveness. *Advances in Pharmacology*, 1967, **5**, 79–108.
403. Vaughan, E., & Fisher, A. E. Male sexual behavior induced by intracranial electrical stimulation. *Science*, 1962, **137**, 758–760.
404. Vergnes, M., & Karli, P. Déclenchement du comportement d'agression interspécifique rat-souris par ablation bilatérale des bulbes olfactifs. Action de l'hydroxyzine sur cete agressivité provoquée. *Comptes Rendus des Séances de la Société de Biologie*, 1963, **157**, 1061.
405. Vergnes, M., & Karli, P. Etude des voies nerveuses de l'influence facilitatrice exercée par les noyaux amygdaliens sur le comportement d'agression interspécifique rat-Souris. *Comptes Rendus des Séances de le Société de Biologie*, 1964, **158**, 856.
406. Vergnes, M., & Karli, P. Etude des voies nervauses d'une influence inhibitrice s'exercant sur l'agressivité interspécifique du rat. *Comptes Rendus des Séances de la Société de Biologie*, 1965, **159**, 972.
407. Vonderahe, A. R. The anatomic substratum of emotion. *The New Scolasticism*, 1944, **18**, 76–95.
408. Ward, A. A. The cingular gyrus: Area 24. *Journal of Neurophysiology*, 1948, **11**, 13–23.
409. Wasman, M., & Flynn, J. P. Directed attack elicited from hypothalamus. *Archives of Neurology*, 1962, **6**, 220–227.
410. Watson, J. B. *Behaviorism.* New York: Norton, 1925.
411. Waxenberg, S. E., Drellich, M. D., & Sutherland, A. M. The role of hormones in human behavior: I. Changes in female sexuality after adrenalectomy. *Journal of Clinical Endocrinology and Metabolism*, 1959, **19**, 193–202.
412. Weiskrantz, L. Behavioral changes associated with ablation of the amygdaloid complex in monkeys. *Journal of Comparative and Physiological Psychology*, 1956, **49**, 381–394.
413. Welch, B. L. Discussion of "Aggression, defense, and neurohumors" by Rothballer, A. B. In C. D. Clements and D. B. Lindsley (Eds.), *Aggression and defense: Neural mechanisms*

and social patterns, Volume five, *Brain function.* Los Angeles: University of California Press, 1967. Pp. 150–164.
414. Welch, B. L., & Welch, A. S. Aggression and the biogenic amine neurohumors. In S. Garattini and E. B. Sigg (Eds.), *Aggressive behaviour.* New York: Wiley, 1969.
415. Whalen, R. E. Sexual motivation. *Psychological Review,* 1966, **73,** 151–163.
416. Whalen, R. E., & Fehr, H. The devolpment of the mouse killing response in rats. *Psychonomic Science,* 1964, **1,** 77–78.
417. Wheatley, M. D. The hypothalamus and affective behavior in cats. *Archives of Neurology and Psychiatry,* 1944, **52,** 296–316.
418. Whitty, C. W., Duffield, J. E., Tow, P. M., & Cairns, H. Anterior cingulectomy in the treatment of mental disease. *Lancet,* 1952, **1,** 475–481.
419. Wilder, B. J. The clinical neurophysiology of epilepsy, a survey of current research. Public Health Service, NINDB monograph No. 8. 1968.
420. Wilder, J. Sugar metabolism in its relation to criminology. In Linduer and Seliger (Eds.), *Handbook of correctional psychology.* New York: Philosophical Library, 1947.
421. Williams, D. Neural Factors related to habitual aggression: Consideration of differences between those habitual aggressives and others who have committed crimes of violence. *Brain,* 1969, **92,** 503–520.
422. Williams, D. R., & Teitelbaum, P. Control of drinking behavior by means of an operant-conditioning technique. *Science,* 1956, **124,** 1294–1296.
423. Williams, R. J. *Biochemical individuality.* New York: Wiley, 1956.
424. Wolpowitz, E. The use of thioridazine (Melleril) in cases of epileptic psychosis. *South African Medical Journal,* 1966, **40,** 143–144.
425. Wood, C. D. Behavioral changes following discrete lesions of temporal lobe structures. *Neurology,* 1958, **8,** supplement 1, 215–220.
426. Woods, J. W. "Taming" of the wild Norway rat by rhinencephalic lesions. *Nature,* 1956, **178,** 869.
427. Woods, S. M. Adolescent violence and homocide: Ego disruption and the 6 and 14 dysrhythmia. *Archives of General Psychiatry,* 1961, **5,** 528–534.
428. Woringer, E., Thomalske, G., & Klingler, J. Les rapports anatomiques du noyau amygdalien et la technique de son extirpation neurochirurgicale. *Revue Neurologique,* 1953, **89,** 553–560.
429. Wright, J. H. Test for a learned drive based on the hunger drive. *Journal of Experimental Psychology,* 1965, **70,** 580–584.

430. Wynne-Edwards, V. C. *Animal dispersion in relation to social behaviour.* New York: Hafner, 1962.
431. Wyrwicka, W., & Dobrzecka, C. Relationship between feeding and satiation centers of the hypothalamus. *Science,* 1960, **123,** 805–806.
432. Yasukochi, G. Emotional responses elicited by electrical stimulation of the hypothalamus in cat. *Folia Psychiatrica et Neurologica Japonica,* 1960, **14,** 260–267.
433. Yen, H. C. Y., Day, C. A., & Siggs, E. B. Influence of endocrine factors on development of fighting behavior in rodents. *Pharmacologist,* 1962, 173.
434. Yerkees, R. M. The heredity of savageness and wildness in rats. *Journal of Animal Behavior,* 1913, **3,** 286–296.
435. Yutzey, D. A., Meyer, P. M., & Meyer, D. R. Emotionality changes following septal and neocortical ablations in rats. *Journal of Comparative and Physiological Psychology,* 1964, **58,** 463–465.
436. Zbinden, G., & Randall, L. O. Measurement of drug effects using approach-avoidance behavior. *Advances Pharmacological,* 1967, **5,** 213.
437. Zeman, W., & King, F. A. Tumors of the septum pellucidum and adjacent structures with abnormal affective behavior: An anterior midline structure syndrome. *Journal of Nervous and Mental Disease,* 1958, **127,** 490–502.
438. Zimmerman, F. T. Explosive behavior anomalies in children of an epileptic basis. *New York State Journal of Medicine,* 1956, **56,** 2537–2543.

Author Index

Adams, D. B., 40, 63, 147
Addison, R. G., 20, 47, 99, 164
Addition, H., 20, 47, 99, 164
Ader, R., 142, 147
Adey, W. R., 36, 85, 147
Adrianov, O., 2, 3, 4
Akert, K., 15, 37, 147
Alderton, H., 103, 147
Alexander, M., 57, 73, 166
Allee, W. C., 39, 156
Allikments, L., 42, 147
Alonso-de Florida, F., 8, 147
Alpers, B. J., 88, 147
Altman, J., 13, 147
Amader, L., 90, 156
Anand, B. K., 37, 40, 41, 42, 45, 87, 147, 148
Andersen, P., 136, 159
Appley, M. H., 14, 39, 152
Ardery, R., 47, 148
Arita, M., 17, 23, 90, 167
Azrin, N. H., 39, 46, 66, 71, 72, 148

Bach-Y-Rita, 59, 95, 153
Baenninger, R., 49, 148
Bagdon, R. E., 8, 165
Bagshaw, M., 85, 165
Bailey, P., 90, 148
Baker, D., 64, 170
Ball, J., 35, 148
Balzas, T., 136, 142, 157
Ban, T. A., 103, 104, 105, 122, 148
Bandler, R. J., viii, 15, 31, 56, 57, 63, 69, 128, 133, 148
Barclay, A. M., 30, 148
Bard, P., 41, 85, 148
Barker, P., 104, 149
Barnett, S. A., 27, 34, 111, 112, 113, 129, 149
Barsa, J., 105, 149
Bartholomew, A. A., 103, 149
Beach, F. A., 19, 20, 35, 97, 120, 129, 149, 160
Beauchesne, H., 103, 163

Beeman, E. A., 6, 19, 32, 35, 62, 97, 144, 149
Bemporad, J. R., 37, 151
Bender, M., 87, 161
Bennett, M. A., 48, 149
Berger, F. M., 105, 149
Berkowitz, L., 13, 22, 38, 39, 72, 83, 125, 149
Bernstein, H., 32, 135, 150
Bevan, J. M., 35, 150
Bevan, W., 26, 35, 150
Bianchi, A., 97, 162
Birch, H. G., 97, 151
Bloom, W., 39, 66, 87, 170
Boelhouwer, 104, 156
Boff, E., 24, 105, 122, 167
Bolles, R. C., 13, 150
Bonsignori, A., 19, 97, 170
Borman, A., 97, 162
Boshka, S. C., 39, 66, 150
Bovard, E. W., 122, 150
Bowne, G., 57, 73, 166
Bradley, C., 104, 150
Bradley, R. J., 93, 153
Brady, J. V., 37, 150
Bremer, J., 120, 150
Bridges, C. C., 47, 163
Brobeck, J. R., 40, 147
Brown, J. L., 40, 56, 57, 87, 150
Brutkowski, S., 41, 87, 150
Bucy, P. C., 84, 85, 91, 122, 161
Buddington, W., 104, 158
Buki, R. A., 103, 151
Bunnell, B. N., 35, 37, 49, 72, 118, 151, 169
Bunney, W. E., 112, 163
Burdock, E. I., 40, 156
Burkett, E. E., 49, 151
Burnand, G., 64, 151
Buss, A., 38, 151

Caggiula, A. R., 113, 114, 151
Cairns, H., 36, 41, 87, 90, 156, 173
Carpenter, C. R., 47, 48, 151

175

Carthy, J. D., 31, 143, 151
Chagas, C., 2, 3
Chamber, W. W., 32, 169
Chamberlain, G. H. A., 20, 46, 167
Christian, J. J., 46, 50, 151
Clark, G., 64, 97, 151, 170
Clark, L. D., 33, 151
Clark, S. M., 146, 151
Cleghorn, R. A., 21, 46, 152
Clemente, C. D., 34, 45, 87, 157
Cofer, C. N., 14, 39, 152
Cohen, S., 103, 152
Cole, J., 36, 87, 156
Collias, N. E., 6, 152
Colombo, C., 35, 68, 169
Conner, R. L., 64, 152
Cook, L., 105, 152
Coppen, A., 99, 152
Crabtree, M., viii
Cunningham, M. A., 105, 152

Dalton, K., 20, 23, 46, 98, 99, 152, 157
Daly, D., 87, 164
Danowski, T. S., 121, 152
Darwin, C., 34, 152
Daugherty, M., 34, 152
DaVanzo, J. P., 34, 152
Daves, W. F., 26, 150
Davis, D. E., 46, 50, 151
Davis, F. C., 39, 66, 152
Day, C. A., 35, 68, 169, 174
De Craene, O., 105, 152
DeGroot, J., 34, 45, 87, 157
Delgado, J. M. R., 7, 19, 23, 31, 39, 40, 42, 45, 49, 59, 63, 72, 86, 92, 93, 95, 96, 114, 117, 121, 143, 147, 152, 153, 158, 162, 163, 165
Denhan, J., 105, 153
DeSisto, M. J., 31, 128, 153
Deutsch, D., 118, 120, 153
Deutsch, J. A., 118, 120, 153
Dickey, C., 96
Dicks, D., 85, 118, 153
Didiergeorges, F., 31, 32, 56, 87, 136, 143, 144, 153, 154, 160
Dobrzecka, C., 19, 174
Dollard, J., 38, 154
Doob, L. W., 38, 154
Drellich, M. D., 121, 172
Drolette, M. E., 46, 155
Dua, S., 37, 41, 42, 45, 87, 148

Duffield, J. E., 41, 90, 173
Duisberg, R. E. H., 90, 157
Dunn, G. W., 20, 23, 46, 98, 154

Ebling, F. J., 31, 143, 151
Edwards, D. A., 65, 154
Edwards, S., 56, 66, 155
Egger, M. D., 5, 15, 19, 31, 41, 44, 65, 143, 154
Ehrlich, A., 18, 154
Eibl-Eibesfeldt, I., 27, 34, 154
Eisenberg, J., 34, 154
Elger, W., 97, 165
Endroczi, E., 6, 20, 23, 48, 128, 129, 131, 133, 134, 154, 162
Epstein, A. N., 17, 35, 170
Ervin, F. R., 16, 59, 60, 61, 88, 92, 95, 116, 153, 154, 163, 167, 170

Falconer, M. A., 90, 154
Fehr, H., 33, 173
Fernandez de Molina, A., 2, 37, 41, 154, 155
Feshbach, S., 13, 30, 49, 155
Fish, B., 104, 155
Fisher, A. E., 114, 119, 155, 172
Flesher, C. K., 37, 151
Flynn, J. P., 5, 15, 19, 26, 27, 31, 32, 33, 34, 40, 41, 44, 45, 56, 58, 62, 65, 66, 68, 86, 136, 143, 147, 154, 155, 162, 168, 172
Fonberg, E., 41, 42, 44, 86, 87, 150, 155
Foote, W., 56, 66, 155
Foss, G. L., 121, 155
Fraser, I. A. A., 104, 149
Frederichs, C., 100, 155
Fredericson, E., 14, 21, 27, 34, 48, 69, 70, 155, 168
Freed, H., 17, 169
Fuller, J. L., 85, 155
Funkenstein, D. H., 46, 155

Galef, B. G., 86, 155
Garattini, S., 68, 155
Geiger, S. C., 7, 16, 21, 63, 72, 168
Geist, S. H., 121, 167
Gellhorn, E., 122, 155
Giacalone, E., 68, 155
Gibbs, F. A., 16, 88, 90, 155, 156
Gibson, J. G., 21, 46, 156
Gilchrist, 2

Author Index 177

Gill, J. H., 142, 156
Gilman, A., 103, 157
Ginsburg, B., 39, 156
Glees, P., 36, 87, 156
Gloor, P., 86, 88, 100, 156
Glueck, 104, 156
Glusman, M., 40, 156
Goddard, G. V., 44, 45, 156
Gol, A., 86, 156
Goodman, H., 100, 155
Goodman, L., 103, 157
Gorney, R., 99, 159
Gourley, B., viii
Graff, H., 18, 157
Green, J. D., 34, 45, 87, 157
Green, J. R., 90, 157
Greene, R., 20, 23, 98, 99, 157
Grice, H. C., 136, 142, 145, 157
Griffiths, W. J., Jr., 142, 157
Grossman, S. P., 118, 120, 157
Guerrero-Figueroa, 88, 166
Guhl, A. M., 46, 49, 50, 157
Gyland, S., 100

Haber, R. N., 30, 148
Hafez, E. S., 48, 157
Hagiwara, R., 59, 95, 153
Hake, D. F., 39, 66, 148
Hall, C. S., 64, 157
Hamburg, D. A., 98, 99, 157
Hamilton, W. J., III, 13, 34, 163
Hamlin, H., 117, 158
Harada, T., 17, 23, 90, 167
Hardy, K. R., 120, 157
Harlow, H. F., 112, 157, 166
Harris, G. W., 116, 157
Hartman, C. G., 112, 171
Hatch, A., 136, 142, 157
Hawke, C. C., 20, 46, 97, 157
Heath, R. G., 7, 8, 19, 45, 58, 59, 88, 94, 95, 96, 104, 116, 122, 123, 157, 158
Heimburger, R. F., 91, 92, 126, 158
Heimstra, N. W., 33, 158
Heise, G. A., 8, 165
Hendley, C. D., 105, 158
Hess, E. H., 113, 158
Hess, W. R., 5, 37, 158
Higgins, J. W., 117, 158
Hill, D., 60, 90, 154, 158
Hinde, R. A., 13, 22, 158
Hoddinott, B. A., 103, 147

Hoebel, B. G., 31, 57, 113, 114, 151, 160, 169
Hoggart, K., 64, 151
Huffman, J. W., 35, 159
Hunsperger, R. W., 5, 37, 40, 41, 56, 57, 87, 150, 154, 155
Hunt, L., 20, 47, 99, 164
Hunter, H., 64, 151
Hurst, C. M., 86, 156
Huston, J. P., 31, 128, 153
Hutchinson, R. R., 26, 31, 33, 39, 46, 66, 71, 136, 148, 159

Ingram, W. R., 40, 159
Ishijima, B., 7, 17, 90, 167

Jackson, V. A. B., 104, 167
Jacobsen, E., 26, 159
Janowsky, E. S., 99, 159
Jansen, J., 136, 159
Jarrard, L. E., viii, 25, 49, 141, 151
Jasper, H., 165
Jenkins, R. L., 60, 159
Johnston, V. S., 93, 153
Jonas, A. D., 17, 88, 159
Jones, L. U., 139, 159

Kaada, B. R., 42, 56, 122, 136, 159, 172
Kaelber, W. W., 40, 41, 85, 159, 163, 170
Kahn, M. W., 72, 159
Kalina, R. K., 8, 24, 105, 159
Kalsbeck, J. E., 91, 92, 126, 158
Kang, L., 34, 152
Karli, P., 2, 3, 4, 6, 7, 31, 32, 33, 36, 41, 44, 56, 63, 71, 86, 87, 123, 136, 142, 143, 144, 153, 154, 159, 160, 172
Kaufman, C., 111, 160
Kaufman, I. C., 112, 160
Keith, E. F., 8, 165
Kellaway, P., 86, 156
Kelleher, R. T., 105, 152
Kennard, M. A., 36, 41, 87, 160
Kennedy, G. C., 19, 160
Keschner, M., 87, 170
Kessel, N., 99, 152
Kessler, S., 64, 160
Kielberg, R. N., 92, 167
Kiess, H. O., 16, 26, 31, 71, 166
King, F. A., 37, 88, 160, 174

King, H. E., 5, 6, 16, 44, 58, 116, 125, 160
King, J. A., 19, 35, 62, 144, 162, 171
King, M. B., 31, 57, 160, 169
King, S. H., 46, 155
Kislak, J. W., 19, 20, 97, 120, 160
Kitahata, L. M., 86, 153
Klein, S. J., 64, 157
Kline, N., 103, 161
Kling, A., 7, 17, 36, 37, 41, 45, 85, 86, 87, 118, 153, 161, 167
Klingler, J., 90, 173
Kluver, H., 84, 85, 91, 122, 161
Komisaruk, B. R., 63, 161
Korn, J. H., viii, 25, 136, 142, 145, 161, 164
Kreschner, M., 87, 161
Kulkarni, A. S., 125, 161
Kuo, Z. Y., 32, 161

Lagerspetz, K., 13, 64, 72, 161
Laties, V. G., 39, 66, 161
Le Beau, J., 7, 18, 41, 90, 161
LeMaire, L., 20, 46, 97, 161
Lennox, W. G., 64, 161
Lerner, L. J., 23, 97, 161, 162
Levine, S., 64, 152
Levison, P. K., 15, 27, 31, 33, 162
Levy, G. W., 26, 35, 150
Levy, J., 19, 35, 62, 144, 162
Lichtenstein, P. E., 21, 70, 72, 162
Liddell, D. W., 91, 162
Lisk, R. D., 116, 162
Lissak, K., 6, 20, 23, 48, 128, 129, 131, 133, 154, 162
Lorenz, K., 11, 13, 22, 34, 124, 125, 162
Lyght, C. E., 100, 162

Mabry, J. H., 70, 169, 170
MacDonnell, M. F., 31, 34, 62, 65, 68, 136, 162
MacLean, P. D., 42, 45, 162
Mahal, G. F., 117, 158
Mallick, S. K., 125, 162
Mandell, A. J., 99, 159
Mark, V., 59, 60, 61, 88, 92, 95, 116, 153, 154, 163, 167, 170
Marler, P., 13, 34, 112, 113, 163
Marrone, R. L., 47, 163
Masserman, J. H., 21, 70, 163
Mayer, J., 17, 19, 163, 164

McAdam, D. W., 40, 163
McCandless, B. R., 125, 162
McConnell, H. J., 8
McGrath, W. B., 90, 157
McKinney, W. T., 112, 163
McLaughlin, R., 71, 148
McWhirter, N., 114, 163
McWhirter, R., 114, 163
Mempel, E., 41, 87, 150
Merrilless, N. C. R., 36, 85, 147
Meyer, A., 90, 154
Meyer, D. R., 146, 151, 174
Meyer, P. M., 37, 146, 151, 160, 174
Michael, R. P., 116, 157
Mickle, W. A., 94, 96, 123, 158
Miller, H. R., 135, 169
Miller, N. E., 9, 15, 38, 154, 163
Miller, R. E., 72, 163
Milner, B., 90, 168
Mirsky, A. F., 36, 41, 72, 86, 167
Mirsky, I. A., 72, 163
Mises, R., 103, 163
Mitchell, C. L., 40, 159
Mitchell, G. D., 113, 163
Monroe, R. R., 88, 163
Montagu, M. F. A., 105, 106, 124, 163, 164
Moos, R. H., 64, 99, 157, 160
Morrison, S. D., 17, 164
Morton, J. H., 20, 47, 99, 164
Mountcastle, V. B., 85, 148
Mowrer, O. H., 38, 154
Moyer, K. E., 17, 18, 32, 48, 60, 63, 69, 71, 84, 86, 111, 113, 117, 119, 121, 122, 123, 126, 128, 133, 136, 141, 142, 143, 144, 145, 146, 148, 150, 164, 166
Mulder, D., 87, 164
Murphy, J. V., 72, 163
Myer, J. S., 27, 33, 72, 136, 142, 164
Myers, R. D., 85, 118, 153

Nagahata, M., 91, 164
Nagao, T., 91, 164
Nakao, H., 40, 164
Napoleon, L., 82
Narabayashi, H., 91, 164
Nauta, W. J. H., 37, 150
Neri, R. O., 97, 166
Neuman, F., 97, 165
Newton, G., 33, 158
Nuttin, 4

Author Index

Ogashiwa, M., 7, 17, 90, 167
Ohye, C., 7, 17, 90, 167
Olds, J., 63, 161
Oppenheimer, M. J., 135, 169
Orchinik, C., 17, 169
Ore, G. D., 89, 170

Pacella, B. I., 60, 159
Parkman, J., viii, 106
Pearson, O. P., 92, 165
Peele, J., 36, 41, 86, 168
Pegrassi, L., 19, 97, 170
Penfield, W., 165
Pennington, V. M., 103, 165
Pillai, V., 105, 152
Plotnik, R., 72, 85, 165
Pool, J. L., 17, 90, 165
Porter, P. S., 142, 156
Pray, S. L., 47, 163
Pribram, K. H., 36, 41, 72, 85, 86, 155, 165, 167
Price, W. H., 64, 165

Randall, L. O., 8, 165
Randolph, T. G., 101, 165
Ransohoff, J., 40, 156
Reid, L. D., 142, 156
Reiss, M., 46, 165
Renfrew, J. W., 26, 31, 33, 159
Resnick, O., 102, 104, 106, 166
Revlis, R., 48, 128, 166
Reynolds, H. H., 142, 166
Rich, C., 90, 156
Richardson, C. E., 64, 170
Richardson, F., 109, 110
Richter, C. P., 21, 166
Roberts, W. W., 16, 26, 31, 71, 166
Robinson, A. M., 20, 46, 170
Robinson, B. W., 57, 73, 166
Robinson, W. G., 88, 166
Rocky, S., 97, 166
Rodgers, D. A., 46, 50, 170
Rogers, W. J. B., 105, 152
Roisin, L., 40, 156
Romaniuk, A., 37, 166
Ropartz, P., 34, 136, 166
Rosenberg, P. H., 18, 103, 166
Rosenblum, L. A., 112, 160, 166
Rosenfeld, A., 24, 103, 166
Rosenzweig, M. R., 136, 166
Ross, A. T., 104, 167

Rosvold, H., 36, 41, 72, 85, 155, 167
Ruckert, R., 34, 152

Saito, Y., 91, 164
Salazar, J. M., 145, 167
Salmon, U. J., 121, 167
Salzer, H., 100
Sandberg, J. H., 12
Sands, D. E., 20, 23, 46, 98, 167, 170
Sano, K., 7, 17, 87, 88, 90, 91, 167
Saunder, J. C., 105, 149
Sawa, M., 17, 23, 90, 167
Schallek, W., 8, 165
Scheckel, C. L., 24, 105, 122, 167
Schreiner, L., 7, 17, 36, 41, 45, 85, 86, 87, 167
Schwab, R. S., 92, 167
Schwade, E. D., 7, 16, 21, 63, 72, 168
Scott, P. P., 13, 14, 21, 22, 26, 27, 34, 39, 46, 48, 51, 63, 66, 69, 70, 89, 116, 157, 168
Scoville, W. B., 90, 168
Sears, R. R., 38, 154
Sem-Jacobsen, C. W., 93, 168
Serafetinides, E. A., 88, 168
Seward, J. P., 19, 34, 97, 168
Shalloway, D. M., 118, 151
Shapiro, M., 86, 156
Shealy, C., 36, 41, 86, 168
Sheard, M. H., 32, 40, 45, 65, 168
Siegel, A., 86, 168
Sigg, E. B., 19, 35, 68, 97, 169, 174
Singer, J., 82
Skinner, B. F., 2, 3
Skultety, F. M., 40, 169
Smith, D. E., 31, 57, 169
Smith, M. H., 37, 151
Sodetz, F. J., 35, 49, 72, 118, 151, 169
Soulairac, A., 118, 169
Soulairac, M. L., 118, 169
Southwick, C. H., 39, 169
Spiegal, E. A., 17, 87, 91, 135, 169
Sprague, J. M., 32, 169
Stachnik, T. J., 70, 169, 170
Stamm, J. S., 118, 170
Steinbeck, H., 97, 165
Stellar, E., 18, 32, 157, 169
Stevens, J., 59, 88, 116, 154
Stevenson, W. A., 20, 46, 170

Stone, C. P., 64, 170
Storr, A., 1, 170
Strauss, E. B., 20, 46, 170
Strauss, I., 87, 161, 170
Suchowsky, G. K., 19, 97, 170
Sullivan, J. J., 20, 47, 99, 164
Summers, T. B., 41, 85, 170
Sunderland, S., 36, 85, 147
Sutherland, A. M., 121, 172
Sutton, J. H., 39, 171
Sweet, W. H., 59, 61, 92, 95, 153, 163, 167

Tansella, M., 68, 155
Teitelbaum, P., 17, 21, 35, 70, 170, 173
Telegdy, G., 6, 20, 23, 48, 128, 129, 131, 133, 154
Telfer, M. A., 64, 170
Terzian, H., 89, 90, 170
Thapar, R., 2, 3
Thiessen, D. D., 46, 50, 170
Thomalske, G., 90, 173
Thompson, A., 85, 170
Thompson, T., 39, 66, 87, 170
Thor, D. H., 39, 66, 150
Tidwell, J., 39, 171
Tilly, C., 82, 171
Tinbergen, N., 14, 22, 27, 71, 171
Tindall, W. J., 20, 46, 170
Tinklepaugh, O. L., 112, 171
Tobach, E., 13
Tobias, C. A., 23, 171
Toch, H. H., 83, 171
Tolman, J., 35, 144, 171
Torkildesen, A., 93, 168
Tow, P. M., 17, 41, 90, 171, 173
Treffert, D. A., 16, 63, 171
Turner, E. A., 19, 36, 171
Turner, W. J., 24, 104, 171

Ueki, Y., 17, 23, 90, 167
Ulrich, R. E., 39, 46, 66, 70, 71, 72, 136, 159, 169, 170, 171
Umbach, W., 117, 171
Uno, M., 91, 164
Urich, J., 19, 35, 97, 172
Ursin, H., 7, 17, 42, 44, 86, 87, 172

Valzelli, L., 26, 68, 102, 155, 172
Vanegas, H., 56, 66, 155

Vaughan, E., 114, 172
Vergnes, M., 31, 32, 33, 44, 56, 87, 136, 143, 144, 154, 160, 172
Von Berswordt-Wallrabe, R., 97, 165
Vonderahe, A. R., 18, 40, 87, 172

Walker, E. A., 85, 170
Wallace, J. D., 93, 153
Ward, A. A., 36, 87, 117, 172
Wasman, M., 15, 26, 27, 31, 40, 58, 65, 143, 172
Watson, J. B., 124, 172
Watterson, D., 60, 158
Waxenberg, S. E., 121, 172
Way, J. S., 40, 159
Weiskrantz, L., 36, 172
Weisman, H. M., 39, 66, 150
Weiss, G., 59, 93, 95, 153
Welch, A. S., 68, 173
Welch, B. L., 68, 69, 172, 173
Whalen, R. E., 33, 120, 121, 173
Whatmore, P. B., 64, 165
Wheatley, M. D., 6, 18, 37, 40, 173
White, R. T., 27, 33, 164
Whitehouse, J. M., 35, 150
Whitlock, C. C., 91, 92, 126, 158
Whitty, C., 17, 36, 41, 87, 90, 156, 171, 173
Wiberg, G. S., 136, 142, 157
Wilder, B. J., 88, 173
Wilder, J., 100, 173
Wilkes, E., viii
Williams, B. F., 35, 150
Williams, D., 21, 60, 70, 173
Williams, R. J., 64, 173
Wilson, J. L., 90, 154
Wolpowitz, E., 103, 173
Won, W., 40, 156
Wood, C. D., 6, 18, 36, 41, 42, 44, 173
Woods, J. W., 17, 86, 173
Woods, S. M., 16, 63, 173
Woringer, E., 90, 173
Wright, J. H., 21, 173
Wycis, H. T., 17, 87, 91, 169
Wynne-Edwards, V. C., 111, 174
Wyrwicka, W., 19, 174

Yalom, J. D., 99, 157
Yasukochi, G., 37, 40, 57, 174

Yen, H. C. Y., 35, 174
Yerkees, R. M., 64, 174
Yoshida, M., 91, 164
Yoshioka, M., 7, 17, 90, 167
Young, P., 14

Yutzey, D. A., 146, 151, 174

Zbinden, G., 8
Zeman, W., 88, 174
Zimmerman, F. T., 103, 174

Subject Index

Acetylcholine, 94
Adolescent, disturbed, 103
Adrenal
  adrenalectomy
    inter-male aggression, 35
    mouse killing, 144
    predatory aggression, 32
    women, sexual tendencies, 121
  androgens, 98
  cortex, 20, 46
    dysfunction, 121
  weight, 46
Adrenalin, 47
Adrenocortical steroids, 100
Affect, negative, 104
Affective aggression, 26
  olfactory lesions, 143
Affective arousal, 14
Affective states, incompatible, 123
Affiliation, 109
  neural system, 114
  physiological mechanisms, 113
Affiliative responses, 112, 113, 124
Affiliative tendencies, 109, 111, 122, 124
  inhibition of from lesions, 117
Affluence, 3
Aggression
  chemistry, 9
  circuits, 5, 6, 8, 14, 65
  classification, 27, 28, 54
  control
    agitated behavior, human, 90
    brain lesion, 23, 61, 84, 87, 91, 106
    brain stimulation, 7, 92, 95, 106, 126
    cortical, 3, 4
    diet, 100
    drugs, 101, 106, 126
    environmental manipulation, 126
    frustration elimination, 126
    hormone therapy, 96, 106, 126
    implications of model for, 2, 13, 80
    learning, 23
    nonphysiological methods, 83
    physiological methods, 7, 8, 106, 126
    potential, 6
    radio, brain stimulation, 7, 95
    single physiological manipulation, 126
    stress elimination, 126
    theoretical position, 22
    training, 126
  definition, 26
  explosion, 126
  facilitation, 86, 90, 102, 145
  inhibition
    amygdala, 86
    brain lesion in animals, 84
    brain lesion in humans, 87
    brain stimulation, 95
    drugs, 102
    education, 4
    learning, 7, 83
    septal stimulation, 94
  interactions, 30, 49, 50
  model, 2, 5, 6, 52, 54, 83, 96, 119
  spontaneous, 104
  threshold, lowering by septal lesion, 37
  types, 5, 25, 27, 54, 65, 68, 75, 84, 86, 102, 111, 113, 126, 129, 136, 145, 146
  neurological basis, 41
  interactions, 49, 50
  summary, 51
Aggression-inhibiting drugs, 102, 105
Aggression syndrome, 105
Aggressive
  alcoholics, 103
  behavior, 1, 3, 16, 18, 104, 106, 122, 145
    incompatible with escape, 122
    intractable, 126
    multiple causes, 3
  energy, 22
  excitability, 105
  fantasy, 63

Subject Index

mental defectives, 103
pathological tendencies, 8
sex behavior, 16, 22
strains of rats, 64
tendencies, 8, 22, 124
thoughts, 63
Agitation, 7, 18, 58, 89–91
Agonistic behavior, 21
Agouti, 17, 36, 41, 86
Aldosterone, 99
Allergy-induced aggression, 100, 101
Ambition, 9, 22, 125
Amitriptyline, 103
Ammonium chloride, 47, 100
Amphetamine
  hyperactivity control, 104
  predatory attack, 32, 65, 68
Amygdala
  aggression-facilitating nuclei, 86
  aggression-inhibiting nuclei, 86
  amygdalectomy, 46
    aggression facilitation, 85
    effects, 41
    irritable aggression, 51
    lynx, 7, 14
    predatory aggression, 57
  irritable aggression, 47
  lesion, 41–44, 86
    aggression inhibition facilitation, 36, 85, 91
    basal nuclei, 18
    central nuclei, 18
    fear-induced aggression, 51
    maternal aggression, 48
  predatory aggression, 32, 66
  nuclei involved in aggression, 42
  stimulation inducing aggression, 5, 16, 44, 59, 60, 95
    central nuclei, escape, 66
    facilitation, 56, 63
    inhibition, 19
    seizure pattern, 63
Analysis of variance, 132
Androgens
  antagonists, 23, 97
  female irritability, 35
  inter-male aggression, 19, 34, 68, 97, 144
  irritable aggression, 45, 68, 97, 144
  masked by estrogens, 19
  modulation of neural substrates, 64
  predatory aggression, 144
  reduction by amygdalectomy, 46
  reduction by castration, 6, 97
  sexual arousability in women, 121
Androgenital syndrome, 121
Anger
  amygdala stimulation in man, 44, 59
  animals, 40
  drug control, 104
  episodic, 95
  inhibition by fear, 73
  irrational, 2
  irritable aggression, 29
  neural system activity, 63, 73
  reduction by
    cingulectomy, 7, 18
    temporal lobe lesions, 7, 84
    temporal lobe epilepsy, 88
  "slow to anger," 127
"Anger out" response, 47
Annoyance, 38
A-norprogesterone, 97
Antidepressant, 103
Antihostility
  agent, 8, 9, 106
  button, 8, 95
  drugs, 8, 9, 106, 107
Antisocial behavior, 100, 104
Anxiety, 37, 91, 102, 105
Arousal, 84, 91
  sympathetic, 27, 40
Asocial behavior, 100
Assaultive behavior, 16, 59, 61, 74, 81, 92, 95, 103
Ataxia, 105
Atropine, 58
  sulfate, 57
Attack
  affective, 3, 15, 26, 27
  aggressive and violent, 89
  amygdaloid lesions, 18, 42
  boss monkey, 7
  brain stimulation
    animal, 5, 56, 57
    human, 59, 60
  cat, on experimenter, 5, 31
  cat, on objects, 15, 27, 33
  cat, on rat, 5, 15, 27
  extinction-produced, 39

fear-induced, 28
on hallucination, 57
inhibition, 73
  by habituation, 142
instrumental, 70, 71
irritable aggression, 29, 38
mouse, on mouse, 27
neural system sensitivity, 62
persistence and sensory feedback, 33
predatory, 26, 28, 31, 33
  suppression by atropine, 57
rat, on frog, 6, 128, 129
rat, on mouse, 27
spontaneous, 70
territorial aggression, 29
unlearned preference, 15
Avalanche syndrome, 42
Aversive control, 82
Aversive stimulation, 112
  irritable aggression, 39, 40, 66
Avoidance, 72

B complex therapy, 47
Baboon, 85, 86
Basic behavior, 14, 21
Behavior control, 1, 2, 107
  abuse, 82
Behavior disorders, children, 103, 104
Behaviorism, 124
Benadryl, 104
Benzodiazepines, 105
  aggression inhibition, 105, 122
  friendly behavior, 122
Betta splendens, 47
Blood chemistry
  affiliative tendencies, 120, 121
  aggression, 19, 25, 67, 68, 74, 97, 100, 101, 119
  consummatory behavior, 19, 25
  neural sensitivity, 120, 124
Blood constituents, 6
Blood pressure, 59
Blood sugar, 100
Body contact tendencies, 112
Brain chemistry, 68
Brain dysfunction, 87
Brain lesion
  affiliation inhibition, 117
  aggression control, 23, 58, 61, 84, 87

aggression facilitation, 18
aggression reduction, 17
consummatory behavior reduction, 17
See also Amygdala; Amygdalectomy; Bulbectomy; Central grey; Cingulum; Cryosurgery; Fornix; Frontal lobe; Hippocampus; Hypothalamus; Lesion; Medial lemniscus; Mesencephalon; Midbrain; Olfactory bulb; Pyriform area; Temporal lobe; Thalamus; Uncus
Brain mechanisms in aggression, 56
Brain research, 2, 3, 5, 8, 9, 10
Brain stimulation
  affiliation, 116
  aggression control, 23
  aggression induction, 72
  aggressive behavior, 15
    inhibition, 18
    reinforcement, 70, 94
  consummatory behavior, 15
    inhibition, 18
  nonsurgical, 23, 96
  See also Amygdala; Caudate nuclei; Central grey; Cingulum; Forel's Field; Fornix; Frontal lobe; Hippocampus; Hypothalamus; Medial forebrain bundle; Mesencephalon; Midbrain; Reticular formation; Septum; Superior colliculus; Tegmentum; Temporal lobe; Thalamus
Bulbectomy, aggression inhibition, 136
Bulimia, 89
Bulls, 6, 46

Calming effects, 23, 90, 91, 93, 94
Carbachol, 15, 31, 56, 57
Castration
  androgen level reduction, 97
  bulls, 6
  chemical, 98
  humans
    altered sexual activity, 120
    penalty for sex crimes, 20
  inter-male aggression, 62
  irritable aggression, 45, 46

isolation-induced aggression, 68
mouse killing, 32, 144
neonatal, 64, 65
Catacholaminergic stimulation of septum, 35
Cataleptic state, 37
Cats, 5, 15–18, 26, 27, 31, 33, 34, 36, 41–43, 45, 56, 58, 62, 63, 65, 70, 71, 86, 87, 105, 119, 122, 131, 133, 136, 143
Caudate nuclei stimulation, aggression inhibition, 7, 19, 23, 45, 51, 92, 93
Central grey
  lesion, docility, 40
  stimulation, 45
Chick killing, 63
Chimpanzee, 93, 97
Chloral hydrate, 103
Chlordizepoxide, 8, 23, 105
Chlormadinone acetate, 97
Cholinergic stimulation, septum, 35
Cholinergic system for predatory aggression, 56
Chromosomal abnormalities in man, 64
Cingulum lesion
  affiliation inhibition, 117
  aggression facilitation, 18, 41
  aggression reduction, 41, 87, 90
  anterior in man, aggression control, 7, 17, 18, 41, 90
  fear reduction, 36, 41
  maternal behavior, inhibition, 118
Cingulum stimulation
  aggression facilitation, 41
  irritability, 37
Clinical endocrinology, 20
Cognitive processing, 58
Colonial species, 111
Colored vision in man from electrical brain stimulation, 95
Competition, 33, 39
Compulsive behavior, 101, 104
Concentration in man from brain stimulation, 95
Concentration, poor, 104
Conditioned aggression, 71
Conditioned attack, 70
Conditioned emotional response, 50

Conditioned fear, amygdalectomy effect on, 36
Conflict, 2, 111
Conspecific, 28, 29, 34, 45, 47, 112
Consummatory behavior, 14, 17, 25
  learning, 21
  of prey, 143
Contraceptives, oral, reduced irritability, 99
Control, 107
Cooperation, innate tendencies, 124
Copulation, brain stimulation, 114
Cortical control, 3
Crime, 20, 24, 60, 98, 99, 100
Cruelty, 100
Cryosurgery, 91

Decerebration, 18
Decortication, 58
Deer, 27
Defeat, as punishment, 34
Defense, 27, 42, 56
Dehydroisoandrosterone, 20, 46
Delinquency, 60
Denervation sensitivity, 40
Depression, 102, 103, 112, 116
  animal model, 112
  inhibition by septal stimulation, 122
  premenstrual, 99
Deprivation, 14, 15, 33, 51, 66, 69, 70, 71, 72, 74
Depth electrodes, human, 88
Destructiveness, 91, 103
Diandrone, 20, 46
Diazepam, 105, 106
  aggression control in man, 8, 23
Dibucaine, 86
Diet, 100
Diethylstilbestrol, 45
Dilantin, 23, 103, 104
Diphenylhydantoin, 24, 103
Disobedience, 104
Dispersion of species, 111
Diuretic, 99
Docility, 90
  cingulectomy, 36, 41
  electrical stimulation, 92
  temporal lobe lesions, 84, 85, 89
Dogs, 41, 42, 85
Dominance, 19, 34, 35, 49, 57, 69, 70, 72, 73, 85, 90, 145

Dopamine, 68
Double-blind study, 104
Doves, 48
Drinking behavior, 11, 25
Drive, 13, 14, 22, 39, 47, 49
Drugs, 8, 23, 24, 89
  See also specific drugs
Dyscontrol syndrome, 24, 88

Eating, 11, 13, 14, 15, 18, 19, 21, 25, 32, 33, 70, 72
Education, 3, 4, 7
EEG, 59
  abnormal, 60, 61, 88, 104
  14/sec. and 6/sec. positive spikes, 16, 21, 60
  seizure patterns, 63
Egocentrics, 101
Ejaculation, as result of electrical brain stimulation, 114
Elation, as result of electrical brain stimulation, 95
Electrical stimulation of the brain
  aggression inhibition, 18
  aggressive behavior, 15, 27, 74
  attack, 56
  consummatory behavior, 15
    inhibition, 18
  radio controlled, 7, 57, 59, 93, 95, 107
  sensations and behaviors, 107, 108
Electrodes, implanted, 7, 92, 93, 95
  in man, 8, 16, 59, 92
Emotional display, affective aggression, 27
Emotional excitability, 91
Emotionality, olfactory lesions, 143
Emotionally disturbed children, 104
Encephalization, 5
Endocrine
  aggression and affiliative behavior, 118
  fear-induced aggression, 38
  innate organization, 106
  irritable aggression, 46, 47, 66
  levels of aggressiveness, 75
  neural development, 64, 74
  neural system sensitivity, 68
  premenstrual tension, 125
Endocrinology, clinical, 46
Energy, 125

Epilepsy, 60, 64, 74
  aggression, 88
  cingulectomy control, 90
  psychomotor, 94
  temporal lobe, 88, 89
Epileptic, psychotic, 103
Epileptic seizures, 16, 21
  control by temporal lobectomy, 89
Epileptigenic focus, 88
Episodic anger, 95
Episodic behavior disorder, 88
Ergotropic circuits, 90
Erotic tendencies from electrical brain stimulation, 116, 117
erratic behavior, 104
Escape, 28, 29–38, 40–42, 51, 66, 67, 86, 138, 139, 140, 142, 145, 147
  incompatible with aggressive behavior, 122
  threshold lowered, septal lesions, 37
Estradiol, 97
Estrogen, 20, 97, 98
  androgen effect, 19, 97
  maternal aggression inhibition, 6, 23, 26, 48
  maternal behavior inhibition, 120
  sexual behavior, 120
Estrus, 19, 45
  continuous, stilbestrol implant in hypothalamus, 115
Ethological studies, 13, 14
Euphoria, 74
  medial forebrain bundle, stimulation of in man, 116
  septum, stimulation of in man, 19, 45, 67, 94, 123
Experience, 70, 72, 73
Exploratory behavior, 62, 119
  brain stimulation induced, 15
Explosiveness, 104
Extinction, 39

Fatigue, 69
  irritability from, 39
Fear, 29
  amygdala, 42, 84, 86
  anger-inhibiting, 74
  cingulate lesions, 36, 41
  conditioned, 36

Subject Index

learned, 49
    measures of, 145
    reduction by temporal lobe lesion, 89
Fear-induced aggression, 73
    amygdala, 42, 44, 86
    defensive behavior, 56
    definition, 28
    neural basis, 38
    physiology of, 36, 37, 38
    relation to irritable aggression, 29, 36
    summary, 51
Feedback, sensory, 33
Female irritability, 19
Fighting, 13, 34, 46, 62, 63, 64, 65, 69, 72, 89, 97, 136
Flight, 56
Force, 83
Forel's field, stimulation of, 45
Fornix
    electrical stimulation, erotic ideation, 117
    lesion, aggression inhibition, 91
Friendly behavior, 8, 18, 23, 91, 106
    benzodiazepines, 122
    temporal lobe lesions, 91, 122
    temporal lobe stimulation, 117
Frog killing, 20, 31, 48, 56, 63, 69, 128, 131, 132, 138, 139, 143–46
Frogs, 20, 132
Frontal lobe
    lesion
        aggression facilitation, 18
        aggression inhibition, 91
        predatory aggression, 32, 51
    tumor, 87
    ventromedial stimulation, aggression inhibition, human, 93, 94
Frustration, 6, 20, 38, 47, 51, 57, 74, 83
    low tolerance for, 104

Genetic differences, 64
Glucose, 19
Gonad, 64
    hormones
        inter-male aggression, 119
        male mating response, 119
        predatory aggression, 51

Gonadectomy, territorial aggression, 48
Gonadotropic hormone, 98
Grasping hand test, 137, 138, 143, 147
Grooming, 112, 115, 117
Group living, 111
Guinea pigs, 19, 20, 120

Habit, 49, 72
Habitual aggressive, human, 60, 61
Habituation, 34, 142
Hallucination, attack by cat, 40, 57
Haloperidol, 104, 105
Hamster, 17, 35, 97, 118
Happiness, induced by electrical stimulation of septum, 19, 45, 67, 94, 123
Head injury, 60
Hedonism, 14
Heredity, 21, 63, 64, 74
Hippocampus
    chemical stimulation
        aggression facilitation, 45
        aggression inhibition, 86
        irritability in man, 58
    electrical stimulation
        aggression in man, 59
        predatory aggression, inhibition in cat, 66
        rage in man, 59
    lesion, 84, 86, 89
        agression facilitation, 18, 45, 87
Hoffmann-La-Roche Laboratories, 8
Homicide, 81, 87, 88, 100
Hopelessness
    premenstrual, 99
    inhibition of by septal stimulation, 122
Hormones
    aggression control, 23, 97, 99
    balance, 6, 20, 23, 68, 75, 118, 125, 129
    gonadal, territorial aggression, 48
    maternal aggression, 128
    neural sensitivity, 74
    reproductive
        maternal aggression, 51
        maternal behavior, 120
        sex behavior, 120
        territorial behavior, 51
    See also specific hormones

Hostility, 4–8, 44, 60, 67, 83, 91, 106
  affiliation, 125
  brain stimulation induced, 5, 6
  control, 106, 127
    brain lesion, 7, 17, 84, 85, 89, 91
    brain stimulation, 8, 95, 96
    drugs, 9, 101–5
    endocrine therapy, 97
    innate, 124
    role-playing, 83
  drug facilitation, 103
  EEG during, 60
  energy, 125
  homicidal, 87
  hypoglycemia, 100
  impulses, 89, 106
  induction by brain stimulation, 58, 116
  limbic system, 4
  neural system, 63
  physiology, 109
  premenstrual, 98, 99
  sleep deprivation, 39
Hunger, 33, 72
Hydrocortisone, maternal aggression, 6, 20, 129
Hydrolic model of aggression, 124
Hyperactivity, 91, 103, 105, 118
Hyperemotionality, septal lesion, 37
Hyperexcitability, 103
Hyperkinetic child, 104
Hyperphagia, 18
Hypersexuality, 46, 85
Hypoglycemia and hostility, 99, 100
Hypomania, 84, 91
Hypophysectomy, 35
Hypothalamus
  anterior-posterior reciprocal inhibition, 122
  chemical stimulation, lateral nuclei, 15, 31, 57
  electrical stimulation
    aggression, 56
    anterior, inter-male aggression, 57
    eating, 15
    fear-induced aggression, 51
    lateral, 5, 15, 19, 31, 33, 57, 62, 71, 143
    medial, 5, 15, 31, 40, 143
    posterior, 58, 114
    preoptic, sex behavior, 114
    ventromedial, 19, 40, 47, 51
  lesion
    lateral, 17, 33, 87
    posterior, aggression control in man, 7, 17, 87, 90
    ventromedial aggression facilitation, 18, 37, 40, 51
    ventromedial hyperphagia, 18
  predatory aggression, 32, 33, 51, 57
  tumor, 87, 88
Hysteria, 102

Ictal, 88
Implications of aggression control, 8, 9
Implications of physiological control, 4
Imprinting, 113
Impulse control, 61, 64
Impulsivity, 104
Inactive neural system, 61
Incompatible neural systems, 122
Inhibitory mechanisms, 18
Innate
  behavior tendencies, 11
  depravity, 124
  mechanisms for aggression, 64, 74, 113
  neural systems, 54
Insensitive neural systems, 61
Instinct, 22
Instrumental aggression, 28, 73
  definition, 30
  dominance, 49
  habit, 60
  mouse killing, 71
  reinforcing brain stimulation, 70
  summary, 51
  war, 122
Intellect, 9, 124
Inter-ictal symptoms, 88
Inter-male aggression, 27, 137, 145, 146
  androgens, 68, 97
  bulbectomy, inhibition, 136
  definition, 28
  dominance, 73
  gonadal hormones, 119
  heredity, 63, 64

physiology, 34, 35, 36
satiation, 69
summary, 51
test, 137, 138
testosterone, 32, 62, 65
Internal environment, 83
  manipulation, 22, 23, 24
Internal impulses, 11
  affiliation, 109
  aggression, 11, 13, 22, 66, 73, 109
International Brain Research Organization, 2
Intervening variable, 13
Irritable aggression, 28
  amygdala, 42
  androgens, 68, 97
  anger, 73
  cingulum stimulation, 41
  control, stilboestrol, 20, 23, 98
  definition, 29
  factors facilitating, 66
  and fear-induced aggression, 36, 38
  hypothalamus, 37
  inhibition, 73
  interaction with predatory aggression, 50
  isolation, 144
  neural basis, 39
  neural inhibition, 66, 67
  neural sensitivity, 65
  neurology, 56
  olfactory lesions, 32, 143, 144, 146
  physiology, 38-47
Irritability, 50
  aldosterone, 99
  allergy, 101
  brain lesions, 40, 42, 87
  brain stimulation, 37, 59, 116
  control, by drugs, 23, 99, 104, 105
  cyclical, in female, 19
  diandrone, 20
  endocrine dysfunction, 20, 21, 46
  fatigue, 39
  females given androgens, 35
  frustration-induced, 20
  generalized, 57
  irrational, 9
  maternal aggressions, 48
  neural systems, 125

normal, 88
  premenstrual tension, 20, 23, 98, 99, 125
  stress, 39
  summary, 51
  tumors, 87, 88
Islet cell tumors, 100
Isolation, 35, 65, 135, 136, 137, 139, 141, 145, 146
  aggression toward handler, 136
  emotionality, 142
  irritable aggression, 144
  mouse killing, 142, 147
  olfactory lesions interaction, 136
  shock-induced aggression, 136
Isolation-induced aggression, 35, 68, 97

Jactation, nocturnal, 89

Klinefelter's syndrome, 64
Kluver-Bucy syndrome, 89, 91

Lactation, 6, 20, 48, 129, 131, 133
Lateral olfactory stria, predatory aggression, 32
Laughter, 125, 126
Law of effect, 70
Learning, 11
  affiliation and hostility, 111, 123, 124
  aggression control, 23, 73, 83
  aggressive behavior, 21, 70, 75
  consummatory behavior, 21, 83
  dominance, 34, 72
  instrumental aggressions, 30, 49
  interaction with internal states, 72
  in man, 73
  mouse killing, 71
Lesion
  aggression, 58, 72
  consummatory behavior, 18
  See also Brain lesion
Libido, 98
Librium, 8
Limbic system, 4, 91
Lipidol, 91
Lipids, 19
Lithium, 99
Lynx rufus, 7, 17, 36, 41, 86

Maternal
  aggression, 6, 20, 23, 28, 29, 48, 49, 51, 73, 128, 129, 133, 134
  behavior, 113, 118, 133
  brain stimulation, 115
  fantasy, 120
  inhibition by brain stimulation, 121
  hormones, 120
Mating response, 119
Maze, 16, 71
Medial lemniscus lesion, produced docility, 40
Memory, 89
Menstruation, 20, 98
Mental hospital, 87, 91, 103
Mental retardation, 60
Meprobamate, 105
Mesencephalon
  electrical stimulation, 58, 121
  lesion, aggression inhibition, 91
Microminiaturization, 96
Midbrain
  cells active during fighting, 63
  electrical stimulation, 40, 45, 56, 65
  lesion, aggression inhibition, 32, 40, 87
  predatory aggression, 32, 66
Mind-body interactions, 14
Modulating systems, 66, 67
Monkeys, 7, 8, 17, 19, 23, 36, 37, 41, 45, 57, 70, 71, 72, 84–87, 90–93, 95, 105, 106, 112, 114, 117, 118, 121, 122
Mood swings, 104
Moral insanity, 100
Morphine withdrawal, 39, 66
Motivation, 30, 70
Motiveless behavior, 102
Motor system, 89
Mice, 13, 19, 27, 33–35, 64, 68, 69, 70, 71, 97, 129, 132, 136
Mouse killing, 15, 31, 32, 44, 50, 56, 57, 63, 71, 136–40, 142–46
Murder, 16, 123, 124
Mutilation of animals, 22

Narcoleptic, 95
Negative affect, 127
Negative reinforcement, 21
Neural facilitation, 65, 74

Neural inhibition, 4, 44, 66, 74, 92, 121, 123, 127
Neural model, 123
Neural organization, 106
Neural sensitivity, 62
  hormone influence, 119
  neural influence, 65, 66, 121
Neural substrates for aggression, 56, 64
Neural system incompatibilities, 67, 74, 119, 122
Neural systems for affiliation, 111–19
Neural systems for aggression, 54, 58, 61–63, 66, 68, 72–74, 84, 87, 100, 111, 119, 123, 125, 126
Neuro-endocrine interactions, 6
Neuro-humoral substrates, aggressions and seizures, 16
Neurology of predatory aggression, 3
Neuronal irritability, 99
Neurosis, 104
Neurotransmitter, 68
Noradrenaline, 47, 68

Obesity, 21, 83
Obsessive compulsive states, 90, 102
Odor in inter-male aggression, 34, 136
Oesterone, maternal aggression, 129, 131, 132, 133
Olfaction, 34
Olfactory bulbs
  inter-male aggression, 34
  lesions, 135, 136, 139
    affective aggression, 143
    irritable aggression, 143, 146
    predation, 136
    rage, 136
Onychomys, 33
Operational definitions, 25, 27
Oppression, 9
Orality, 85
Ovariectomy, sex arousability in humans, 121
Overactivity, 104, 105
Oxazepam, 105

Pain
  in animals, 40

brain stimulation, 57, 58
facilitate aggression, 74
induced aggression, 39, 70
inhibition by septal stimulation, 59, 94, 96
irritable aggression, 47, 51
predatory aggression, 49
Paraldehyde, 103
Paranoid, 8
Parental behavior, 113, 124
Parke, Davis & Co., 24
Pathological aggression, 8
reduction by temporal lobe lesion, 90
Pathology, 8
Perphenazine, 103
Persecution, feelings of, 123
inhibition by septal stimulation, 123
Personality
androgenital syndrome, 121
immature, 104
improvement after temporal lobe lesion, 90
Phalanger, 36
Pharmacotherapy for aggression, 102
Phenobarbital, 86
Phenothiazines, 102
Pigeons, 39, 48, 71
Pituitary adrenal axis, 46
Placebo, 100
Play, 84, 91
Pleasant sensation, brain stimulation-induced, 75
Pleasure principle, 14
Population, 46, 50
explosion, 126
Posture, aggression inhibiting, 34
Predation, 131, 143, 144
Predators, 27, 33
protection from, 111
Predatory aggression, 73
amygdala, 41, 44, 86
brain stimulation, 15, 44, 62
definition, 28
and fear-induced aggression, 38
and fear and pain, 49
and frog killing, 131, 137
heredity, 63
and instrumental aggression, 71
and irritable aggression, 29
mouse killing, 137, 143

neural facilitation, 65
neural inhibition, 66
neurology, 56
physiology, 31–34
punishment, 72
satiation, 69
summary, 51
topography, 26
Pregnancy, rat, 129, 130
Pregnane derivatives, 97
Premenstrual
irritability, 125
syndrome, 49, 99
tension, 20, 23, 24, 46, 98, 99, 105
Premenstrum, 98
Prepyriform cortex, predatory aggression, 32
Prey, 28, 29, 31, 33, 69, 143
Prison, 20, 98, 100
Prison management, 104
Prisoner, 47, 104
Progesterone, 99
aggression inhibition, 20, 23, 97
sexual behavior, 120
Prolactin, maternal behavior, 120
Propendiols, 105
Protein diet, 100
Psychiatric disorder, 88
Psychic blindness, 85
Psychological causes of aggression, 3
Psychomotor seizures and aggression, 90
Psychopath, 60
Psychopathology, 104
Psychosis, 104
Psychotic, 8, 19, 24, 105
Psychotic hostility, 102
Punishment, 34, 72, 82, 100
Pyriform area, 48

Radio frequency lesion, 92
Rage
allergy, 101
brain lesion, 42
inhibition, 89
brain stimulation, 19, 37, 58, 59, 95
inhibition, 94, 123
brain tumor, 87
diandrone, 20, 46
EEG, 21, 22
feline, 31

inhibition, 73
irritable aggression, 38
spontaneous neurological, 16, 89
Rana pipiens, 129
Rats, 6, 15, 21, 27, 31, 33–35, 37, 39, 44, 46, 50, 56, 57, 61, 63, 64, 66, 69, 70, 71, 86, 112, 114, 116, 128, 129, 137, 138
cotton, 17
Norway, 17, 36, 41, 63, 86
Reciprocal inhibition of affective states, 122, 126, 127
Reciprocal innervation, 67
Reinforcement, 6, 75
aggression control, 83
contingencies, 4
dominance, 85
instrumental aggression, 30, 49, 51, 70, 71
interaction with drugs, 105
negative, 21, 72
value of aggression, 15, 16, 71
Relaxation, brain stimulation-induced, 95, 116
Responsibility for aggressive acts, 22
Restlessness, 104
Restraint, 87
Reticular formation, electrical stimulation and aggression, 31
Reticular system, 65
Reward, 72
Rhinencephalon, 88
Robbery, 81
Role-playing, 83

Sadness, septal stimulation inhibition, 122
Sarcasm, 124
Satiation, 15
predatory aggression, 69
Satiety center, 19
Schizophrenia, 89, 105
Schools, 81
Scientific endeavors, 125
Sedation, 84, 87, 91, 104, 105
Sedative surgery, 90
Sedatives, 8, 103
Seizures, 103
Selective breeding for aggression, 64
Self-stimulation, 57
Sensory defect, midbrain lesions, 32
Sensory feedback, 33

Septum
chemical stimulation, 35, 58, 94
electrical stimulation
aggression inhibition in man, 8, 19, 23, 45, 51, 94, 123
eating inhibition, 19
erotic tendencies in man, 116
depression, inhibition, 122
hopelessness, inhibition, 122
sexual motive state, 122
inter-male aggression, 51
lesion, 35
aggression, 18, 37, 146
escape, 37
fear-induced aggression, 51
maternal aggression inhibition, 48
slow wave activity, 59, 94
tumor, 88
Serotonin, 68
Sex
activity in humans after castration, 120
crimes, 20, 46, 97
deviated criminals, 103
drive, 97
male response after testosterone in hypothalamus, 115
related aggression, 30, 73
Sexual
arousability, women, androgen, 121
behavior, 11, 13, 14, 21, 112
brain lesions, 118
fantasy during brain stimulation, 120
ideation from septal stimulation, 94
maturity and intermale aggression, 34
response, 30, 98
tendencies, hormones, humans, 112, 120
biological basis, 120
Sham rage, 18, 58
Shock-induced aggression, 136, 137, 138, 144, 145
Shrew, 19
Sleep, 89, 95
Sleep deprivation, 39, 66
Social
behavior, innate tendencies, 23, 124

Subject Index 193

experience, 35
indifference after cingulectomy, 31
interaction, 111
stimulation and mouse killing, 142
Socioeconomic structure, 3
Sociological mechanisms and aggression, 3
Sodium retention, 99
Solitary confinement, 91, 98
Species-specific aggression, 28
Spontaneous aggressive action, 16
Spontaneous episodic anger, 59
Spontaneous neural activity, 7, 16, 60, 62, 74, 87, 89, 119
Spontaneous neurological rage, 16
Spontaneity reduction, hypothalamic lesions, 90
Steers, 6
Stereotaxic
  amygdalotomy, 92
  lesions, 91, 96
Stilboestrol, aggression inhibition, 20, 23, 46, 98
Stimulants, 104
Stimulus-bound affiliative responses, 113
Stimulus-bound aggression, 27, 40, 56, 57, 59, 74, 113
Stimulus-bound eating, 15
Stimulus control of aggression, 34
Stimulus objects for aggression, 14
Stimulus situation, 27, 28, 29, 30, 33, 34, 50, 62
Strain differences, 142
  predatory aggression, 63
Stress, 6, 20, 21, 39, 46, 66, 83
Subictal, 88
Submission, 34, 35, 49, 72, 85, 93
Submissive posture, 37, 51, 118
Sugar tolerance test, 100
Superior colliculus, aggression facilitation from electrical stimulation, 45
Super relaxation from brain stimulation, 95
Suppressor circuits, 6, 40, 92
Suppresor systems, aggression, 7, 121
Surgery, 7, 17, 74, 84, 88, 91, 92, 96, 126
Symbolic behavior, 61, 73

Tantrums, 101, 102, 103, 104
Taxon-specific, 112
Teasing, 105
Tegmentum, stimulation, rage and pain in man, 58
Temperament, 124
Temporal lobe, 44, 89
  abnormal EEG, 61, 88
  electrical stimulation
    aggression facilitation, 45
    aggression inhibition, 94
    erotic ideation, 117
  lesion, 84
    aggression control in man, 17
    fear-induced aggression, inhibition, 36, 51, 85, 122
    friendly behavior facilitated, 122
  spontaneous activity, 16
  tumor, 87, 88
Temporal lobectomy, 88, 89, 90
Tension, 3, 7, 73, 91, 104, 105
Territorial aggression, 47
Territorial defense, 28, 29, 51, 73
Territoriality, 47, 93
Territory, 28, 29, 48
Terror, 107
Testicular atrophy, 46
Testosterone, 32, 35, 62, 64, 65
  irritable aggression, 144
  mouse killing, 144
  preoptic nuclei of hypothalamus, 115
  territorial aggression, 48
Thalamus
  electrical stimulation
    aggression facilitation, 45
    copulation, 114
  lesion
    anterior nuclei aggression inhibition, 87
    dorsomedial nuclei aggression control, 17, 87, 91
  predatory aggression, 66
  spontaneous activity, 16
Theoretical implications, 124
Thioridazine, 103
Thiouracil, 35
Threats, 7, 8, 22, 47, 62, 87, 93, 100, 111
Thyroid, 21, 46
Thyroxine, 35

Tissue irritation, 86
Topography of response, 26, 27, 31, 32, 34, 51, 70, 143, 144
Training, 4, 7, 21
Tranquilizers, 103, 105
Transmitter, radio, 58, 95, 96
Tropotropic circuits, 90
Tumor, brain and aggression, 40, 60, 74, 87
  frontal lobe, 87
  hypothalamus, 87
  septum, 87
  temporal lobe, 87
Tybamate, 105

Uncus, lesion, 84, 85, 89
UNESCO, 2, 9
Unicetomy, 118
United Nations, 9
Unsocial behavior, 100
"Unstable," 102

Value judgment, 4, 106
Violence, 20, 47, 60, 81, 98, 102
  control
    cingulectomy, 7, 18, 19, 90
    punishment, 82
  EEG, 14/sec. and 6/sec., 16, 22
  menstrual cycle, 20, 47
  psychotic, 8
    control of, brain stimulation, 8
  sex-related, 30
  temporal lobe, 16
  thalamus, 16
  threshold, 61
Vision, 34

Water retention, 99
Wildcats, 7, 17

Xylocaine, 86
XYY syndrome, 64

COLL. FOR HUMAN SERVICES LIBR.
201 VARICK ST. N.Y.C. 10014